PLANNING AND MANAGING CHANGE

PLANNING AND MANAGING CHANGE

A Reader edited by Bill Mayon-White
at the Open University

Paul Chapman Publishing
in association with
The Open University

P·C·P
Paul Chapman
Publishing Ltd

Selection and editorial material
copyright © The Open University 1986

First published 1986
by Harper and Row Ltd, London

Reprinted 1988
by Paul Chapman Publishing Ltd,
144 Liverpool Road, London N1 1LA

British Library Cataloguing in Publication Data
Planning and managing change.   (R8VO)
    1. Organizational change
    I. Mayon-White, Bill   II. Open University
    III. Series
    658.4'06   HD58.8

ISBN 1 85396 053 5

Typeset by BookEns, Saffron Walden, Essex
Printed in Great Britain by
St Edmundsbury Press Ltd, Bury St Edmunds, Suffolk

B C D E F G   4 3 2 1 0 9

CONTENTS

Part 1
CHANGE IN PRACTICE

PREFACE

This book of readings is about the management of change, and forms an integral part of an Open University course on the same topic. Typically the process of developing, writing, and printing courses within the university takes anything up to four years from the time at which the proposal starts to wend its way through the approval procedures to the time at which students first start to study the course.

In the case of *Planning and Managing Change*, this has been cut to a target of fifteen months, and at the time of writing it looks as if we will just reach that target!

Managing this process in the institutional environment of a body such as the Open University has been a risky enterprise and could not have been carried through without the commitment of the course team members and the active support of many members of the university. This has been demonstrated in many ways, from a willingness to experiment with new working methods and technologies to a preparedness to cope with the erratic progress of the course authors! In doing this we have tried to practice what we preach, even if imperfectly.

But this small change has to be set against a wider range of similar experiments as the university moves forward to adopt new patterns and ways of working in order to maintain its place at forefront of open learning and higher education. So in this sense as well, the Open University is experiencing the difficulties of managing change which are described in the papers in this book.

The help of my course team colleagues in arriving at this selection of material is gratefully acknowledged as is the patience of Marianne Lagrange and her team at the London office of Harper and Row. They too took on this enterprise cheerfully and efficiently.

As for the book itself I hope that the reader will find the selection satisfying and stimulating. The approach was deliberately eclectic, but with change as the integrating theme. Where the collection falls short of expectations I must accept responsibility.

W.M.M-W.
London
Summer 1986

THE PLANNING AND MANAGING CHANGE COURSE TEAM

OPEN UNIVERSITY
Lewis Watson
David Asch
Sheila Cameron
Bill Mayon-White
Derek Pugh
Rosemary Smith
Valerie Timmis
Nicholas Watson
Jane Thompson

BBC
Alison Tucker

EXTERNAL ASSESSOR
Dr Allan Williams, Centre for Personnel Research and Enterprise Development,
City University Business School

INTRODUCTION AND AIMS

Initially this set of readings was prepared with the needs and requirements of one particular audience in mind—namely, the Open University students studying a management course entitled 'Planning and Managing Change'. However, the role of an editor would not be fulfilled if other audiences were disregarded. So the editorial strategy was essentially one of striving for a balance between the needs of these sudents and other possible groups of readers.

Any manager concerned with change, and today that includes almost all managers, should find the material highly relevant. The book is divided into four parts and progresses from case studies which present change problems in a range of settings through to papers which address concepts and theories about success-ful change management. It is common in a book of this kind to restrict the selec-tion to material from academic journals. This option was rejected, and instead this reader provides a sample of the management literature in selected British and American management monthlies and journals over the last 15 or so years. The practising manager will find some papers here which are short and easily diges-ted, and can reserve the more academic material for more careful deliberation.

The general aims of the book are best described as an attempt to meet the needs of students working on their own in the traditional distance learning mode of the Open University over a six-month period. Thus the book can be regarded as a selective 'mini-library' with four parts covering major themes of the course. All readers should find that this allows them to dip in and out of the book, collecting ideas which can be tested against experience even without the teaching structure of the complete course.

The first part provides a range of examples of change and is designed to give a straightforward entry to the theme of this book. Part 2, 'The Challenge of Change', introduces the problems encountered and paves the way for some of the more academic material in Part 3 which has papers focusing on strategy. The final part deals with implementation, and the papers here remind us of the difficult boundary which exists between theory and practice. Implementation problems traditionally have been ignored by the theoreticians. And consultants are rarely around when the heavy costs and damage generated by badly conceived changes become known. Iterative approaches, evolutionary strategies and incrementalism are all terms which reflect current thinking about implementation. There is a close link between Parts 3 and 4. The separate section on implementation is included to emphasize its importance in all managed change processes.

In the period covered by the papers in the book we have seen a steady increase in the importance of this theme of change with a noticeable increase in the number of articles on the topic appearing in the last few years. This increasing awareness of change as a process to be managed has occurred in the context of a worldwide recession characterized by business failures and the challenge of turnarounds. In the United Kingdom a Conservative government has imposed new goals on both public and private sectors of the economy. To this must be added the explosion of information technology. The combination is presenting all organizations, large and small, with formidable challenges of change.

In both the Open University course and in this reader two particular themes can be identified. The first concerns the school of thought which is usually called Organizational Development and the second is best described by the label Systems Thinking. Both strands are seen as complementary in management education and they form the basis of the teaching in the course. The readings which appear in the later sections of this book provide something of a history on the subject of change over recent years and the course itself reflects an increasing concern for the role of people in organizations and the need for involvement and participation if changes are to be successfully designed and carried through.

The story of change in any organization must always include some examples of their heroic failures. These are perhaps best characterized by the phrase 'I had the answer but they wouldn't listen'. Elegant designs, well-written and well-argued reports recommending changes of all types sit on the shelves unread and disregarded in most organizations. Thus the challenge for management trainers, managers themselves and the members of the 'Planning and Managing Change' course team has been to try to identify those features of change-strategies which can lead to the successful implementation of change in an organizational setting.

To these general aims must be added some more specific requirements, for example, much of the literature on change in the last two to three years focused on the impact of new technologies whether these be the technologies of office automation or their close relatives the new technologies which are changing manufacturing industry. This set of readings is not intended to provide a comprehensive literature on either of these applications of technology. Instead it is designed to offer a much broader range and to look beyond technological change to other types of change and at the driving forces for change which may affect any organization, be it in the manufacturing or services sector; in private ownership or in the public domain. This is reflected in the range of case-study material. It is here that one can perhaps see the clearest indication that the successful management of change requires an approach that is both sensitive to the context in which change is taking place and yet offers 'generalizable' principles and concepts which take account of peoples' needs. The course and this book provide material that will enable the reader to gain access to those concepts and to gain some understanding of the kinds of process and technique which can be employed in particular organizational contexts.

The later sections of this book provide an introduction to the different schools of thought which are taught in the course, namely, that of organizational development and systems thinking as previously mentioned. The reader is invited to look at the arguments for a particular set of ideas and then to balance these against the views of the other authors.

Before inviting the reader to sample the material itself two further points need to be made. Inevitably for our specialist Open University student reader it is possible through the other teaching materials which have been prepared to direct the reader to specific passages of individual papers. This opportunity resulted in a decision to include the papers largely in their original published form in this collection. This means that the papers as presented here can be taken to reflect the views as expressed by their authors in the original publications from which they were drawn. I have not attempted to edit or reduce or reinterpret the arguments presented at that time. It is intended that the generalist reader will thus be able to use the book as a source and as a means of accessing other literature in this topical field. However, it is recognized that by choosing this strategy there will be times at which the reader may wish for more guidance. The separate introductions to each section provide advice on the role and importance of individual papers.

A further point concerns the cyclical or iterative process by which a selection of this kind is arrived at. In principle it is possible to freeze the selection process at any stage and to say 'we can go no further because any further change will result in the loss of something which is valuable and good and its replacement by something whose value is unknown or untested'. But the contents of a book of this kind has to be agreed on and fixed at some point in time. Thus it must be accepted as a sampling of the literature on the topic of change and is not intended to be an exhaustive treatment. Only North American and United Kingdom journals are covered. The book does not attempt to cover literature from mainland Europe. Even so, many of the examples are of multinational corporations which have global operations and subsidiaries operating in many countries. The interested readers would be well advised to scan the references of individual papers and to extend their study to other publications. (For example, Peters' and Waterman's best-selling book *In Search of Excellence* is a highly readable account of innovation strategies in large American companies.) Alternatively the reader interested in the development of ideas in the field of management may find useful background material in the earlier collection of readings edited by Bennis, Benne and Chin (1961).

A final word of advice: a book of this kind cannot be read easily from cover to cover. Essentially it is a collage of material covering a field of interest and is best used as a source to be sampled regularly. Thus the most useful way of using the book is to sample individual sections and papers and not to attempt a reading from beginning to end. In this sense the material is order-independent. For the lay reader the most interesting material may be the case studies. For the academic reader the later sections provide food for thought about the concepts and methodologies that constitute approaches to the management of change. But the busy executive will have to slow down to digest the material here. The course team's understanding of successful innovation and successful management of change suggests that time spent in diagnosing problems, in reflection, and time spent in consultation is time well spent.

The general teaching strategy of the course to which this book belongs requires the student to build bridges between his/her own experience and the experiences of other organizations. For any reader a series of questions may provide useful triggers for evaluating any of the material in the reader. The questions can be reduced to two or three of the following kind:

How would I put these ideas to work in my organization?

How would I respond to a change which was initiated in this or that way?

What parallels can be drawn between this case study and my own experience?

But I must leave it to you as the reader to enlarge on these ideas for using this book.

REFERENCES

Bennis, W.G., Benne, K.D. and Chin, R. (1969) *The Planning of Change* (2nd edn [1961, 1st edn]), Holt, Reinehart and Winston, New York

Peters, T.J. and Waterman, R.H. (1982) *In Search of Excellence*, Harper and Row, New York

PART 1
CHANGE IN PRACTICE

Case studies and examples open this book as a means of building a bridge between the text and our own experiences of change. There is some variation on the length and depth of the papers here. At the lighter end the pieces by Hancock and Laurance cover issues of which all managers in the UK must be aware. Jaguar's' turnaround is becoming a classic and no-one can be unaware of the plight of the National Health Service.

In contrast the story of Tannoy's fate is relatively unknown, yet the lessons ring true. Stratford Sherman describes change problems in some well-known American companies and seeks to find some common features to explain growth and survival. Whiteside's article on General Motors will be seen by some as building on these features. A single example perhaps seems to be more telling.

The section also includes an easily digested account of reorganization at the Swedish car manufacturers Volvo. The experiments at Volvo which led to these changes were based on an understanding of the systemic nature of many of the problems found in industrial production. It is significant that the changes at Volvo were people-orientated and apparently had little to do with technology.

Part 1 is thus designed to be a platform from which other aspects of change-processes and change-management can be examined.

1 QUALITY BRINGS SALES DIVIDENDS AT JAGUAR

Geoffrey Hancock

When John Egan joined Jaguar in April 1980 as chairman and chief executive, losses had been running at about $3 million a month. The situation was grave. His brief from the British Leyland parent board was blunt—either stop the alarming losses and get on a profit course or close the business. Under Egan's direction, Jaguar set about developing a quality control programme intended to turn the business around. Now, nearly four years later, the dramatic effect of that programme can be seen in Jaguar sales, the raising of morale, and the boost to wages.

Egan explains: 'I knew we had a beautiful, world class car but I also knew we had to introduce massive improvements to our quality.' He sought those improvements by what he called 'the pursuit of perfection'. This effort dealt with identified quality problems and has since been developed to take in all aspects of efficiency in the Jaguar operation. The effect has been electric. Jaguar is booming again and making a profit. This surplus is hidden in the overall BL (British Leyland) accounts, but the Jaguar operation today has a considerable degree of independence.

The quality factor has been reflected in the rise-fall-rise of Jaguar sales figures, from 1976 to 1983. These figures are eloquent testimony to the dividends paid by attention to quality. For hardly any other reason could world sales of Jaguar cars in 1983 have shown such a marked increase over the previous year.

The most outstanding increase was in North America, where the total sales of 16 000 cars were more than 5000 higher than in 1982. US sales of 15 815 put Jaguar Cars Inc. 50 per cent above the previous record annual sales total of 10 349 set in 1982.

The first step in Jaguar's turnaround came when it identified 150 problems related to quality, 60 per cent of them the responsibility of outside suppliers and the rest occurring 'in house' with factory-prepared components and assembly. Task forces were organized and each was given responsibility for curing specific faults.

Hancock, G. (1984) Quality brings sales dividends at Jaguar, *Quality Progress*, May, pp 30–33 © 1984 American Society for Quality Control. Reprinted by permission
Jaguar is now privatised. Ed.

One problem, involving front disc brake noise and vibration, was identified through high warranty costs and customer complaints. The appropriate task force set about diagnosing the problem, finding a remedy and then implementing it. As a result the specification of the brake pad was changed; a new source was found for the disc casting; and new equipment at Jaguar's Radford factory produced matched sets of discs to much finer tolerances. Also, to protect the disc assemblies from grit and water during transit, it was decided to protect them with plastic bags.

The task-force concept proved important when, in 1980, Jaguar became the owner of the former Pressed Steel Fisher body assembly plant and paint shop, and inherited some long-established paint problems. Another Jaguar task force found that the problems arose in the thermoplastic reflow system. This system was revised and re-equipped and the workforce retrained; the effort paid off in significant improvements.

Between its worst year and the start of its revival in 1982, Jaguar dispensed with 40 component suppliers who were unable, or unwilling, to provide the quality demanded. During this period, the company placed the financial onus on its suppliers and made them pay the cost of work arising from their quality failures. The success of this scheme led to the introduction of the Jaguar warranty threshold policy, under which the supplier assumes liability for all labour, handling and materials costs when the fault incidence exceeds 1.5 per cent. By the end of 1984, the suppliers of 73 per cent (by value) of the components will have joined the scheme.

Jaguar's philosophy now is to take its association with suppliers beyond a purely commercial relationship. It aims to develop a long-term relationship and encourage research and development. At regular meetings, Jaguar engineers and the suppliers work towards a situation in which the suppliers warrant their products as being 'fit for purchase and use'.

Suppliers are now graded on the 'fitness for purpose' standard. After a complete audit, they are adjudged either to be first class in every respect of quality, system and procedures or to meet most requirements, although some areas still need remedial treatment or to be suitable for a business action programme which will either move the firm to one of the higher categories or lead Jaguar to find a new source for the component.

Jaguar's new approach helped solve a problem with power-steering faults that had been traced to oil-seal leakage. The supplier had difficulty in eliminating the fault and so Jaguar engineering and quality personnel moved into that factory, helping the company revise the complete manufacturing process and working jointly on a new and higher specification for assembly.

In some cases it was not easy to establish where remedial action was needed, and so customer-tracking proved useful. Telephone calls were made to 150 Jaguar buyers in the US and 150 buyers in Britain, and were followed up after 30 days and again after nine months. One point that emerged was the surprisingly high number of owners experiencing headlamp-bulb failures. This had not shown up in warranty returns for the simple reason that dealers had replaced the faulty bulbs without claiming for the new ones. As a result of the calls to customers, the bulb fault was referred back to the supplier, who took action to improve the quality.

Quality also comes into the reckoning in the standard of dealerships, of which Jaguar has about 200 in the US. As Neil Johnson, Jaguar's director of sales and marketing, explains, dealers are very often the only point of personal contact with customers, and looking after Jaguar customers is a highly specialized job.

Like many other car firms, Jaguar has to part company with dealers from time to time, although in the US terminations have been counterbalanced by new signings. Decisions to end agreements are based on assessments that suggest minimum standards have not been met and are unlikely to be achieved. In Britain in the past few years Jaguar terminated agreements with dealers that had not come up to expectations, but some 220 other dealers met the standards required.

Jaguar's success is, in large part, because during the most severe period of a worldwide trade depression, the company was able to motivate a dispirited workforce to join in a concerted effort to put matters right at Jaguar. During a two-year period, Jaguar's payroll was reduced at all levels by 30 per cent. Nevertheless, both quality and productivity rose during that period. The upshot is that while 10 500 employees made 14 105 cars in 1980 only 7400 employees produced 22 046 cars in 1982. And the 28 000 cars built in 1983 are the most Jaguar has produced since 1974.

2 EIGHT MASTERS OF INNOVATION
Stratford P. Sherman

New, fast-growing, high-tech businesses by no means have a monopoly on new ideas, as I discovered when I studied eight large, long-established and notably successful American corporations, operating in many different industries, that have managed to keep alive the vital innovatory spark. Among their common features: strong corporate cultures, decentralized structures, lean management, rapid communications and a compulsion to keep new ideas coming to keep from falling behind.

The world has fallen in love with innovation. Ask a technocrat in Paris or a middle manager in Dayton who the heroes of contemporary capitalism are. You will hear excited tales about Silicon Valley, but few words about those heads of giant corporations who used to be known as the captains of industry.

But does big business have to be slow and stodgy? How does the management of a corporate colossus keep new ideas coming and nurture them into new ways of making money? Given the tendency of the innovation cult to consign most of the *Fortune* '1000' to the dustbin of history, these seemed questions well worth asking. In search of answers, I went looking for large, innovative American companies.

Using *Fortune*'s lists of the 500 largest industrial and service companies as a base, I asked business school professors, management consultants and security analysts for nominations. Each nominee was measured against peers in the same industry according to such objective criteria as research-spending and the number of new product introductions. The final cut was necessarily subjective, particularly on the question of what constitutes a true innovation. Does Honey Nut Cheerios, a so-called brandline extension of the original cereal, represent as much of an advance as a new microprocessor? I don't think so. I then interviewed managers at the companies on the list of finalists, in part to confirm my choices, in part to find out how they achieved and sustained such inventiveness. One finalist, Citicorp, declined to be interviewed.

THE CHOSEN FEW

Judged by these methods, eight of the most innovative giants of US industry are American Airlines, Apple Computer, Campbell Soup, General Electric (GE), Intel, Merck, Minnesota Mining & Manufacturing (3M), and Philip Morris. They are nimble enough to put smaller companies to shame. While the eight differ in many ways, the techniques they use to foster innovation are sufficiently similar to provide clear-cut lessons. These techniques combine a 'let a thousand flowers bloom' zest for new ideas with a rigid, almost martial discipline bred, finally, of fear.

The management of each of the eight is convinced of the *need* to innovate, regarding new ideas as the essence of long-term survival. No matter how dependent the companies are on purely technological advances, they are uniformly devoted to marketing. Their people believe that markets can speak, and routinely treat bureaucratic considerations—who works for what division—as entirely subservient to the goal of listening carefully to their customers. All the companies have clearly defined corporate cultures through which their strategic aims are widely, and convincingly, promulgated.

Not satisfied simply to indoctrinate employees in such 'mom and flag' values as product quality, market leadership and the necessity of invention—although they loudly preach these values—the eight companies also ruthlessly limit the search for new ideas to areas they are competent to exploit. Not one of these corporations is a gambler: financially disciplined sometimes to the point of parsimony, their top executives are convinced that the risk of experimentation can carefully be controlled.

COMPANY CHARACTERISTICS

The eight innovators are uniformly profitable and most are fast-growing compared with their competitors—even though their average age is a hoary 102 years. All are large enough to have tested the proposition that size necessitates idea-stifling bureaucracy: their 1983 sales range from Apple's $983 million to GE's $27 billion.

Two companies, Apple and Intel, were early entrants in the high-tech boom of the last decade. Intel has dominated key segments of the $1.9-billion-a-year market for microprocessors by staying on the leading edge of technology. Apple, declining to follow IBM's example in microcomputer design, is winning customers with its easy-to-use Macintosh technology.

Three companies won their place on the list by shedding conservative ways. Since the airlines were deregulated in 1978, American Airlines (owned by the holding company AMR Corp.) has consistently found ingenious solutions to the difficulties facing all the old trunk carriers. For example, it introduced rewards for frequent fliers, creating brand loyalty in the commodity business of air travel. Campbell Soup, once a lumbering dinosaur of the food industry, last year introduced more new and successful products than any competitor. General Electric, which files more new patents each year than any other US company, seems finally to have learned how to transform its good ideas rapidly into big and growing businesses.

The remaining three companies have longer histories of inventiveness. Minnesota Mining & Manufacturing, generally known as 3M, often meets its ambitious goal—explicit since 1981—of getting 25 per cent of its sales from products less than five years old. Philip Morris, famed as an inventive marketer of cigarettes, soft drinks and beer, is also an imaginative manufacturer whose 'state of the art' plants have helped increase the company's profit margin in the cigarette business from 17 per cent of operating revenue to 24 per cent in the last decade. Merck, the Rahway, New Jersey-based pharmaceuticals company, has maintained its edge as what one analyst calls 'the class act' in drug research, most recently in the emerging field of biotechnology.

DRIVING FORCES

Costly and chaotic, the process of innovation requires powerful motivation—and it turns out that the most common motivator is old-fashioned fear. At all these companies, resting on the status quo is perceived as a sure way to corporate disaster. Says Leslie Vadasz, 48, the tense, Hungarian-born senior vice president for planning at Intel: 'Two things drive this business, technology and paranoia.' Intel faces domestic and international competition with the potential to render its products obsolete virtually overnight. Management keeps driving the point home by insisting that deadlines for the delivery of new products be met religiously.

American Airlines persuaded its unionized workers to accept the industry's first two-tier wage pact—new hires are paid 30 to 50 per cent less than veteran employees for the same work—by educating them in how much lower costs are at competing start-up airlines. And however inspired workers at Apple may be by the idealistic exhortations of Chairman Steven Jobs, 29, none is ever very far from spine-stiffening awareness of IBM's rise to near dominance in microprocessors.

General Electric's management created a sense of urgency largely through its own efforts. In the late 1970s GE was one of the nation's 10 largest industrial corporations, with most of its sales coming from relatively slow-moving technologies. Employees had little reason to think of the company as imperiled until John Welch, Jr, 49, became chief executive in 1981. He began trumpeting the message that he wanted GE to concentrate on faster-growing fields, many in high tech, and would get rid of any operation that did not fit the plan. Managers throughout the company watched, and trembled, as Welch sold off over a hundred businesses, from small appliances to air-conditioning, that failed to meet his standards.

To keep their products in the GE portfolio, managers of slow-growing lines have been impelled to find new ways to revitalize their businesses. For example, when court decisions opened the way for companies to make more of their own electricity from the heat produced in manufacturing—a process called *co-*

generation—GE's electrical-equipment people positively jumped on the opportunity. They devised a whole new method of doing business, shifting from merely selling equipment to a more complex service approach that promises to make life easier for customers while boosting GE's margins. Now GE will build, finance, own, operate and even provide fuel for customers' plants. 'When challenged,' says Welch, 'the bureaucracy will bring together the technical resources and creative thinking to rally around.'

ORGANIZATION AND COMMUNICATION

New models of corporate organization are emerging at the innovative companies. To retain an entrepreneurial feel for their markets, most of them work hard to stay highly centralized. For example, 3M encourages a process analogous to cell mitosis: as they develop new products, units of the organization subdivide into new units. At Campbell Soup, $3.3 billion in sales is spread among 52 so-called strategic business units.

The ability to make use of the market information gleaned by decentralized operations seems to depend on compressing the lines of communication between the chief executive and the middle manager. Apple achieved this by flattening its organization chart: fully 15 people report to Chief Executive John Sculley, and a line manager of modest responsibility is rarely more than three reporting levels away.

All these companies believe in keeping their management ranks lean, but even those with relatively thick layers of management have developed ways of keeping top management in touch. Perhaps the simplest solution is that of Campbell Chief Executive Gordon McGovern, 57, who picks up the phone whenever he has a question and calls the employee most competent to answer it, no matter how lowly. 'I talk to Gordon at least once every six weeks', says Paul Masaracchio, 35, a marketing manager who has developed such successful new products as Prego spaghetti sauce and Casa Brava frozen Mexican dinners. He goes on: 'When I was at General Foods I saw the president of the company once in five years.'

Communications is the glue that holds these structures together. People in different disciplines are simply not allowed to remain in isolation. Business units are kept small, in part to throw engineers, marketers and finance experts together into the sort of tight groups most often found in start-up companies. When the interaction fails to arise naturally, it is engineered: all these companies require their workers to spend a great deal of time at meetings where information is shared and plans are discussed. Every year Intel brings secretaries from around the US together for meetings: they discuss such matters as the optimum use of word processors and formats for memos. The 'get in there and reason together' imperative extends even to the top ranks: at American Airlines, all major decisions are made by an 11-member planning group whose members include the heads of marketing, finance, operations and personnel.

GENERATING IDEAS

A company open to new ideas risks being deluged by them, and directions for channeling the flood have to come from the top. Among the chief executive's most important responsibilities at each of the eight companies is to define a corporate mission clearly enough to enable even low-level employees to sort opportunity from insanity. Intel's engineers, for example, know that the company is determined not only to replace its own products before the competition can render them obsolete but to meet its customers' demand that succeeding generations of chips retain design continuity. Such clear strategic guidelines are almost self-enforcing, since they enable middle managers to quickly identify and kill ideas that do not fit. That in turn can cut down dramatically on the need for innovation-deadening supervision.

The cost of disciplining the innovation process can be high in people and business opportunities lost. Many of the ideas Intel rejects for strategic reasons are perfectly sound. They are so sound, in fact, that many highly qualified engineers have left the company to develop them elsewhere.

At the same time, a sense of corporate mission can have wonderfully rousing effects. Since he became chief executive in 1980, Gordon McGovern has devoted much of his energy to selling his employees on the idea that Campbell Soup is no longer merely a processor of inexpensive foods. Before he arrived, virtually all new products were required to reach breakeven within a year; McGovern encouraged the development of several new products, including Le Menu premium-priced frozen dinners, with breakevens projected as far as three years ahead. The guiding principle behind this change is that Campbell is not, in McGovern's phrase, a 'well-being company'. Brand managers there understand this to mean that all Campbell's products, old and new, must appeal to a target market of health-conscious and sophisticated consumers.

On their own initiative, brand managers have reformulated the company's Swanson's TV dinners to appeal to more discriminating palates, replacing soggy french fries with fettuccine Alfredo. Sales of the line are up for the first time in years. A 29-year-old marketing manager named Patti Goodman came up with Juice Works, a new line of children's drinks. One flavour mimics the overwhelmingly sweet taste of R. J Reynolds Industries' Hawaiian Punch. Unlike its competitor, Juice Works is made entirely of natural fruit juices and without added sugar. Security analysts expect concerned mothers to buy about $90 million of the new product this year, compared with Hawaiian Punch's annual sales, estimated to be $130 million after four decades.

THE WINNOWING PROCESS

A sense of mission, by itself, may not be enough in sorting out possible new directions: most of the eight companies also rely on a tough internal testing process to produce the necessary winnowing of ideas. Intel strongly encourages engineers to attend frequent meetings with their peers at which ideas are examined in the harsh light of what the company calls 'constructive confrontation'. Intel believes that when employees put their heads together, they can not only eliminate bad ideas but strengthen good ones.

Jack Welch of GE and Robert Crandall of American Airlines are known for demanding that managers petitioning for capital meticulously prepare formal business plans defining the scope of the profit opportunity and showing step-by-step procedures for building the new business. Dennis Crosby, 39, a director of marketing services at American Airlines, survived the process, starting a new unit to use idle telephone capacity at American's reservations facilities to sell other companies' products by phone. 'We all learned to have our *t*s crossed and our *i*s dotted,' says Crosby. 'If we don't, the deficiency is, er, highlighted.'

Even these tough bosses, though, are not sticklers for return-on-investment projections carried out to the last decimal place. The time it takes to bring a new product to market—as long as a decade in some instances—can make that sort of projection absurd. Formal business plans are used instead to force middle managers to think their projects through, to provide evidence of the scope of the opportunity and to present credible scenarios for retrenchment in case they are wrong.

STARTING SMALL

While they will leap when necessary, these companies typically approach new businesses in a cautious, incremental way, that lowers the cost of failure. 'It's a lot easier to get me to invest $50,000 than $1 million,' says Lester Krogh, senior vice president for research and development at 3M. A key aspect of the corporate culture there is the idea of 'make a little, sell a little'. That policy has one major drawback: security analysts note that 3M's new products, aimed at relatively small market niches, rarely break the $100-million sales barrier. That's an inefficient way to expand a company that already has sales of $7 billion.

Even when a business is ill-suited to the little-by-little approach, the innovative companies strain to find ways to cut down their financial exposure. Merck, for example, must often invest heavily in manufacturing facilities for a new remedy well before the Food and Drug Administration has authorized its sale. To reduce risk, the company relies on computer modeling to find ways to reduce that investment to a minimum. Instead of building a $200-million plant for its new Primaxin, a neutron bomb of an antibiotic that kills just about every bacterium known to man, Merck makes it in 10 complex steps at existing plants spread across the United States.

Innovative companies typically enter new markets on a small scale, so that failures can be quickly identified and killed, while winners can prove their worth. GE invested $20 million—not much for a company of its size—in facilities to back up an extended market test of a new, extraordinary heat-resistant specialty plastic called Ultem, which could be used in the manufacture of computer circuit boards. Now that the plastic has won the approval of IBM and other customers, GE is studying every aspect of investing another $59 million in a full-scale plant. Explains Dr Roland Schmitt, chief of the research labs where the product was invented: 'Marketing people are wrong as often as technical people. It is important to approach markets as well as science experimentally. In the long run even expensive failures that teach you something are cheaper than lots of market research that teaches you nothing at all.'

IN-HOUSE TESTING

Some companies test-market products internally. Apple gives every one of its employees an Apple computer—not as a perk, but as a way of gathering consumer information. Says Jobs, 'One time a bunch of people came back after opening the box and said, "There are six manuals! It's intimidating and we don't know which one to read first!" That comment was worth more than $100,000 of market research.'

GE, which has thus far had little success selling its line of factory automation systems, is showcasing them while refining their design in the company's own plants. GE's automated dishwasher plant in Louisville, Kentucky, has yielded reams of favourable press coverage as well as a product good enough to increase GE's market share in dishwashers by eight points to 40 per cent. And before making a commitment to sell so-called expert systems—computer programs that attempt to replicate the thought processes of human experts—GE designed an expert system for use in its locomotive-engine repair facility in Erie, Pennsylvania.

UNOFFICIAL TINKERING

The pressure to experiment in-house extends even to individual workers at the innovative eight. While their controls may be tight otherwise, these companies often turn a blind eye to employees' attempts to sneak around bureaucratic roadblocks. Formally or informally, innovative companies with research staffs encourage scientists to devote up to 15 per cent of their time to projects that have not been passed on by the company. And 3M promotes the practice by promulgating cherished company tales such as the story of the engineer who kept slipping back into the lab even after he was fired: his success there led to an improved asphalt shingle and his eventual promotion to vice president. Managers generally allow more latitude to researchers with strong track records, and they are quick to withdraw the tinkering privilege temporarily when deadlines are tight. Even so, a certain amount of time is wasted—innovative companies regard that as a cost of doing business.

Financing for such projects frequently comes in the form of 'bootlegged' funds: padding that business-unit managers build into budgets and then distribute without formal reviews. Since top management can never give more than tacit approval of such practices, middle managers rely on their sense of the corporate culture to tell them how far they can go. Such informal mechanisms nurtured the first four years of the development of 3M's Post-it notepaper, whose gently adhesive backing allows users to stick notes on almost any surface without thumbtacks or tape. Post-it is now estimated to be a $50 million-a-year business.

ENSURING A BALANCE

The toughest job of all at an innovative company is ensuring that the risks and rewards are balanced in a way that prods employees toward prudent experimentation. One crucial protection big companies offer their workers is the assumption of financial risk: engineers do not have to hock their homes to finance their work. Probably more important, managers at innovative companies have learned to leave their subordinates' failures unpunished—except, of course, in cases of sheer incompetence.

This is not just a matter of not yelling at people. The best organizational solution to the challenge seems to be what management consultants call 'syndication of risk'. A derivative of management by consensus, it basically means drawing plenty of people into any risky decision—including, whenever possible, the chief executive. Says American's Crandall, 'In the end, if something doesn't work it is the resident and the chairman who are responsible.'

In one way or another, the eight companies reinforce the fear of stagnation with rewards for success. 'We want our people to focus on the upside', says GE's Welch, who annually doles out $2 million in special bonuses for extraordinary contributions. Others rely less on money than on ego-boosters: 3M gives prizes— trophies and certificates—while Intel gives its design engineers the gratifying opportunity to present their new products to engineers at client companies.

But all these companies act on the belief that their employees enjoy the act of creativity for its own sake. Discoverers of new drugs covet the admiration of their peers—says Dr Edward Scolnick, head of basic research at Merck, 'I wouldn't want to hire anyone who doesn't want to be famous.' It is not balderdash to say that employees at any of the eight innovators have real opportunities to change the world—or at least transform their companies. The 100 people who developed Apple's Macintosh have seen the computer's sales grow since its January 1984 introduction to an annual rate of nearly $1 billion—about as much as the whole company, with 4600 employees, sold in 1983. That kind of opportunity may just be the most powerful motivation in the world.

3 LESSONS FROM EXPERIENCE
Mary Weir and Jim Hughes

Looking back over the years from February 1976, when the factory at Coatbridge first opened, what are the lessons from Tannoy's experience which are relevant to other organizations moving towards greater participation and to the wider scene of British industrial relations?

To a large extent, any lessons can only be based on subjective views and therefore this chapter highlights what the present authors learned from this experience with Tannoy. These lessons are listed here and each will be discussed in detail:

Starting from where people are
Involving the trade union
Demonstrating commitment to changes
Having realistic expectations
Maintaining consistency
Integrating participation into management
Developing an evolutionary process
Using learning opportunites
Allowing the freedom to fail
Balancing hard vs soft management
Staying in touch with reality
Planning time and resources

Clearly, others who were involved may have different views, from their own perspectives, which are equally valid as part of the debate on participation.

STARTING FROM WHERE PEOPLE ARE

The very fact that we are stating our subjective views emphasizes the first and one of the most important lessons. Any effort to introduce changes or to operate in different ways must start from where people really are and not where those initiat-

Weir M. and Hughes J. (1983) Lessons from experience, *International Journal of Manpower*, Vol. 6, No. 1/2, pp 80-102. Reprinted by permission of MCB University Press

ing the change would like to think they are. While this may seem obvious, it is only too easy to make assumptions about other people's views and preferences, without properly checking out those assumptions. Everyone makes his/her own assumptions about how the world works, whether it is a kind or a cruel place, and behaves accordingly. But unless these subjective assumptions are checked out against the realities of the situation, it is possible to misread totally the attitudes, expectations and behaviour of other people. There are several reasons why checking out assumptions is important.

Different Value Systems

The meaning of actions and ideas may be quite different when interpreted through value systems based on very different life experiences. It is important to recognize and accept the realities of other people's culture and circumstances rather than impose a personal value system on them.

Personal Experience

Most people rely on their past experience when making assumptions about a current situation. But even personal experience is a rapidly perishing commodity and may be quickly out of date. When a manager says 'when I was in that department' and a supervisor says 'when I was on the shop floor', they are making an assumption that their experience is still valid and may not be fully aware of how much things have changed unless they first check out their assumptions.

Hierarchical Structures

The organizational hierarchy is one of the most effective mechanisms for filtering out bad news on the way up. Senior managers may not realize how out of touch they are with the views of the grass roots, unless they go and talk regularly and directly with the people there.

INVOLVING THE TRADE UNION

One of the clearest examples in Tannoy of the kind of problems which can arise from not checking out assumptions was in the initial refusal by the work force to join the union. In a strongly unionized area such as Coatbridge the management assumed that the response to the approach from the union would be enthusiastic, so it was taken by surprise at the strength of feelings against unions. The subsequent agreement owed a great deal to the efforts of the local union officials in convincing the workers that they had the opportunity to run things differently within their own branch.

In our industrial environment, it is essential to involve the trade union movement as completely as possible in the change process. This proved absolutely fundamental in the Coatbridge situation. We may question the wisdom of some of the other decisions, but on this there can be no doubt whatsoever. Some of the most impressive changes took place within the trade union structure and attitudes. The shop stewards quickly took over responsibility for their own negotiations and the regional officials were very supportive of the growing independence of the branch. A great deal of creative thought and energy came from the stewards' partners in the process, both at the daily nuts-and-bolts level as well as on major issues such as the Absence Committee and handling redundancy.

DEMONSTRATING COMMITMENT TO CHANGES

The second lesson learned, again well-rehearsed and obvious, is the need for continuing, demonstrated commitment from senior management to the principles in their philosophy—not just a speech now and then. The regressive forces inherent in every individual and organization are such that reinforcement by constant encouragement of progress, however small, is essential. The jungle moves back into the clearing very fast. There is a temptation to abandon new ideas when the going gets rough and to revert back to old habits. This is especially true, for example, when the pressures of production limit the time and energy available. Finding time for the work-group meetings was often a problem in Tannoy, but it was only through the discipline of keeping the meetings going on a regular basis that they became credible and useful. This also applies generally. If management only calls a meeting with the workers to tell them bad news, 'communication' falls into disrepute and is not believed or taken seriously.

We also learned it is important for management to be *seen* to be committed. The visible demonstration of members' commitment, even in quite small ways, is far more convincing than all the missives from behind the 'mahogany door'. At the time when the Work Improvement Committee became so overwhelmed with ideas coming up from the work groups that nothing seemed to be getting done, the strength of management commitment was called into question. The system of patron managers which was set up at that time got all the senior managers talking with the groups on a regular basis and went a long way towards getting both more action and clearly demonstrating their commitment to the whole process.

HAVING REALISTIC EXPECTATIONS

One of the dangers of starting out with a long-term goal is that it will create high expectations which cannot readily be fulfilled. It is obviously important to create a high level of enthusiasm—an essential ingredient of the spirit of the project—without also creating the false expectation that Utopia is just around the corner. This is similar, of course, to the normal management practice of defining goals which require 'stretch' but are within reach.

There is inevitably a tension between healthy impatience and the rate at which individuals and organizations can change and grow—the tension between the 'prophetic' and the 'pedestrian'. We found that it was necessary to give adequate attention to keeping long-term objectives visible, as well as the short-term administration and discipline of maintaining momentum.

If initial high expectations are not fulfilled this can inevitably lead to cynicism and frustration. So while the level of expectations needs to be realistic, we also believe that cynicism should be seen as legitimate and used constructively to understand why expectations are not being met.

MAINTAINING CONSISTENCY

Closely linked with the question of expectations is the need for consistency between words and action—not only to say it but *do* it. Given the natural cynicism of most people, there is a tendency to take a 'wait and see' attitude towards new approaches, to see how long it lasts before the old patterns of behaviour reassert themselves. Indeed Pat Lowry, chairman of ACAS stated:

> . . . I am convinced that a cornerstone of good industrial relations is management consistency—the knowledge that whatever the circumstances and pressures the management will so far as is possible react in the same way to a particular situation whenever it arises. The knowledge that management always responds consistently and fairly as well is an even more essential ingredient to good industrial relations than a well-drafted grievance procedure or an equitable pay system.
>
> The future challenge to managers is that having become more consistent in their attitude and approach during the recession, they will be prepared to remain so when the commercial pressures return again. Will new-found principles continue to be observed or will old-fashioned expediency rule again?

In Tannoy, one of the areas where any inconsistency was quickly challenged was in its policy of single status.

Even quite minor incidents were interpreted as symbolic regressions and created great feeling. For example, when yellow curtains were put up for the first time in Hughes's office, as well as the conference room in an effort to improve their appearance for visitors and customers, the wrath and dismay reverberated round the factory.

But resisting such apparent inconsistencies was a two-way process. For example, when there was pressure to move back from monthly to two-weekly pay the management resisted it as the thin end of the wedge against the single-status policy. Instead, by running parallel courses on personal finances and company budgets, it used the pressure constructively to achieve a better understanding of the company's financial position and policies.

On a much more fundamental level, the inconsistency over the policy of self-inspection of quality resulting from the pressure to get into production with the new products was damaging both to the concept of individual craftsmanship and to the image of the company itself.

INTEGRATING PARTICIPATION INTO MANAGEMENT

There is sometimes a tendency to view participation as something separate from the problems and pressures of organizational life. Participation may be considered the best way of solving *this* problem, but not that one. Such a selective view of participation is, in our opinion, likely to be seen as instrumental and insincere. The business of changing the working environment must always be (and be seen as) an integral part of the operating objectives of the company and not as an extra tool to be used when appropriate or as a compensation for the less popular elements of its operating philosophy. It must be fundamental to the whole way of managing the organization, rather than being prepared to participate on some issues but not others.

For Tannoy, operating in a participative way was seen by the management as a relevant response to the tough economic threats it faced. By involving everyone in an understanding of the company's financial situation and by sharing difficult as well as easy decisions, the ownership of the process gradually moved down the organization. The fact that the company faced grave financial difficulties and yet has survived is evidence of the resilience and determination that has resulted from everyone being closely involved in the operation.

DEVELOPING AN EVOLUTIONARY PROCESS

From the start-up at Coatbridge we saw the development of participation as a slow evolutionary process and our experience confirmed this view. While it was important to have firm philosophical principles, the day-to-day process was highly pragmatic in nature. Although some use was made of particular technniques—such as job design or semiautonomous work groups—the emphasis was always on an organic process, developing according to its own perceived needs rather than according to a preset or specific programme.

The value of this approach, we found, was that it encouraged a way of thinking through problems, using the four principles, rather than advocating particular solutions to problems. In their meetings, the workgroups were encouraged to look at problems and evaluate alternative solutions according to the principles so that they became directly involved in the diagnostic and planning process themselves. As the groups became slowly more proficient in learning how to solve problems and to plan out the steps needed for implementation, they gradually became more confident of their abilities to contribute usefully to improving their own working situation. At the same time, they became much more aware of the organizational structure and learned about the decision-making responsibilities of the different levels and departments within the company. Gradually, the methodology of problem-solving and learning have been built into the company structure in a way which will enable these processes to be maintained.

USING LEARNING OPPORTUNITIES

Closely allied to this is the importance of seeing learning and development opportunities in small situations as well as large. There is a potential opportunity for development in almost every decision-making process. The learning material is there every day, but the skill is to recognize and use opportunities for learning. To facilitate such learning, there must be an awareness of this at all levels in the organization, so that they see in the many detailed incidents and decision-making new ways forward.

We also found it was important to see the learning opportunities in conflict situations. If conflict and cynicism are regarded as healthy and legitimate, it is possible to use these feelings positively as a learning opportunity to move forward rather than just a negative 'them and us' situation.

Overtime was one issue which often caused conflict. While people were prepared to be constructive during regular working hours, overtime was regarded as a perk and a privilege which brought out the old practices. One problem was that when overtime was needed on the subassemblies, many of the women working there were reluctant to come in to work. However, the men were usually keen to have all the overtime they could and resented the occasions when the women got overtime but the men on final assembly were not needed. The problem was resolved by setting up a training course for the men to learn some of the jobs on the subassemblies, especially the simpler jobs which required less dexterity. The women who were second-wage earners could then spend more time with their families, while the men had acquired a wider range of skills and therefore more opportunity of being able to do overtime.

The question of who was selected for overtime was gradually handed over by the supervisors to the work groups themselves. The supervisor specified how many people were needed and let the group members decide among themselves who should come in. Although the supervisors were sometimes accused of favouritism, the groups came to realize the difficulties involved in administering the overtime rota.

This approach to learning implies a significant change of role for managers and supervisors to realize that they are important developing agents and to make an adequate allocation of their time and energy to this training/educational role. They also enable people to feel legitimate about stopping and saying 'Let's look at how we did that' so that they have the opportunity to learn things for themselves at their own pace.

But managers and supervisors have to be involved in the growth process as well and feel that they are getting some personal benefit for themselves. By trying to work in a more participative way, they developed their own personal skills and opened up their frames of reference. The concept of patron managers, whereby each manager was linked with two or three work groups on a consulting basis, proved a very effective means of developing counselling competence. The need to explain ideas and policies directly to the groups has also encouraged them to become far more articulate as well as prepared to voice their own views up the line. As individuals they are prepared to take more risks and to take on bigger decisions themselves without feeling they have to refer back to 'Dad'.

ALLOWING THE FREEDOM TO FAIL

Making mistakes is, of course, one of the most important learning processes. While it is obviously essential that competence and success are encouraged and rewarded, it is also important to create an environment in which openness about mistakes and learning from them is equally valid. One of the most inhibiting restrictions of managers is their feeling that it is not permitted for them to admit failure or confusion to their subordinates so they collude with them in maintaining the 'infallibility' fantasy. We believe that one of the conditions that is essential if this kind of process is to succeed is the freedom to fail—the freedom to learn from things which go wrong and to try again. This freedom enables people to learn for themselves in a way which would be impossible in a tightly structured or prepackaged programme.

In Tannoy, the openness and freedom with which people allowed learning to take place, both in themselves and in others, stemmed largely from the personal openness of the managers themselves. They developed a capacity for handling and accepting criticism which was unusual. By building the sense of security for people to try out new ideas or to tell a manager he/she is wrong brought out a great deal of creativity in people, something that tends to be inhibited in hierarchical organizations.

But being prepared to admit mistakes also earned the manager's respect and authority. For example, when a popular newspaper approached Tannoy to write an article, the request was put to the work improvement committee. Although the members were doubtful, the convenor asked Hughes whether it would be good for business. When Hughes said it would, the committee agreed to the visit on condition that the loud speakers were given prominence in a photograph. When the newspaper published an oversimplified misleading story, everyone felt embarrassed and let down. Hughes realized he had been wrong in believing that the publicity would be good for sales, but felt the freedom to say to the work force, 'I made a mistake' and apologize to them.

Business life does not usually encourage managers to be open to criticism and prepared to admit mistakes, but as Marchington suggests, this may be an essential precondition for participation to be effective.[2]

BALANCING HARD vs SOFT MANAGEMENT

But open management does not imply soft management. Indeed it is often more difficult to achieve an open style of management, which might be interpreted as being soft, than to rely on hard tactics and a 'macho' style to get things done. Maccoby clearly highlights this dilemma from his interviews with managers:

> Most people still believe that the alternative to hardening one's heart or detaching one's feelings is being soft and letting others have their way. One reason why attempts at more participative management fail is that soft-hearted managers shrink from being leaders, setting limits, opposing bad ideas that have support from the people and answering legitimate criticisms. They are too insecure. They want to be liked and respected. They would rather rely on anonymous authority, bureaucratic rules and 'objective measurements' that rob them of real respect and authority but protect them from having to make difficult and sometimes mistaken decisions and being thought arbitrary, hard or nasty.[3]

There is a fine line between giving people the freedom to learn how to take responsibility for their own decisions on the one hand and, on the other, being too permissive, so they feel they are 'getting away with it'. For Tannoy, two issues which were constantly on this tight rope were absenteeism and smoking.

Although five people were dismissed for absenteeism after the first year, there was a widespread feeling that some workers were abusing the sick-pay scheme and putting it at risk for everyone else. Initially, when the joint absence committee was proposed, the workers refused to take part. However, they came to accept the joint responsibility and the committee played a very effective role in controlling absenteeism and later in the redundancy.

A similar sequence happened in relation to smoking which was not allowed on the factory floor. A special area had been set aside where smokers could go and have a cigarette when they felt the urge. But while they were smoking, they were not working. The work groups wanted management to take action because it meant that smokers were having more breaks that nonsmokers. The management said it was up to the groups to decide how to allocate work between smokers and nonsmokers to achieve the group target. The problem remained unresolved for a long time, but eventually the time taken for smoking became less and less as the smokers came under pressure from their groups.

By allowing people space to take authority the management did pragmatically what Barnes calls 'creativity pursuing the unexpected'. He highlights the almost unnoticed role of paradox in organizational behaviour:

> To buy when others are selling, to ask questions when others expect answers or to give new autonomy when subordinates expect tighter controls are all actions that make sense under certain conditions. . . . Managers need to replace the hard vs soft behavior with paradoxical actions that cope with new information, confront important disciplines and care for individual people and issues. The goal is not to do one or the other; it is to weave them into a pattern of separate behavior that sets the basis for new reciprocal patterns.[4]

We believe that finding the appropriate balance between hard vs soft behaviour is one of the main challenges in developing participative management. It is important to be able to say 'No' clearly. Managers must not pretend they are going to give an idea further consideration when they know full well they are not even going to entertain it. For example, there should be no hesitation in vetoing a recommendation which would put customers at a disadvantage. Equally, though, it is important to be open, to be prepared for genuine discussion and criticism and to provide the support and freedom for people to learn for themselves how to take responsibility. Although in Tannoy it was a constant struggle to maintain a balance between hard and soft behaviour, the consensus was 'at least we're trying'.

STAYING IN TOUCH WITH REALITY

To make good use of the experience of other companies means staying in touch with the outside world, not only learning from it in the early months of the start-up of a new factory. It is all too easy to become organizationally introverted; we found it was important to have an external frame of reference to which the internal changes in Tannoy could be related. An internal development process like this must be kept in touch with the realities of the outside world and especially with political, commercial, social, educational and technological developments.

The involvement of an external research consultant who was independent and seen to be independent was, in our experience, a useful way of maintaining such links with the outside world. This contact brought an element of objectivity, as well as encouragement and information, from others engaged in similar ventures. The network of contacts through the Work Research Unit, the Harvard Project on Technology, Work and Character and the Scottish Workshop were extremely valuable in giving a perspective to the changes in Tannoy. We also had direct contacts with other companies introducing similar policies, such as Tate and Lyle, May and Baker, Digital Equipment and QC Colour. By putting Tannoy's efforts into the wider context, it was possible constantly to question the change processes which were taking place internally, and also to contribute to some extent to their learning from our experience.

PLANNING TIME AND RESOURCES

Last but not least, and in some ways most important of all, is the question of time and resources. We learned that it is easy to underestimate the amount of time and effort needed to begin and maintain a viable change process. Introducing a more participative style of working means a fundamental change of attitudes on the part of both managers and workers. It seems realistic to us to think of participation as a five- to ten-year gradual evolutionary process, rather than something which can be introduced this year, next year, or by legislation. There are no quick and ready answers, but practical day-to-day pressures create the temptation to speed the process up by taking seemingly simple short cuts. Such short-term expediency, we found is likely to set things back rather than speed them up and only makes the whole process more difficult in the long run.

The corollary of such a time-scale is the need to devote sufficient resources to the development process. The commitment to keep carrying on, by achieving change cumulatively in small ways, means that resources have to be planned and budgeted for to support a lengthy change process. To many companies this may seem an unusual idea, with the result that such changes are introduced on the side rather than being seen as a central issue for the future growth and survival of the company. The same companies may well invest 3–4 per cent of turnover in research and development for redesigning their products to keep abreast of competitors and maintain their market share. Yet the idea of formally budgeting resources to redesign their organization structure, to keep it up-to-date, would be seen as unnecessary.

RELEVANCE OF TANNOY'S EXPERIENCE

Are these lessons in any way relevant to the wider scene of British industrial relations, or is the resilience and continuity of the Tannoy venture dependent on factors which were, and are, unique? Three factors in particular encouraged the development of participation at Tannoy:

Greenfield site
Smallness
Leadership

Greenfield Site

There is certainly a fundamental difference between developing participative management in new greenfield plants, such as Tannoy, and in existing plants. The frequent reaction of managers hearing about ideas which are being tried in new factories is that anything is possible, even easy, in a greenfield site. With a blank canvas on which to draw, they claim, there is no limit to the advances which can be made. To some extent this is true. With no old prejudices to sweep away and no entrenched attitudes to change, the task in the early stages was to define the meaning of participation for that particular plant.

But the effort needed simply to turn four empty walls into a busy factory left very little time and energy to think how everyday actions were giving meaning to the definition of participation. Yet without the discipline and commitment to be constantly relating decisions back to the framework of participation, it would have been all too easy to find that the many different elements of the organizational structure were not internally consistent with each other and with the principles which had been agreed.

Smallness

The small scale of the Tannoy venture could, of course, be regarded as a unique advantage, particularly in terms of communication. But equally, the plant suffered the disadvantages of a manufacturing unit which was functionally and physically separated from the rest of the organization. On the other hand, it is clear that 'small is beautiful' conditions can be reproduced within large organizations by restructuring around coherent product and profit centres of a few hundred people.

Leadership

Did the leadership and enthusiasm of a few key people constitute a unique factor? Certainly, in the initial stages, the commitment and enthusiasm of the present authors and others provided energy and direction without which the venture might well have foundered or become more conventional. But the speed with which the emotional involvement with the venture moved through the organization soon dispelled this fear. Indeed the vigour with which this process took place created the healthy conditions in which continued 100 per cent involvement and intervention by the authors would have been counterproductive and would have created unhelpful and collusive dependence.

If the process then is not unique, where is the evidence of its relevance?

When this chapter first went to press, there was limited evidence in the UK of constructive, creative efforts to find new ways forward or of radical initiatives.

The keynote in the industrial relations environment seems to be regression to the 'simple' solutions of power stuggle and confrontation—heavily influenced by the economic gloom and the struggle for survival.

This very preoccupation with survival may, in fact, contain the seeds of hope for healthier development in the longer term. For the Tannoy venture was certainly about survival—about rapid response to threats and opportunities, about a resilient organization which made fast internal change possible to match the rapid outside change, and about living with the consequent strain and tension of such frequent changes.

Huxley said that the closing years of this century would see us in economic wars for survival far more deadly than the military wars which occupied the first half of the century. The severity of this economic conflict can shake loose the rigid constraints of industrial thinking and compel a challenging of the assumptions which have limited organizational imagination. We hope that what we describe demonstrates a little of what is possible when imagination is combined with professional commitment.

REFERENCES

1.   Lowry, J.P. (1981) British industrial relations: Some personal reflections. Glasgow Shell Lecture
2.   Marchington, M. (1980) *Responses to Participation at Work*, Gower, Farnborough
3.   Maccoby, M. (1981) *The Leader: A New Face for American Management*. Simon and Schuster, New York
4.   Barnes, L.B. (1981) Managing the paradox of organizational trust, *Harvard Business Review*, March-April

4 REGROUPED SUCCESS AT VOLVO
H. G. Jones

At a time when many of the world's car firms are still reporting sales declines, which European company has increased its market share steadily over the past five years, while moving from loss to a 9 per cent return of capital? The answer, surprisingly, is Volvo—surprisingly because the oil crisis of the 1970s left Volvo exposed and vulnerable, with the wrong models selling (thanks to Sweden's strong currency) at the wrong price. Yet in the first three-quarters of 1982, Volvo sold 8 per cent more cars in all, against the background of a 5 per cent decline in the world market. As a manager at Olofström says, with quiet satisfaction, 'The last two years have been good to Volvo.'

His plant is one of those where the famous Volvo developments of group working have been applied. These much-publicized developments inevitably became overshadowed by Volvo's business difficulties after 1973 and by its intense efforts (twice abortive) to merge its way out of these troubles. But in 1982, the solution was found in merger with Beijerinvest; what has been described as Sweden's biggest commercial transaction at a stroke reduced car sales from half the group total to a quarter. From this greatly strengthened base, the car side has proceeded to exploit the benefits of obtaining, largely through group working, the quality-conscious labour force which is so valuable to a manufacturing firm selling into the top end of the market.

In Olofström, for example, quality control was once, to some extent, regarded as a police function: if defects were not actually concealed from the policing inspectors, they were none too actively disclosed. Now that the operators themselves are largely responsible for quality, the quality control people are regarded as colleagues; the change is much appreciated—not least by the quality controllers. At the Torslanda plant, Volvo has gone further still; it is experimenting with a scoring system linked to a quality bonus (of less than 5 per cent of total pay). The blue-collar union is watching this experiment very closely, because of possible repercussions on its members; but in the early days of the scheme Volvo

Jones, H. G. (1983) Regrouped success at Volvo, *Management Today*, Feb, 78–82 seemed to be getting about 3.5 per cent more 'quality-free' (that is, flawless) output. It is a good psychological point that bonus payments are linked to the positive aspect of 'quality-free', rather than to a negative penalty system depending on number of defects.

Continuity of production with a strike-free labour force is also a valuable asset. (In fact, there was a strike early in 1982 by white-collar workers claiming that their pay rises were lagging relative to blue-collars, but it was settled in a week; over a 10-year period the two groups have now actually had very similar percentage increases.) Group-working is a major factor in preserving good relations throughout a labour force whose members identify with the company, while gaining personal job satisfaction from increased responsibility.

The benefit in economic terms is real, though impossible to quantify. However, even without the inclusion of Beijerinvest (an oil-trading and food conglomerate), sales have shown steady growth over all the past few years save 1980; giving a yield on the group's own capital of 13 per cent in 1981, or 14.5 per cent if Beijerinvest is included. No wonder that Managing Director Pehr Gyllenhammar, the spiritual and practical father of group-working, can claim with some pride that 'there is a continuously higher level of quality . . . and there is the ability to produce efficiently'.

Group-working, of course, is not confined to Volvo in Sweden. Since 1970 it has become widespread in many Swedish industries. The initial objective was to overcome absenteeism and heavy labour turnover (sometimes amounting to more than 50 per cent) by increasing job satisfaction through work variety. This was expected to lead to involvement and then identification with the job and the company. In some areas at least, there is now a continual process of development and rising expectations.

The basic idea is unchanged—to expand the work content for an individual operator by making a group of between, say, four and 20 people responsible as a team for a recognizable subassembly, instead of each undertaking a series of repetitive tasks. The work content of the subassembly might take, say, 20 minutes, compared with two minutes for the repetitive task. Alternatively, in a continuous process such as a chemical plant, the group could take on responsibility for a whole section, including maintenance and the forward planning of raw materials, as well as day-to-day operations.

In the Swedish car industry, which has been prominent in group-working, Volvo Olofström is a particularly interesting example. The works in southern Sweden employ about 4000 people spread over a press shop and associated assembly shops, which fabricate a range of subassemblies for Volvo cars. The work is potentially noisy and heavy; it also lacks the glamour of an immediately evident, sophisticated end-product. Labour turnover at Olofström, which has been as high as 40 per cent, has now been reduced to an average of less than 10 per cent—and in some sections to between 2 per cent and 3 per cent.

As for productivity, an important measure in a metal-working shop is the number of press strokes per hour: throughout the period of group-working at Olofström, there has been a steady improvement in the works average from 290 to 350, with no sign yet of levelling off. However, this performance could be vitiated if change-over time deteriorated. In fact, though, steady improvement here as well has reduced change-over time by 44 per cent for the works average and no less than 51 per cent for one line where group-working is at an advanced state.

A discovery confirmed over several years is that, in a suitable environment, many of the people engaged in group-working progressively expand their job capacity. At first, they limit themselves to learning how to work as a group on the fairly obvious tasks directly concerned with the physical aspects of the job. The next stage is often for the group members to enlarge the scope of their job by undertaking various adjustments of the equipment that previously might have needed the attention of a different operator or even a skilled one.

One of the objectives has always been for the group to develop autonomy in doing its job: increasingly, this has been regarded as an important feature of industrial democracy. Once a degree of autonomy has been achieved, it is a natural step for some groups to have ambitions in the direction of planning. However, experience indicates that, at any point in time, working groups are not all at the same level of performance. At Olofström, five different levels of performance have been defined: they build up as a number of specified activities are carried out.

For production operators, Level One is the lowest: they add more activities to reach higher levels. Thus, the Level One activities are production, questions of safety and order, reporting activities and control of production. For Level Two, the operator adds die-setting, contact at breakdowns, talking with work study people about payment, manning the line and introducing new line group members. The Level Three additions are: making adjustments and maintenance, preventive maintenance, planning and coordinating resources, contact with planning department, classifying parts which need either adjustment or scrapping and dividing manpower within the allotted time. Three more activities raise performance to Level four: quality control, reporting on production and pay and rotating jobs. Finally, the Level Five operator will take on reporting functions, training needs, choosing and training reserves and economic matters.

In 1978, 10 groups were 'working as a group' (Level One), 58 had undergone job enlargement (Two), 30 had increased responsibility for planning (Three), 2 groups were working on job rotation (Four) and 1 group was in a better position to make independent decisions and develop its range of responsibility (Five). By the late summer of 1982, after a slight drop in 1980, the figures for most levels had increased substantially. By 1983 they hoped that the total number of groups for Levels Three, Four and Five would have more than doubled since 1978. A drop between the end-1980 target and the 1982 actuals came in Levels Three and Four; that was because, during 1980, an outside consultant was employed with the intention of speeding up the move towards group-working. In retrospect, an overambitious target seems to have been set for the number of groups moving up from Level Two to Level Three.

The number of working groups is not constant, but varied between 92 and 112 in the period under review. This reflects the personnel situation; a group consists (usually) of four or five people who may change; some people may not wish to work as a group, and some may even change their minds. Alternatively, the group may become so disorganized that a problem of definition arises, as in 1980, when the company had to review the position. Also, the jobs themselves are very flexible in Sweden, and this too might lead to change.

Up to the beginning of 1981, the initiative for change was in fact management-inspired. As a result of events in the spring of 1981, the initiative for forming new groups and for their advance through the different levels of achievement now rests with the workers, in what is described as a 'self-regulating' system. Further steady progress is expected. Already the number of groups achieving a worthwhile measure of success through group-working has almost doubled since 1978.

The operators say their work is now more satisfying because it is more varied and also because of the increased awareness of quality. Working in a group demands cooperation between all its members and gives them an important feeling of having influence. Cooperation between groups is a natural outcome. A group, it is claimed, can have influence upwards throughout the entire company in matters of the working environment as well as in manufacturing procedures.

Swedish companies have always been eager for their staff to be well-trained. Before group-working, the training for production operators at Olofström amounted to two weeks. Because of the spread of tasks and the greater expectations, the training has been extended to at least 26 weeks in the workshop, followed by 17 weeks on the care of the equipment. A new employee first learns work techniques and then some 25 work applications, the emphasis throughout being on accuracy and precision. The aim is for the operator to understand the function of the different types of equipment, to be able to undertake routine adjustments without having to call for a skilled mechanic.

As might be expected from a background in which personnel development looms so large, the training includes theoretical sessions in which there is a fair amount of discussion. The additional training does not arise entirely because of group-working, but is an on-cost that has to be considered. Leaving aside any question of reducing labour turnover, the point is that because the works produce components with a high-quality surface finish aimed at the top end of the market, Volvo management believes that its training costs are fully justified.

As an incentive to speed up the development of group-working, the management at Olofström as early as 1976 proposed a bonus amounting to between 5 per cent and 7 per cent of the group's gross pay depending on the level achieved. The actual make-up of the pay in the bonus scheme is as follows: basic pay for production workers, determined by job evaluation, 75–84 per cent of the total; individual merit and training, 1–3 per cent; 5–7 per cent depending on level of working group; with 10–15 per cent reserved for productivity and quality. All the proposals were opposed by the unions. Both the confederation of the Blue-collar Workers (LO) and the Metal Industries Union (METALL) have long followed a policy of pay solidarity, with the key aim of reducing pay differentials, which have fallen markedly since 1959. LO has also usually argued in favour of a straight day-rate. So union opposition to a pay structure that deliberately created differentials was not surprising—especially with the differentials existing in the same plant.

However, workers at local level were anxious to obtain the additional payments, which amounted to nearly 5 per cent, and pressed for a change in policy. Gradually, attitudes did alter. Currently the LO position is that provided pay is above the nationally negotiated minimum, small differentials are acceptable. Anyway, wage drift has always occurred in some plants, and this bonus scheme is regarded as a particular form of wage drift. METALL, too, has adopted a similar position, with the reservation that the scheme must be carefully controlled—particularly as it relates to productivity and quality: the union thinks a bonus element of 15 per cent of total pay is on the high side.

During the latter part of 1980, with the company and the local unions immersed in these negotiations, development of group-working came to a halt. The hiatus was perhaps worsened by skilled and ancillary workers who saw the advantages won by those directly employed in production and then wanted similar benefits. Management was obviously not averse to extending the scheme; but for these other workers the definition problem is more difficult. In production, recurring patterns of tasks emerge for similar processes in groups making components which superficially may look quite different; this similarity makes it comparatively easy to construct a set of common conditions to define levels of group working. It is also relatively easy to get agreement on the validity of such a checklist as a measure against which to judge performance.

How can a comprehensive set of criteria be designed for nonproduction workers, say, in a service function where the task differs from day to day? Toolmakers will obviously have different levels of skill as well as different kinds of opportunity for enriching their working life, as opposed to, say, plumbers or fork-lift truck drivers.The Olofström scheme for skilled workers is currently based on a set of 20 activities, starting with (1) service work, and continuing as follows: (2) daily operation report (3) care of equipment (4) general housekeeping (5) occupational safety (6) time-accounting (7) materials (8) planning of tasks (9) contact with other units (10) questions concerning the general amount of work (11) work result follow-up (12) training (13) personnel contacts (14) resource planning (15) work rotation (16) altering tasks (17) personnel questions (18) finances (19) work with special projects.

The culminating activity in this chain of 'self-regulation' is (20) planning. For Level One of group-working, the first three activities in the preceding list must be done satisfactorily. For Level Two, five more activities are required, of which two must be activities (4) and (5). Additional activities can be selected from the list to raise the performance level: Level Three demands five additional activities, while four more are needed for Level Four and three for Level Five (making up the total of 20).

These levels for skilled workers are believed to be broadly comparable with the five levels for production operators, although some of the activities on the list are open to extremely wide interpretation. At the present stage, this is understandable—the aim is to provide an opportunity for self-regulation as widely as possible; still, activity 20 (planning) could plainly overlap with activity

8 (planning of tasks) or with activity 14 (resource planning) or even with 16 (altering tasks).

A mechanism has thus been set up to agree on the level of activity, with the foreman playing a leading role. Subjective judgements are involved in assessing some of the activities, aided by cross-reference to other groups of workers. It is too early yet to analyze the effectiveness of group-working for the skilled and ancillary workers, but the opportunity of participation has certainly been given a warm welcome. The scheme is expected to take one or two years to get under way, with a further two years needed to build up a reasonable number of groups on Levels Three and Four.

The other aspect of the 1981 negotiations involved a productivity bonus. Speedy and remarkable progress has been made in this area; by 1982 only a fifth of the labour force was still being paid on a time rate, with no productivity element, against 65 per cent in 1980. Recently office staff have been included in the scheme, so they can now earn up to a quarter of the production premium.

All this has inevitably affected the position of the foremen. Some of the upgraded activities of the production operators (such as planning and coordinating resources, contact with the planning department, or undertaking quality checks) are clearly the type of tasks which used to be in the foremen's domain. Most of the operators involved have welcomed the changes as an upwards move in function and interest. The LO union, too, has recognized the increased spread of responsibility of its members, arguing that changes brought about by group-working have made the foremen redundant.

The Volvo management firmly rejects any such suggestion, although it agrees that the foremen's job will change considerably—often with part of their own reponsibility also moving 'upwards' into realms where earlier the manager had reigned. In fact, much of the foremen's job is still on the shop floor in close contact with the groups; but instead of perhaps being the driver, they have now become team leaders—and are so called officially.

The foremen have their own union, SALF. Initially, both men and union had considerable misgivings on where group working would leave the foremen. It was clearly recognized that attitudes and tasks would change. In addition to any question of redundancy, the foremen had the psychological problem of their own reactions to the unknown. To meet these fears, in addition to the normal desire to ensure a good outcome, the company instituted a training scheme largely devoted to encouraging and developing leadership qualities. In such a context, the course is steered only loosely; much of the content as well as the form, is decided by the members, under the old dictum that 'the more you put in, the more you get out'. The training scheme has been both ambitious and successful.

Numbers of foremen (or team leaders) have fallen somewhat, but most are now on top of their new status. They are fully committed to the concept of evolutionary development represented by group-working—so much so that a similar scheme for foremen is being initiated. Instead of the five levels for the blue-collar workers, a 'staircase' with four steps has been introduced, plus a productivity bonus similar to that for the operators.

The company has devoted a major effort to a review of the modern function of a foreman. The four steps in the development of a foreman's skills can be summarized as: (1) direct on-line functions concerned with maintaining output (2) indirect functions such as minimizing downtime and passing on goals (3) goal-setting and team development (4) high degree of independence, creation of good morale, initiation of cost-cutting and general ability to stand in for a superior. The activities in the steps, as implied in the description of a staircase, are added together to achieve progress up the stairs.

The mechanism is that the team leaders first analyze their own position, adding if appropriate other functions to the checklist, or deleting some activities if these are inappropriate to the job. The assessment is then discussed with the immediate superior and after that with the next manager up the line of command. By way of illustration, development Step Two is 'inform about goals and plans as well as increased efforts in personnel questions and measures for increasing production'. It includes: (a) *initiate, arrange and participate in regular production team meetings, at least four times a year* (b) *participate in preparation of expense budget and in its follow-up* (c) *check equipment for reliability* (d) *follow up downtimes and take measures to reduce these* (e) handle questions about wages as well as explain current wages (f) cooperate with other units (g) be responsible for developing personnel resources, for example, through planning discussions (h) work with social problems concerning personnel. (*The activities italicized are obligatory for the step.*)

Collectively, the activity checklists outline a system of development calculated to increase job satisfaction and at the same time make Swedish industry progressive and efficient in its operations. The search for the right system has involved critical self-examination by the management and will have taken about a decade to reach fruition. It has also devoured much time and talk, both in selling the ideas and obtaining feedback for modifications; but the end-results are regarded as a good return for the effort.

POTENTIAL FOR BRITAIN

The Olofström method is unlikely to be directly or immediately applicable in the UK, though it is full of possibilities which the British could explore if they were so inclined. But group-working is only part of the Olofström story. The labour force went down from 5000 to 4000 from 1979 to 1983 (by natural wastage), but output went up by 8 per cent. Group-working played a significant part in these changes; but so has major reorganization of the production facilities.

Assembly in 1973 was labour-intensive, with people working at more or less individual benches with much heavy work in lifting, turning over parts, welding and so on. The aim was to improve the working environment by organizing the work into a number of short production lines, each dedicated to a particular component, such as a car boot-lid.

Such a line is not cheap: the line for the boot-lid had a capital cost of some £900 000 and requires four or five operators. In fact, to provide contact between the members of the team (which is an essential feature of group-working), the line has been designed as three sides of a rectangle, with the loading, unloading and inspection functions on the long arms of the rectangle, and the processing (welding, application of adhesive, matching parts, clinching, metal finishing) located in the relatively short cross-member. The operators themselves are on the 'inside' of the rectangle.

It would be wrong to give the impression that these special purpose lines are in a state of flux; but the equipment and the concept behind the use of the equipment are under constant review. Part of the effort is concerned with fostering the growth of the working group, possibly through using locally designed 'live' stock magazines to free the operator more from the discipline of the machine. Simulation on a computer is used at the design stage to ensure that an overall systems view is taken of a proposed change.

The technical life of the main components in such a production line is expected to be about seven years, and the pay-back period for any new feature is usually between one and two years. For most applications, a return on capital of at least 30 per cent is required, but for environmental improvement a smaller return is acceptable. Automation now plays a large part in many of the special purpose lines and is a key element in the integration of a human-machine system where the emphasis is on the person as part of a thinking team. The equipment used in automation can be considered under three headings: mechanical handling, computer control and robotics.

Mechanical handling, for example, is an important element in this high degree of automation, used to locate and to move parts along the line; the equipment needs to be specially designed for the tasks, and any changes require at least some form of mechanical adjustment or even a complete redesign. One device, a press loader, has been designed by Olofström and marketed to 35 different press shops throughout the world. The synchronization and moving of the parts along the line is usually computer-controlled, as are any special welding cycles.

The welding also has its built-in diagnostics analyzed by the computer; feedback to the computer means that the process will be stopped by any untoward happenings (such as a welding rod running out): and the production data is stored for analysis. The computer aspect of automation is closely linked with the higher levels of group working, where process control and analysis, followed by the appropriate action, are essential activities. To involve the operator as well as the foreman is a decisive step towards a self-regulating system.

THE CASE FOR ROBOTS

The case for the installation of a robot at Olofström rests on six factors:

1. improved yield in the use of materials
2. improved quality—in glueing especially, where the robot maintains a consistent repetitive pattern of movement
3. greater speed
4. improved environmental conditions for the operator
5. economy in use of manpower—while the cost of a robot has doubled over 10 years (with technical improvements included), the future cost is expected to increase at only 80 per cent of the rise in labour costs
6. possibility of reuse.

The application of robots has grown rapidly—with a big increase in 1980 to a figure of 74 for Olofström alone in 1982. The total numbers of robots in use throughout Volvo is 260, a figure which compares, ominously enough, with about 375 throughout the entire UK in 1980.

The union attitude, and also that of local workers, is that the robots (and all automation for that matter) are just other machines. To be competitive, it is argued, the workers must have the best machines, so the changes at Olofström have been welcome. The loss of jobs was not welcome, of course, but it was accepted as necessary for competitiveness and thus future job security. In fact, automation is only opposed by LO if working conditions are likely to be worsened thereby.

The specially designed production lines and their automation features have helped to make feasible the higher levels of group-working; they relieve the operators of much heavy manual work and also liberate them from the demands of machines that require continual reponse. In exchange, the existence of group-working and the progressive attitudes associated with it have facilitated the introduction of automation. Jointly, the combination makes Volvo a very formidable competitor for the UK.

5 FEAR AND EXCITEMENT: THE PRICE OF CHANGE AT GENERAL MOTORS
David Whiteside

Saturn Corporation's new headquarters building is a study in modernity: a stylish grey-and-burgundy lobby, guarded by a high-tech security station complete with computer terminal that automatically logs in visitors, checks them for clearance and prints out temporary badges. It is crisply pleasant, especially with the morning sun streaming into its three-storey atrium.

Outside, a bright blue-and-white striped circus tent billows lightly in the wind as apprehensive public relations staff spot Roger Bonham Smith's slate-grey Cadillac Fleetwood Grand Brougham limousine rolling up. The chauffeur holds a door open for the grey-suited chairman of General Motors Corporation. A rousing march blares over loudspeakers as white banners emblazoned 'Saturn' flap overhead. The same breeze ruffles Smith's greying sandy hair.

It is dedication day for Saturn Corporation's new headquarters building in suburban Troy, Michigan, and the diminutive chief executive officer of the world's largest industrial corporation is here to wish his favourite new subsidiary well.

The ceremony is standard fare. Smith declares it to be a great day 'for those of us who have watched Saturn develop into a project of cosmic dimensions. If Saturn does what I believe it can, it will be something that the whole world will benefit from'. Saturn employees seated in the tent respond to his grandiose claims with controlled enthusiasm. As always, the chairman's voice squeaks, and his delivery, while measured and clear, is uninspiring.

FAST AND FURIOUS CHANGES

But what Smith has done to giant GM *is* inspired. Indeed, he is fast emerging from the shadow of his more charismatic rival across town, Chrysler Chairman Lee A. Iacocca, as the most widely admired CEO in industry. Even if he makes no more major moves in the years remaining before he retires, most observers agree he has already done more to alter the course of GM and the US auto industry than anyone since the legendary Alfred P. Sloan Jr.

Whiteside D. (1985) Fear and excitement: the price of change at General Motors, Dec, pp 49–56. Reprinted with special permission from *International Management* copyright © McGraw-Hill International Publications.

The changes have come fast and furiously in the brief space of only five years, breaking up time-honoured structures in a company that already was widely admired for the quality of its management. The new GM culture is a management professor's dream—fearless, sweeping, creative moves into new business and reshuffling of old units to pursue established markets, never allowing complacency to set in.

The results have some GM executives on edge, but most seem charged up and stimulated, which obviously is part of Smith's objective.

'Roger Smith has brought the excitement back to this business,' says Saturn President William E. Hoglund.

Indeed, beneath Smith's lacklustre delivery lurks an important change—for GM if not for the world—and there is a coherent plan behind the pyrotechnics.

First to create a fertile field in which to plant the seeds of change, Smith dislodged nearly every major aspect of how a car is designed, manufactured, marketed, sold and serviced from old habits by consolidating GM's domestic car operations into two so-called super groups. 'In the old days, we were glad just to have a job and glad to fall in behind a charging general,' admits one veteran engineer. 'I don't know if he talked to God or to the marketing guys, but he told us the direction.' Adds Lloyd E. Reuss, GM vice president and group executive in charge of the Chevrolet–Pontiac–Canada group. 'You have to be receptive to change. In fact, you have to go out and welcome change.'

Second, Smith arranged more than a half-dozen high-technology companies—including new acquisitions, minority equity investments and joint ventures—around this core business bubbling with activity. Some, such as Electronic Data Systems Corporation (EDS), are designed to take over peripheral, if vital, functions so that the carmakers can concentrate on their main job. Others, such as Hughes Aircraft Corporation and five vision companies in which GM has taken a stake, are designed to speed the adoption of new technologies—primarily electronic—in GM's products and plants.

The plan is to become what GM President F. James McDonald likes to describe as an 'agglomerate corporation'. That is, these acquisitions and investments serve a dual purpose. They will help revitalize GM's core business, but they also contribute new sources of earnings and provide some countercyclical balance to the mature auto industry. 'Eventually, more mature companies must renew themselves,' McDonald says. 'Usually, this is brought on by severe competitive pressures—or by the insight of an unusual leader.'

In GM's case, it appears to be a little of both—intense competition from the Japanese auto industry and Smith's odd but effective mode of leadership. 'It's really fun to come to work because you're not quite sure what you'll read in the papers the next day,' says Saturn President Hoglund, whose urbane good humour contrasts markedly with his chairman's usual demeanour.

It's also increasingly difficult for GM managers to predict who will attend a meeting or join them on a speakers' programme. GM Vice Chairman Howard H. Kehrl recalls being mildly chided by a union member during what he thought was supposed to be a closed-door management review of Saturn. Today, Smith and

Hoglund share the blue-and-white stand with two others, both dressed in conservative business suits. One is the babyfaced governor of Michigan, James Blanchard. The other is Donald Ephlin, a United Auto Workers (UAW) vice president and head of its GM department.

'Roger Smith and I were just talking,' Governor Blanchard tells the crowd, 'and I said that the chairman of GM couldn't have shared a platform with a UAW leader 20 years ago. He replies, "We couldn't have done it five years ago".' For a moment, the sweet breeze of change seems to be blowing through Detroit.

Nonetheless, the nagging question remains whether Smith can rally his troops for the 'mountain of hard work' that he admits lies ahead. In fact, the months following Smith's election as chairman in 1981 are memorable mainly for his gaffes. He offended most of the automotive press corps with impatient answers. More importantly, he torpedoed his own concession-bargaining effort with the UAW by awarding large executive bonuses during the negotiations. After one particularly agonizing sequence of newspaper reports, the now-worshipful Hoglund, then head of GM's Pontiac division, was moved to remark in an interview, 'It may be time we selected a different type (of executive) for chairman.'

Some claim that Smith has grown into his position. But later today he snaps testily at a veteran reporter who asks about quality problems that have slowed production at one GM plant: 'Now, you've been around this business long enough to know that you don't start a new model down the line at 60 (units) an hour!'

Further, his abrasive personal style is not saved solely for outsiders. GM insiders say Smith recently became so enraged over the resignation of a key senior manager that he stormed out of a meeting in mid-agenda, delaying a number of promotions. And when asked what GM is doing to help middle managers over the confusion caused by the reorganization, he flatly denies such a problem exists: 'I don't know anybody that's confused,' he is quoted as retorting.

On Wall Street, more than one analyst now questions Smith's financial wisdom as well. Although GM earned net income of $517 million in the third quarter, the profits came from its finance subsidiary, tax credits and foreign exchange. It lost money on car operations.

GM's gross margins have dwindled to some 16 per cent, down from 18.9 per cent in 1978. Even Anne Knight, auto analyst at Paine Webber Inc. and generally pro-GM, figures net margins for all of 1985 will be a slim 3.9 per cent down from 5.5 per cent in 1978 and 5.4 per cent [in 1984].

In addition, earnings per share shrunk under $11 in the most recent 12 months, down from $14.22 in fiscal 1984. Most analysts revised their earnings estimates downward several times [in 1985], with most putting their forecasts in the $12 range compared with a typical forecast of over $14 jut six months ago. Drexel Burnham Lambert Inc. auto analyst David Healy's most recent published forecast put GM's 1986 earnings at a dismal $9.75 to $10.00.

'Because of corporate reorganization, acquisitions, heavy new-model, plant-conversion and engineering expenses, GM's costs look out of control,' Healy warns. It's not clear yet how much of the damage is temporary, how much permanent. Indeed, while most Wall Street analysts believe that GM is a sound, well-managed company in the long run, there is an increasing number of detractors who question Smith's resolve to get the corporation's costs under control and rebuild profits. One analyst estimates that stockholders are paying about $9 per share for high-tech acquisitions.

That, of course, is the risk that Roger Smith is taking. In time, he hopes, the investments will pay off. And, in any case, for GM to prosper in the emerging world auto market, some bold move was required. Over the years GM had increasingly centralized portions of the car business. Component systems required to meet US safety exhaust-emission and fuel-economy standards were created by project centres rather than by the operating divisions. Moreover, Fisher Body Division and General Motors Assembly Division (GMAD) had become centralized and unwieldy body-stamping and assembly operations separated from the business of selling cars.

The reorganization wiped that out in one stroke. Moreover, the two 'super groups' were freed to create their own management systems. Under the cerebral Lloyd Reuss, the CPC group opted for a highly centralized organization which he hopes to make flexible via a massive training programme in the techniques and virtues of matrix-style management.

In stark contrast Buick-Oldsmobile-Cadillac (B-O-C) group, led by the more freewheeling Robert C. Stempel, has emerged as a decentralized operation. Each B-O-C product programme is organized as an independent business unit with everything from engineering to financial and manufacturing responsibility. And Saturn—which reports through CPC—is following a similarly decentralized path, creating business units to handle each major component development programme. Saturn is taking the concept a step further by assigning some UAW members to its business units in 1985, three years before any of them will actually produce a car.

The point of all this is to institutionalize the process of change. 'It's not change for change's sake.' Kehrl says. 'But if you're not sure, maybe you ought to try it.' But today there are quite a few inside GM who don't want it. In particular, they don't relish the risk-reward style of management and compensation. And while few dare openly criticize the CEO, some are genuinely distraught.

The staccato pace of acquisitions, reorganizations and wholesale staff moves, some say, has been too much to absorb. Just physically relocating the offices of staff affected by the car operation reorganization encountered what insiders describe as a 'facilities gridlock'. Many staff moved, only to find unfinished or unfurnished offices awaiting them. Others were left behind in isolation from their new colleagues. And perhaps most disturbingly, many managers in the all-important technical areas, where GM must regain both competitive product designs and manufacturing costs, complained of confusion over their new responsibilities. 'No one's sure who is responsible for what any more,' one management-level engineer confided.

Indeed, some critics claim that the reorganization was launched with too little advance preparation. 'How is the reorganization going?' B-O-C's Bob Stempel asks rhetorically, laughing: 'It's do-it-yourself management.' Adds Reuss, 'There has been a lot of uneasiness—change is always a little uneasy.'

INNOVATIVE SPIRIT

Stempel and Reuss both obviously take to change well, and have the innovative spirit to create their own new management structures and cultures within each car group. But for others, change is unacceptable. When GM acquired EDS, it moved too fast, they say, and encountered serious problems. For example, GM managers returning from their New Year holiday break found bright orange stickers on all their personal computers and peripherals. Upon inquiry, they learned that EDS had become their owner of record for all GM computers. EDS staff unceremoniously took inventory, leaving their mark behind, while the rest of GM relaxed.

But the worst shock was to those GM employees who suddenly became EDS workers. Two things shocked these troops. The first was the conservative dress and behaviour code imposed by EDS's tough leader, H. Ross Perot. The second was the change from GM's clear-cut salary and benefit programme to EDS's performance-based compensation plan.

Moreover, EDS's style tends to be confrontational, a rarity in GM's mainstream culture. 'We don't believe in confrontation of people,' says Kehrl. 'There will be a confrontation of ideas, but it takes a rare person to see the good in another person's ideas, so it has to be real interchange.'

Predictably, many GM data processors rebelled, the UAW started organizing, and EDS eventually had to back down from its uncompromising posture. In the aftermath, one high-level EDS executive who was prominent in the *brouhaha* went to greener pastures at Ford Motor Company. Insiders speculate that the hard-charging manager left in frustration over GM's belated go-slow policies. Among traditional GM employees who now work for EDS, resentment reportedly smoulders below the calm surface.

To avoid such problems at Hughes Aircraft, Smith's senior management team worked out a new structure. Not only will Hughes Aircraft remain a separate subsidiary, its employees have been told in advance that there will be no change in compensation and benefit programme. There will be no wholesale transfers of Hughes personnel to Detroit or to other GM operations. Moreover, the distance of the arm's-length relationship is extended by making Hughes Aircraft a subsidiary of a subsidiary, albeit one with close ties to GM's fourteenth-floor headquarters building.

This is GM Hughes Electronics. In addition to protecting Hughes's existing staff from culture shock—'We don't want to do anything that will interfere with their high-technology, scientific research culture,' declares Donald J. Atwood, chairman of GM Hughes Electronics. The structure also will insulate traditional GM employees from Hughes. That's important because the other half of GM Hughes is Delco Electronics Corporation, another new subsidiary made up of existing automotive electronics operations within several GM divisions. Learning from its EDS experience, GM also told these employees that their GM compensation and benefit packages would not be affected.

But more than any other Smith move, the Hughes acquisition raises questions about the agglomerate concept. Failing to find any synergism between the electronics systems used in advanced aerospace products and mundane automobiles, many analysts declared this a pure diversification move. In fact, some argue that GM is close to becoming a holding company with a broad portfolio of interests. Adding credence to the theory, GMAC acquired a small mortgage operation and Smith admitted he might consider issuing yet another special class of GMAC stock.

Atwood denied it. In fact, GM and Hughes already were exploring five or six projects they will tackle together. He ticks off the key areas of interest: integrated circuits, multiplexing, communications (especially of technical data) and instrumentation and displays. Moreover, Robert J. Eaton, vice president in charge of the corporate advanced product and manufacturing engineering staff, confirms his interest in Hughes's experience with electronics and systems engineering. 'I already have my eye on one or two systems engineers I want to bring over there from Hughes,' he says.

Indeed, people transfers are becoming a key issue for GM. Like Hughes, Saturn is being very careful about bringing traditional managers and workers alike into its organizaiton. Risk-reward schemes are in the works for both hourly and nonunion employees. A preliminary agreement with the UAW envisions workers earning only 80 per cent as much in hourly wages as the industry average, with bonuses based on performance and profitability to make up the rest.

AN EFFECTIVE FILTER

Although Saturn had not yet worked out the details of the formula it would use for managerial employees, a similar concept would be applied. 'It is a very effective filter' to make sure only 'the right kinds of people join Saturn,' says Eaton, whose staff created the original Saturn project. 'Risk-reward is a filter,that's why we put it in,' adds Reid Rundell, a former Eaton executive and now executive vice president for strategic business planning at Saturn.

But merely letting a hundred flowers bloom in isolation does little to change an organization as large as GM. That's why it was important to reorganize the core car business and institutionalize change. And to move new technologies and cultures around, GM is also relying on a plethora of methods. By creating joint development centres that concentrate on specific projects, technological knowhow can be moved from one group to another, such as from Hughes to Delco.

But GM managers universally agree that the key to spreading the best parts of EDS, Hughes, or Saturn culture will be the movement of people back to the mainline organization. 'Ultimately, the movement of people is the best way to move technology, be it management technology or technical technology,' says

Saturn's Hoglund. 'There will be good cross-fertilization throughout General Motors.'

So what counts in the end is not the fears of some 'strict disciplinarians who want to stay in the same field all their careers', as Reuss puts it. 'Those days are over.' Nor will the ruffled feathers of Detroits pampered press corps tip the scales weighing Roger Smith's contribution to industrial history. Rather it will be how successful he is at giving leadership to a stuffy mature organization trying to regain its former vigour. 'He seems to make our blood run a little bit faster,' Bill Hoglund smoothly declares. 'We're all marching the same way together,' Smith snaps peevishly, 'I can't think of anything I'd change.'

HOW TO KEEP EVERYBODY GUESSING

In rapid-fire succession, Roger Smith has made nine major moves to transform General Motors Corporation from a car company to an 'agglomerate corporation', as one ranking GM executive calls it, since 1981. Others worry that GM is close to becoming a holding company for a portfolio of businesses operating virtually independently of each other. The chronology of change has been relentless:

1981: GM creates a worldwide truck and bus group, for the first time giving a single unit full cradle-to-grave responsibility for all its truck and bus business, a change that later presages a reorganized car operation.

1982: Smith restructures GM's corporate engineering and manufacturing staffs to break down barriers between product engineers and manufacturing engineers.

1983: He stuns the automotive world by creating a joint venture with Japan's Toyota Motor Corporation to produce a small Chevrolet car in GM's idle Fremont, California, plant. The avowed goal: to learn how the Japanese build such good cars at a substantially lower cost.

In the same year, Smith unveils the Saturn project, aimed squarely at beating the Japanese in costs of production and quality. GM further breaks with tradition and brings the UAW into the product-planning phase via a joint study centre.

1984: He launches a sweeping reorganization of the car business into two integrated car groups, each a self-contained business unit including engineering, manufacturing, assembly and marketing. The five existing car divisions become marketing organizations under the two 'super groups'. GM's unwieldy assembly division (GMAD) and Fisher Body Divison are dissolved, their facilities and staffs distributed to the two groups.

1984: GM acquires Electronic Data Systems (EDS) for $2.5 billion. Wall Street quakes, along with Detroit, as Smith reveals his plan to issue a special cl₍ss of GM common stock with dividends based on EDS's performance.

1984: GM also announces equity investments in five machine-vision companies and an artificial intelligence company.

1985: Smith rocks the industry again by announcing that the Saturn project would become Saturn Corporation, yet another consolidated subsidiary. A separate contract would be negotiated with the UAW.

1985: He ends endless speculation in the press about his often-rumoured 'Lulu' of a project by acquiring, for $5 billion, the coveted Hughes Aircraft Corporation. Yet another special brand of GM stock will be issued for GM Hughes Electronics Corporation, a consolidated subsidiary that will include Hughes as well as Delco Electronics Corporation, a new subsidiary created out of parts of GM's existing electronic and electrical components business units.

6   THE DOCTOR DILEMMA
Jeremy Laurance

Consider this paradox. Over the first five years of the present government, spending on the health service rose 17 per cent in real terms. The number of doctors and nurses has risen, and so has the number of patients treated. Yet according to those who work in it, the health service is in crisis. Just about everyone—doctors, nurses, administrators, trade unionists—points to falling standards, inadequate services and poor conditions, and warns that the service is heading for disaster.

This is nothing new. Ever since its creation in 1948, the NHS has been in a state of crisis. One reason, as Enoch Powell pointed out almost 20 years ago in his reflections on his period as Minister of Health, is that those working in the NHS have 'a vested interested in denigration', a phrase quoted approvingly by the Royal Commission on the NHS in 1978. The only way that those working in the service can get more funds is by publicizing its inadequacies and thereby mobilizing public opinion to shame the government into providing more money. Hence, in Powell's words, we see 'the unique spectacle of an undertaking that is run down by everyone engaged in it'.

But why is the crisis so acute now? First, because the government's claimed 17 per cent growth in the five years to 1983–84 is not all it seems. The claim has been closely scrutinized by the all-party Commons Select Committee on Social Services, which concluded that it does not stand up. The problem is that pay and prices in the health service have risen faster than the general rate of inflation. So the real growth in the service has been not 17 per cent but 7.2 per cent. In the hospital service it has been only 4 per cent, because spending has grown more rapidly on the general practitioner service.

Yet demands on the service have been increasing, both because an ageing population requires more medical care, and because of technological advances in treatment (the more that can be done, the more *is* done). The Department of Health and Social Security concedes that real growth in the hospital service of 3.8 per cent over the five-year period was necessary to meet the additional age

Laurance, J. (1984) The Doctor Dilemma, *Management Today*, Dec pp 5155 demand, and another 2.5 per cent to pay for technological advance. That's 6.3 per cent just to stand still. Since the hospital service actually grew by 4 per cent, it has in effect suffered a cut in real terms of almost 0.5 per cent a year below the officially perceived level of need, for each year that the government has been in office. Small wonder that things look so grim to those in the front line.

VAST WHITE ELEPHANTS

But the second reason why the crisis is acute now is that the big spending plans made in the early 1970s, at a time of economic optimism, are proving unaffordable in today's climate of economic pessimism. Brand new hospitals are completed, but remain unopened because there is no money to staff or run them—vast white elephants. The crisis of the NHS, as Rudolph Klein, professor of social administration at Bath University and a noted commentator on the NHS, has written, is a microcosm of the crisis of Britain. Health care standards are international. Doctors and nurses are mobile, so they see what other countries are doing. They see Britain sliding down the scale of provision and they feel deprived. In many ways, the UK performance is wanting by comparison with the US, Germany and Sweden. The country treats a smaller proportion of patients with kidney failure, for example. It turns people away to die who could benefit from kidney machines.

This is not only because the US, Germany and Sweden are wealthier but because they spend a higher proportion of their gross national product on health. If the UK decided to spend as much per head as Sweden, it would have to triple (roughly) the proportion of GNP devoted to the NHS, from around 6 per cent to almost 18 per cent. In fact, according to Klein, it would take much less than that to bring the *standards* nearer to Sweden's—which shows how efficient the British system is. A more sobering point is that a proper comparison for Britain's health service should be with countries in a similar economic position—Spain or Italy—rather than Sweden or West Germany.

It is true that every country in the Western world faces a crisis in health spending. Expenditure in all the EEC countries rose from 4.1 per cent of GNP in 1960 to 7.3 per cent in 1978. In Britain, as long ago as 1956, the Guillebaud committee—set up to inquire into what were then perceived to be the excessive costs of the NHS—pointed out that there would always be a gap between available resources and what could be done in an ideal world. There was no way of defining even an 'adequate service'. Today's high technology becomes tomorrow's routine procedure.

All governments are now making efforts to control their health costs. In 1979, the French put a tithe on doctors and dentists. The Germans, too, have tried to hold down doctors' pay, circumscribe the illnesses for which the govenrment will pay the costs of treatment and restrict the grants for building hospitals to those that comply with the State plan. In the US, analysis of the treatment provided to thousands of patients has enabled Medicare and Medicaid, the main medical insurers, to introduce preset budgets for treating different conditions. If a doctor spends too much on one patient he/she has to save on the next, or the hospital will be out of pocket.

In Britain, because the government not only controls the *payment* for medical services but also controls the *provision* of them owning the facilities and employing the health workers, it is much better placed to control costs than in other countries. This is the chief reason why, surprising as it may seem to some people, the UK has a relatively cheap and efficient service. In France, health costs rose seven times between 1950 an 1977; in Britain only 2.6 times. Even the French admit there is no evidence that our health care is worse than theirs.

But the process of cutting costs is not easy. Those threatened by change—in the big inner city hospitals—are the producers of health care: doctors, nurses, porters and so on, who are well-organized, powerful lobbies for the status quo. Those who might benefit from change are the potential consumers—in other parts of the country which have been historically underfunded—or those needing the less glamorous specialities like psychiatry and geriatrics. They are not organized; often they are not even identifiable.

Yet despite the cheapness of the NHS, there *is* still scope for saving. This comes on the best authority, from the regional administrators of the NHS. Talking to the 1978 Royal Commission, they said:

> The NHS has become accustomed . . . to the prospect of continual growth in the financial resources available to it. Though agreeable, the result has been to allow slack management, with no incentive to examine obsolete patterns of spending, or to develop a coherent pattern for the future.

'Efficiency savings' and 'improved management' have thus become buzz phrases for the present government. It is seeking them, first, by privatization: that is, by opening up the NHS to competition from the private sector for the provision of all manner of services, from laundry to catering, and maybe later even some medical and surgical services. But, second, and of more significance to the future shape and style of the NHS, it is proposing a major change in the way the service is run.

At the beginning of 1982, Norman Fowler, secretary of state for social services, asked a small group of experienced businessmen and a trade unionist, under the chairmanship of Roy Griffiths, managing director of J. Sainsbury, to see how the NHS might be made more efficient. The terms of reference of the Griffiths inquiry were almost identical with those of the royal commission four years earlier. Yet its members were given only a few months to complete their work, which they did in October 1983. In June 1984, after a period of consultation, Norman Fowler announced that general managers would be appointed at all levels of the service, as recommended by Griffiths, from the individual hospital right up to the top of the hierarchy: general manager of the NHS. They planned for the new appointments to be made by the end of 1985.

'THE HEIGHT OF FOLLY'

In following Griffiths's proposals, Fowler is flying in the face of the British Medical Association (BMA), the Royal College of Nursing, the National Association of Health Authorities and the TUC. The Commons Select Committee on Social

Services described the plan to introduce managers at hospital level as 'the height of folly', because hospitals are still trying to sort themselves out after the last NHS reorganization in 1982, when one tier of administration—the area health authorities—was removed. Fowler may be taking a dangerous gamble.

Interestingly, the reaction has gradually hardened over the months. When the Griffiths report was published, it received a tentative welcome from most quarters, hostility gradually building up as the implications sank in. The reason appears to be that while there is a good measure of agreement over Griffiths's *diagnosis* of the NHS's ills, the *treatment* he recommends is thought more likely to kill the patient than to cure it.

The main problem with running the NHS, according to Griffiths, is precisely that there is not anyone doing it. The doctors spend the money, but they have no responsibility for, and often no awareness of, their budgets. On the other hand, the administrators who control the budgets have no authority over their medical and nursing colleagues. The policy has been to provide the medical staff with resources and let them get on with it. Guaranteeing them their clinical freedom is said to ensure that every patient gets the treatment he or she needs—the fundamental aim of the NHS.

But in the real world, things do not quite work this way. The result of the system of free clinical enterprise is that the NHS has grown less according to need, more according to the political clout of those who work in it. This has led to inequalities between regions (and hence widely varying waiting lists) and inequalities between specialities (psychiatry, geriatrics and community medicine come a poor second in an increasingly fierce scramble for resources).

If you need a hip operation in Solihull, for instance, you will have to wait years longer, in pain, than elsewhere in the country. The waiting list for gynaecological operations is measured in days in London, in months in Kidderminster. Coronary bypasses (for heart disease) are performed on 30 patients per million in Birmingham. In London the figure is 160 per million. An article in the medical press suggested recently that there was little point in GPs referring patients for the operation in Birmingham, because the waiting list was so long. Very likely, the risk of dying on the waiting list is now higher than the risk of dying on the operating table.

Equality of access to the NHS—its founding principle—is a myth. It depends on where you live, your age and social class, what you are suffering from and probably also whether you are black, gay, unemployed, alcoholic or otherwise liable to be judged an undesirable. In general, the provision of resources in the NHS varies *inversely* with the need, as Julian Tudor Hart, GP to a poor Welsh community, pointed out more than a dozen years ago. Clinical freedom has been a two-edged sword—helping some people, but depriving others, usually those most deprived already.

It has also led to inefficiency. The NHS has grown by accretion. For instance, a new whole body scanner for diagnosing cancer, installed at the behest of some consultant, makes a whole range of other tests redundant. But too often, instead of replacing them, it is simply added to them.

Sometimes a consultant's enthusiasm can throw a whole hospital into chaos.

When the heart transplant programme started 'out of the blue' at Harefield Hospital in 1980, it caused 'a major panic all round', according to the area medical officer at the time. Special plans for barrier-nursing rooms had to be drawn up, the nurses' rotas changed and the level of staffing in intensive care increased. It changed the way the whole hospital functioned.

The trouble is that there are no brownie points for cooperating with the planners. Very often, the best way for a consultant to get extra resources is to do his/her own thing and enlist public support, so that the health authority is forced to follow. As in so many other areas affected by cuts, the reasonable consultant, who is prepared to sit down with administrators and discuss where the cuts should fall, gets clobbered.

WHO'S IN CHARGE HERE?

As boss of Sainsbury, Roy Griffiths found all this exasperating. He wrote in his report: 'If Florence Nightingale were carrying her lamp through the corridors of the NHS today, she would almost certainly be searching for the people in charge.' In their absence, the service has relied on consensus management. It has to be said that it has served the country pretty well. The UK gets a relatively good standard of care for a lower cost than elsewhere. Management costs are low, too—less than 5 per cent of total health spending, compared with more than 20 per cent in the US, for example.

But Griffiths was unimpressed. The trouble is that there is a tendency in seeking a consensus to take the line of least resistance. As one witness put it to the select committee, a good manager in this context is 'one who can solve problems, pour oil on troubled waters, avoid conflict and keep things quiet'. Decisions are avoided, fudged or delayed.

Griffiths's solution involves a shift of emphasis in favour of management ('a change of culture' was how one health administrator rosily described it). He envisages doctors being more involved in the allocation of resources, being given management budgets and contracting with health authorities to turn out a given amount of work. The best way of achieving this would be to appoint general managers at every level of the service. That would streamline decision-making and lead to better planning and greater efficiency.

Griffiths himself told the select committee that he had come across working party reports full of good ideas which had not been implemented. 'Why not?', he wanted to know. Invariably the answer was: because there was no-one to implement them. The new general managers would fill that gap. They would get things done. There is not much argument that this is an appropriate solution at the top of the NHS. But it is as you come down the hierarchy, through the regional and district health authorities to the individual hospitals, that the idea provokes increasing anxiety.

The select committee voiced the general concern when it observed that:

All the most sensitive possibilities—a restriction on tests or X-rays, a limitation on the time allowed for post-operative recovery—have to be implemented, if not always decided, at the level of the individual hospital. The potential for conflict at this level is greater than at any other.

This potential is bound to increase as pressure continues to grow inexorably on NHS resources.

UNPOPULAR DECISIONS

Paradoxically, Griffiths argued that this was a weakness of consensus management: it is relatively easy to achieve consensus when all you have to decide is how to spend the extra money, rather more difficult when what you have to decide is where to make cuts. But appointing general managers is hardly likely to ease this problem. Imposing unpopular decisions in a climate of competition for resources would be even more difficult for a general manager than for a team based on consensus.

There is a deeper worry. Is a line-management structure appropriate for the NHS? The difficulty is partly that a hospital, unlike a supermarket, is not profit-motivated, deals with patients rather than things and is immense both in size and complexity. But the chief problem is its professional organization. 'A senior consultant,' the select committee noted,

> may be below the lowest level of unit hospital management, but still independent in his use of resources, not accountable to management for his clinical decisions, and earning more than the Secretary of State.

Nurses, radiographers, physiotherapists, among various others, are similarly independent, responsible to their own profession and making their own, often separate, contribution to patient care. It is hard to see how a line-management structure will cope with this fierce professional diversity.

In short, Griffiths's critics—Sir Alec Merrison, chairman of the royal commission on the NHS, among them—argue that his approach lacks subtlety. A better way of sharpening up consensus management, suggests the select committee, might be to place greater emphasis on the role of chairman, to end the right of each team member to exercise any sort of veto and any right of appeal to the health authority (which they currently enjoy) and to streamline management teams. Indeed, without such reforms, without a change in the whole 'management culture', the general manager will in any case be effectively stymied.

And there's the rub. As two academics from the Nuffield Centre in Leeds have put it:

> Too many people would be in a position to sabotage decisions for the general manager ever to feel secure and comfortable. At the same time, he would be the scapegoat for whatever goes wrong. The Griffiths report says much about responsibility, but nothing about power or authority.

The attitude of the doctors would make or break the thrust of the report, they pointed out with some justification.

And here, in the end, is the key to improving the efficiency of the NHS. It is the doctors who spend the lion's share of the available resources. The overall message coming from all the management inquiries, clinical budgeting experiments and performance reviews now going on in the NHS is the same: the need for a long-term effort to get doctors to look at what they do. It involves a fundamental change in the way they think about their work. But in the end there is no choice: it will have to come.

PART 2
THE CHALLENGE OF CHANGE

The chapters in this part provide a starting point to the theories and concepts which underpin the approaches to the management of change presented in the course as a whole. Thus the paper by Tom Lupton on 'top-down' or 'bottom-up' management, first published in 1971, provides an introduction to some thinking which, at the time, was quite radical. It would be possible to caricature management-thinking in the postwar period as being much concerned with differentials between 'them' and 'us' being concerned with motivation of 'the men/women' or 'the work force'. Lupton's paper clearly poses the question about the nature of the required relationship between the senior and most junior members of any organization if organizational change is to be made successfully. These brief observations made in 1971 may be seen as a way of opening the arguments which have been expanded and refined in much of the more recent work in this area. This chapter is complemented by that from Quinn on 'Managing Strategic Change'. It is a more detailed account of the kind of options which managers in organizational settings face when considering the problems of strategic change. Its length and detail should not deter the reader as it provides a useful introduction to the different models which have emerged and developed in recent years.

The Vickers paper has a special place in this section. He challenges the notion of 'problem-solving' as an appropriate model for managing change, and although at first some of the examples appear dated, a second reading reveals that the lessons of experience apply to today's organizations. Vickers tells us that the systemic properties of the organization cannot be denied and should not be ignored. His message is simple but important.

'A Bias for Action' is a much more recent essay providing an insight into styles of management which Peters and Waterman associate with success in their study of American companies. Their message is the importance of flexibility and adaptiveness. Many of their examples are of experiments carried out to test proposed changes within large companies. These small changes often resulted in major new developments spreading out across the corporations.

7 ORGANIZATIONAL CHANGE: 'TOP-DOWN' OR 'BOTTOM-UP' MANAGEMENT?
Tom Lupton

Most significant organizational changes originate with higher management, and are 'pushed through' in one way or another. Resistance from the 'lower levels' is usually expected and plans are made to overcome it. The phrase 'selling the change' is commonly used to describe a process in which management attempts either to convince those affected that they are likely to gain as a result, or promises them that they will be compensated for any loss of job, pay or status. The task of 'pushing through', 'selling', making the promises and handling the administration of the gains or compensations, often falls to the personnel people, especially the administration part.

'TOP-DOWN' MANAGEMENT THE RULE

Whether the change be the introduction of a new product line, a new machine, a new shop-layout, a new payment system, a new sales organization, a new management structure, a merger, a takeover, a movement to a new location or the introduction of consultants, it is invariably managed from the 'top-down'. The argument for doing it that way sounds reasonable. After all, it is said, senior management is going to be held responsible for what happens to the organization—to the shareholders, to the government or whoever else might own the physical assets. It is up to them, in discharging that responsiblity, to see that at the very least the company survives and at the most grows and develops. They must therefore keep an eye on the competitors, the customers, the suppliers, the unions, the state of technical know-how, the government etc. and make what changes they judge necessary to deal with the situation as they see it. If they judge aright (and whether they do so will depend not only on their own wisdom but on how good the information is on which they base their judgements), then to the extent that they are able to carry through the changes, so will the organization be adaptive and survive and grow, and its management be regarded as successful.

Lupton, T. (1971) Organizational change: 'top-down' or 'bottom-up' management?, *Personnel Review*, Autumn, pp 22–28. Reprinted by permission of MCB University Press

So deeply entrenched is the theory and practice of top-down management of change, and so apparently persuasive the argument in support of it, that most prescriptions for the improvement of organizational performance are variations on it; this includes, odd as it may seem to some, the whole of the 'human relations' school of management thought and research.

McGregor, Blake, Likert and others are, like the 'classical' school and the 'scientific managers' before them, concerned to point out that, if organizations are to be efficient, managers must combine technical and formal administrative competence with skill in getting their subordinates to commit themselves to the goals of the organization (or at least to subgoals that are consistent with those general goals). This managerial skill, it is urged, is based on an understanding of, and a sensitivity to, the needs of subordinates and expresses itself in a willingness to listen to what they have to say by way of criticism and suggestions for improvement; and either to act on these or to be prepared to explain patiently why it is impossible or impractical to do so. Commitment may also be won by management if it makes subordinate jobs more interesting, more demanding, more satisfying; or so it is said.

McGregor's Theory Y, Likert's System 4, Blake's 9/9 Management style are all variations on a simple and familiar theme, namely, that high organization efficiency and human enjoyment of work may be brought about by careful attention on the part of 'superordinates' to the needs of subordinates. To put it more formally, we may say that if subordinate behaviour is to be altered in directions that are consistent with the interests and aims of superordinates then the 'style' of the 'boss' must be participative—Theory Y, 9/9, or something similar. When the boss's behaviour moves along the scale from X to Y then the subordinates' attitudes to him/her change and their behaviour then changes for the better.

When top management wants to make changes, therefore—for example, to diversify the product range, to change the technology, to introduce a job-evaluated grading system, *as well as* doing a good professional job of reshaping the organization's relationships with customers and potential customers or a good job of machine design or job evaluation—the people who are to be affected should be told, or listened to or encouraged to take part in discussion: but it is management, in possession of the attitudes and opinions it has solicited in response to the disclosure of its plans, who decree what is to be changed and how.

The case for top-down management is also argued as follows. Organizations are hierarchical in form. They usually award established competence with higher pay and status. By definition, then, those at the top are more competent than those at the bottom, as well as being more accountable and more responsible. The combination of competence and responsibility is sufficient on this argument, to confer upon management its right to manage; this is the so-called managerial prerogative. By the same token, those who have not become managers have no right to manage. They have other rights, of course: they can, for example, bargain individually and collectively about their terms and conditions of employment. But they have no rights, unless management specifically grants them, to decide what the organization ought to be doing, and how it ought to be doing it. The most that will be allowed is the right to have an opinion about these matters and an opportunity to express it.

MANAGERIAL PREROGATIVE

The notion of organization as a hierarchy dies hard, as does the associated idea of managerial prerogative, ill though these notions seem to have served. Managerial prerogative I take to imply the formal exclusion from decision-making about the disposal of an organization's assets, of any save those named as managers by the owners of the company, or by boards of directors who act on the owner's behalf. The manager's problem is therefore usually stated to be how to preserve managerial prerogatives from too much encroachment by workers, while at the same time motivating those same workers to commit themselves wholeheartedly to the aims of the organization defined by managers.

In fact, workers do a lot of managing on their own account and their behaviour also influences the way managers manage, whether the managers like it or not. The literature on 'restriction of output', not to mention the experience of generations of managers, is replete with examples. Groups of workers are reported to have established a relationship between the effort they put in and the rewards they receive that seems to them fair. They maintain that relationship by controlling the behaviour of individuals through reward and punishment. The work group emerges, in these reports, as a small society, maintaining its identity by transactions with the management system 'outside', and by controlling behaviour 'inside'. In societies such as these, the worker often finds satisfactions that would otherwise be missing from his/her job, satisfactions that arise from having controlled to some extent the social environment and having achieved in the process a bit of 'do it yourself' job-enlargement and job-enrichment.

For at least 60 years this kind of thing has been labelled *limitation* or *restriction* of output, by managers and social scientists alike. The label and the fact that it has persisted indicate a deeply entrenched belief that, somehow, if the workers could be persuaded to stop trying to control things (and succeeding) and to leave it to management, then everything would be done a great deal more efficiently and the workers themselves would be better off. Of course, it is possible for workers to leave decisions in the hands of management and simply to provide information to aid management in making intelligent decisions, on which they will comment and make suggestions: this is what I take the 'human relations' theorists to be recommending.

Human Relations Position

The 'human relations' position is logically very similar to that of the industrial engineer of the old school. Indeed to this day some work-study engineers maintain that if only workers would allow the engineer to plan their work down to the last detail, to set a standard of performance for them and put a cash value on it, then everyone would benefit. For it is argued that the work-study engineer has a set of skills in the observation, measurement and evaluation of work that the worker does not have. Similarly, managers who wish to manage according to the precepts of 'behavioural science' will work with theoretical knowledge of human emotions and thought processes and procedures for influencing behaviour beyond that *formally* in the possession of the worker. The object in both cases is to use these skills as a way of buttressing the prerogatives of management to influence worker behaviour, 'We know more than you, therefore . . .', and in consequence to move those workers to behave in ways that serve the ends of the organization as defined by management.

These considerations apply not only to managers and workers but to any relationship of superordinate-subordinate, except that both the super- and subordinate managers share the prerogative to manage which is formally denied to workers. This is why management by objectives (MBO), which is a method for combining hierarchy and participation, has not been widely applied, to my knowledge, to the first-line supervisor-worker relationship. It would be considered inappropriate in any situation where managers are jealous of their prerogatives. Yet, if managers were to abandon the idea of prerogative, there is no other obstacle that I know of that would prevent a supervisor drawing a worker into systematic periodical discussions of his/her performance, pointing out strengths and weaknesses, indicating areas for improvement and asking the worker to propose reasonable targets for performance on a range of jobs that he/she is likely to do over the next period. If all that were combined with a procedure for systematic promotion and pay appraisal, the whole business would look very much like MBO.

COMPETENCES OF THE UNDERDOG

My contention is *not* that workers are always right and managers always wrong. My own attempts to assist managers to make organizational changes often rest on a diagnosis different from the one those managers usually make. This often leads managers to level the charge of partisanship. That they should do so is understandable. The idea that anyone should hold strongly—as I do—to the view that restriction of output and other such activities, which are clearly a worry to the manager and a seeming reflection on his/her professional competence, are matters for investigation and understanding and intelligent action, rather than *a priori* condemnation, seems to place him/her 'in the other camp'.

As an ex-underdog with long service in that role I start with sympathy for the underdog, but it is logic rather than just sympathy that leads me to the position I shall take up. My position is briefly this (I shall examine what it means for organizational change presently): to become a manager does not automatically confer wisdom greater than that found amongst people who are not, and are never likely to become, managers. A manager might be taught to be, or learn to be, wise about some specialized matters, but he/she cannot be wise about all things all the time; he/she is bound to be considerably less knowledgeable and less wise about the jobs of some of his/her subordinates than they are.

While it is no doubt true that some promoted (or placed) in management are competent in some matters that some workers will never be competent in, this is not the same as saying that all managers are more competent in all things than their subordinates. Indeed, as organizations increase in size and administration and technical complexity, it becomes increasingly difficult for any manager to get a detailed grasp of what is going on, let alone laying legitimate claim to know more about all that is going on than those who are doing a job, whoever they may be. For example. it is simply impossible for a senior manager of an engineering company to have a working day-to-day knowledge of the organization of the whole of the company's production facilities, in the sense that the foremen in each department have, or those who operate machines or carry out assembly work. Such a manager would point out, no doubt with justification, that it would be ridiculous to expect him/her to have that kind of detailed knowledge. But it is difficult to see how he/she could claim to work intelligently in his/her own and the company's interest without easy *access to* such knowledge.

This knowledge is, however, only accessible if those in possession of it are willing to supply it and can see good reason for doing so. If workers perceive that the management's attempts to gain knowledge that they, the workers, have and can use by, for example, introducing participative and consultative procedures, then they will surely refuse to cooperate. What seems surprising is that workers have so often responded to managers' overtures to participate on the managers' terms; that they have been willing to answer the questions of attitude surveyors who are seeking to organize their several opinions, beliefs, and hard knowledge of facts, for the use of management. This could be explained, possibly, by claiming that there are no differences at all between the interests of management and those of workers; only misunderstanding which could be cleared up were the true facts known. Or, one might say that these are real conflicts of interest which are not clearly perceived, or take the view that workers are generous, or sentimental, or ignorant, or disinterested or possibly naïve. Despite all the academic writing and talk about organizations as plural societies, about conflict theory and open-system contingency approaches,[1] the 'misunderstanding' view prevails. The phrase 'it is all a matter of good communications' expresses that view well—'it', in this context, being organizational efficiency and personal satisfaction with work. 'Good communications' ensures them, 'bad communications' do not.

REASONS FOR PROCEEDING

If setting the project up is so risky and difficult, why bother? There are a number of reasons. In the first place, the young have rising expectations; not only expectations of rising material affluence but expectations of an improving quality of life and personal relationships, and meaningful intervention in affairs. These expectations are not confined to the young, either, although it is the young who articulate them best. A response from management which seeks skilfully to manipulate behaviour via participative procedures, consultative machinery, good communications and the like and, in doing so, offers the shadow of involvement rather than the substance, leaving the real control very much where it is already, will not for long be acceptable. Nor will the workers easily settle for the use of a social science-based technology, such as the attitude survey, which makes them merely a source of information with which others may decide what the quality of their working environment will be. Even the most sophisticated forms of paternalism have a limited life-span.

Second, unless men and women can see an opportunity to offer freely, and without fear of the consequences, more of their talents and an opportunity to negotiate the rewards directly with the organization, then the talents will not be on offer and the organization will lose them. It is, however, likely to keep the apathetic persons. To 'invest in people' (that much-abused phrase) means to create an environment in which this freedom and security really exists. The task of management is surely to learn how to work jointly with subordinates, to create such environments, to facilitate, to support, to elicit feedback, to inform and be informed, to involve and to be involved, to listen and, in doing so, to encourage people not only to offer the talents they have but to discover unsuspected talents and opportunities to develop and use them.

Third, the pace of organizational change is speeding up. This is so obvious that it is almost a standard topic for the opening speech at management conferences— 'ladies and gentlemen, we live in times of dynamic change', and so on. The theme is popular, but the understanding of what it involves goes mostly uncomprehended. It is not generally realized that organizations must become increasingly flexible and responsive. Modern technology sometimes (but not always), however, requires a large organization. Given the evident fear that these might get out of the control of the people who own and manage, the latter introduce tight formal organization structures and control procedures. These, in turn, tend to induce the apathetic 'I won't do more than I have to' attitude, the empire-building, the sub-optimization and the rat-racing, which characterize large-scale bureaucracy and the 'resistance to change' it exhibits. This kind of organization is likely to be anything but flexible and adaptive, because its structure places a premium on defensive, play-safe, untrusting people. It is not as if people are inherently defensive, it is the organization that makes them so. A commonly suggested, and sometimes adopted, 'solution' to this problem is to ensure continuing control from the top by making the big organization into a number of smaller ones, giving the managers of the little organizations rope enough either to hang themselves or to pull themselves to safety. This is clearly no solution unless the 'little' manager is willing to take big risks, which is unlikely. We shall have to find a way of building flexibility in organizations from the bottom up. Clearly, to do it from the top down only makes sense if one redefines the role of the 'top' to make it the 'centre' and assigns it a facilitating, supporting, resource-procuring, encouraging role; a role it will not recognize or accept unless a ferment from the bottom makes it imperative.

Fourth, and finally, the increasing complexity of modern technology and the problems of sociotechnical system design that brings (as the jargon puts it) require a rare talent from those managers who work close to the technology. They have not only to manage that technology and the people who man it effectively but to relate to those who work with customers, suppliers, universities, banks and governments; and the last need the talent to work equally effectively with them. Traditional structures of control of the manufacturing processes, as well as traditional methods of designing management structures and coordinating the behaviour of machines, processes and people are likely to prove more and more inadequate to the task of large complex organizations or even small complex ones. Increasingly, the packaged general solution to these problems will have to be abandoned for a method of diagnosing just how flexible, how adaptable, a particular organization (or different parts of it) needs to be, to cope with its environment and its technology of manufacture or service. Which, once again, calls for detailed knowledge and the collaboration of everybody who knows anything that is relevant or can contribute anything that is necessary.

STEPS IN THE CHANGE TO BOTTOM-UP MANAGEMENT

The process of working towards the design of an organization that is sufficiently flexible and adaptable to cope more effectively with its problems (or at least, for finding out whether an organization is or is not flexible and adaptive enough, and what kinds of behaviour might best be encouraged or maintained) can only begin from the 'bottom'—or the 'periphery'—starting with the multidiscipline-change programme already described. The steps that must come after the project team has embarked upon its diagnosis are these:

1. Once an acceptable (to those in it) detailed picture of the functioning of a department, in all its related aspects, has been built up work should begin on a programme for change and a method for monitoring progress. Unless this process and the monitoring method are joint in the fullest sense, namely that everyone who works in the unit is to some extent involved, not only in talking and being talked to but committed to action, then there is little point in continuing. This step is likely to be a lengthy one, simply because the investigators have to work out a common diagnostic framework and, while doing so, develop into a cohesive team. They also have to obtain access to information. This entails the patient establishment of close and friendly relations with the managers, the supervisors and workers in the unit, in an atmosphere where there is bound to be some doubt about the credibility of the project team, probably much scepticism, certainly anxiety, possibly fear and intermittent and impatient nostalgia for the familiar and the conventional.

2. Any action programme that emerges from such a process will probably call for the removal of some of the constraining influences residing in the existing system of managerial policy-making and control. This demand will almost certainly be taken as direct or implied criticism by some superordinate managers. However good the preparation for the reception of such an action programme (and senior management must be thoroughly prepared), there will probably be some resentment, misunderstanding and difficulty in personal relations. Any action programme is also likely to call to the centre resources of cash, of human expertise and physical resources. This is the time when the investigating team and the managers of the unit have to turn outwards for support for what they think they can achieve,

rather than for direction as to what they have to do. The exercise could very well falter seriously at this point, affecting the morale of the team to the point where individuals may wish to return to their old jobs or seek promotion elsewhere in the company. But since the action programme will, among other things, probably show that there will be cost-savings of the conventional kind, sanction to go ahead will probably be forthcoming.

3.   During steps 2 and 3, the aims and methods of the investigating team will have been publicized throughout the organization, so that the ground is prepared for stage 3. This involves taking individual members of the project team to start similar teams in other locations in the company. Some new project members will meanwhile have been recruited and trained in the use of the diagnostic framework used by the team, as well as in its methods of working with managers and workers in the new site in the work of designing programmes for change. Some members of the team will remain behind in the original site to see the action programme through to the point where they will become redundant.

4.   As the scheme gathers momentum, a whole new set of problems will emerge. Clearly, while the move towards a new work-culture has been going its own way in one corner of the company, everything has been going on as it always did in other corners. There will have been negotiations with the unions, work-study investigations, process changes, new products, reorganizations, and so on. But the new work-culture will want to alter the way the old 'agents of change' work, and the way their activities are coordinated and brought into the new scheme of things. It is likely at this stage that some established group, like the personnel managers or the industrial engineers, will make a takeover bid for the programme, on the grounds that it properly belongs with them. They will claim that they would have done it anyway given the opportunity and that, now the time has come for action on a broad front, some high-powered organization controlled from the top is needed so that the whole thing does not get out of control. Now the task for the project team is to study senior management organization and work out with senior management a programme to change it into a small facilitative 'centre' of the organization. The problems of making such a change are obvious and cunning resistance might be expected. However, there must be those in senior management who are inclined to support the programme fully, otherwise it would never have started in the first place.

By a process of diffusion then, or cell division, a new working structure with its own working culture will evolve to replace the old. I have called the old 'top-down' and the new 'bottom-up' management. Perhaps the new mode is better described as 'periphery centre' management, because the emphasis is not on hierarchy but on function. An advantage of the new culture is that it will be flexible and quick in organizational response to environmental change. Also part of the task of everybody is now organizational and personal development, and everybody is now a manager, in the sense of being in a position *legitimately* to influence events, with probably a much larger area of decision than before.

The Result Is No Utopia

Any organization that evolves along these lines is likely to look very unlike Utopia, free of conflict and manned with paragons of virtue at every point. There will still be conflicts about rewards for work done, about access to more responsible better paid positions, and even about what responsibility may now be taken to mean. There will still be specialists whose knowledge has to be used, problems about where they fit and probably some uncooperative individuals. But the hierarchical principle will be much less dominant, as will the attitudes and self-images that are characteristic of those who cherish hierarchy.

One would expect, however, that in a culture that places high priority on problem-recognition, problem-solving and the utilization of competences without regard to hierarchy and traditional prerogative, ways will be found to uncover the likely sources of conflict. And because it is a culture that does not wish problems away, it will probably create effective procedures for solving them.

There are a handful of organizations in the world that are moving in the directions indicated in this chapter, each in their own way, and each in response to different kinds of problems. There are many more however who are working with ready-made packages of one kind or another to get over hurdles as they are perceived by top management. They will soon begin to look old-fashioned.

So, when senior managers holding this view think about change, they tend to assume—partly for want of access to knowledge about their organization, partly for want of a view of organization as an open sociotechnical system,[2] that subordinate people would want to participate in the changes the superordinates want to make, if only they understood why it was so necessary to make them. The choice for managers with this outlook is either to push the change through without seeking to promote understanding, on the grounds that time is short and represents cash; or to seek to promote understanding and collaboration by initiating participation and communication, at great expense, sometimes successfully. Often, though, management gets little result from such efforts.

BOTTOM-UP CHANGE

The theory of top-down management is inadequate, and the practice based upon it inappropriate to the organizations of industrial societies. This is so whether the theory and practice takes the 'classical form', the 'scientific management' form or the 'behavioural science' form. I personally find all variants of the top-down position distasteful. They betray a certain arrogance, where I would prefer humility on grounds both of morals and expediency, and they reflect a view of organization structure and functioning that is an obstacle to understanding what goes on in the world.

'Bottom-up' management is rarely seen. When I refer to it I do *not* have in mind a kind of Utopian 'workers control', nor am I advocating the seizure of the means of production by revolutionary workers, nor workers' councils; nothing like that. Instead, I shall suggest a practical programme which could be started now in any organization, whatever its location or pattern of ownership. Such a programme ought to improve the use of the individual talents at the organization's disposal, heighten cooperation, improve the handling of conflict and make the organization more adaptive.

Most existing organizations draw a fairly sharp line between the managers and the operators (blue collar) and also between managers and routine clerical and administrative workers (white collar); planners, coordinators, controllers and supervisors are in one camp, and 'doers' in the other. Having drawn the distinction, you might expect that the doers will mostly accept it as natural and do what they can to improve their position within the framework that is set. So, somewhat paradoxically perhaps, the move towards bottom-up management must start with a slight push from the top. The push must take the form of releasing some skilled managerial manpower from its job of running the business in traditional ways in order to take on the task of seeking understanding of how the business runs.

The Type of Team Needed

Let us assume that the team requires six people, young, lively, well-trained, ambitious people, who are drawn from specialist activities but who are willing to work with other specialists within a broader multidiscipline framework. These could include, for instance, a person from marketing, one from management sciences, one from research and development, one from personnel and/or industrial relations and one from production, with perhaps a social researcher recruited either from inside or outside the organization. The last one would provide a link to sources of knowledge of organization structure and functioning, in other organizations and in universities, research institutes and the like, as well as being a source of skills in team-building, training, interviewing, and so on.

The chief task of this collection of individuals is to seek understanding of the reasons why things happen in a particular way in the organization. They will not, in the first instance, be expected to say how things ought to be improved. This is *not* another project team to solve problems that someone else has already defined, like 'get the labour turnover down', or 'tighten up the slack standards' or 'get rid of the demoralized payments system' or 'improve the quality'. The object is just to find out in detail, as a first step, what is happening and why it is happening in that particular way. And, while they are doing the job, the collection of individuals must become a team, developing ways of using the expertise of its members and of the rest of the organization, and a common framework for research and diagnosis. Top management must avoid appointing a boss who has 'terms of reference', and is 'held accountable'—such as for reducing costs in a given period, by a given amount. Its only requirement should be that, within a given period (say 6–9 months) it will, in its own way, present to top management what it has been doing, how it set about doing it and what discoveries it has been making.

Such a small group would not be expected to have studied the whole organization in six months. It must start in a small manageable sector of the organization, drawing the managers and supervisors of that unit into its discussions, winning their confidence, smoothing their anxieties. But most of all it must go to the doers—those 'in the other camp'—and involve them fully in the investigation by asking them to put their knowledge, their skills and their experience at the disposal of the team. My experience is that, as might be expected, the task is difficult, time-consuming, sometimes nerve-racking; but entirely possible, given patience, honesty, forbearance and humility. It is certainly absolutely worthwhile.

Workers Will Question

But consider for a moment what is involved. Workers are being asked to collaborate in a venture which is, in the long run, expected to improve the organization's effectiveness and its attractiveness as a place to work, without any guarantee whatever that this will in fact happen, or that their pay and job security will be improved. They are bound to ask questions, such as

Is this a productivity bargain?
What do we get if we suggest ways to reduce costs?
What is the standing of the investigating team?
Are they empowered to make promises, give guarantees, or what?
Who's their boss?
Are they the bosses of our manager and supervisors or not?
How does this investigation differ from the hundreds of head office investigations—technical, work study and so on—that have been carried out here before?

These questions have to be honestly answered.

Risks for the Team Members

The members of the team are being asked to undertake a venture, which is risky for them. It is risky for the career of those who join the team. They will leave the 'normal' career ladder, be expected to work hard to acquire new skills in an atmosphere of great uncertainty, when these new skills will be unrecognizable for a long time as useful to the organization by senior management. Moreover, there is the possibility of failure to produce a diagnosis of the structure and functions of the unit under investigation that will be recognized as superior to any diagnosis that a technical specialist might make. The technical specialists are likely to be somewhat sceptical, even hostile, to attempts to show that a multidiscipline team, using inputs from social science, as well as from established functional specialisms, can do better than them all added together. Especially as the specialists will be able to point to the improvements that have come about in the past as a result of the application of their skills.

Senior Management's Attitudes

The main risk, however, lies in the attitudes and beliefs of senior management. They are likely to hold the view that running a business is a matter of top management getting the best possible advice from its own specialists, acting decisively and then relying on junior management to see that the lower orders cooperate.

Senior managers also tend to rely heavily on formal machinery for communicating their plans and policies to others, whose views they seek so as to incorporate them if they seem useful. They also tend to rely heavily, for their psychological comfort, on the belief that others see them as they see themselves—as rugged, deservedly successful and affluent, but on the whole kindly and well-disposed to the less successful and in favour of all the sound, up-to-date things like good communication, proper bargaining and consultative machinery, business schools, and so on.

Senior management might, however, agree to vote resources to an experiment such as I am suggesting, if they can be persuaded by personnel that they might be missing something to their profit if they completely ignore the findings of social scientists. It will be necessary to overcome their belief that 'people problems' are really something one learns to handle by long experience, not from books or personnel specialists. The obvious must be stressed, namely, that people are a scarce and valuable resource, that the incidence of pay problems, unofficial disputes, low productivity, and the like suggest that the motives behind them are puzzling and might bear examination. Some personnel officers might point out that recent research demonstrates some of the ways in which they are related—the technical, management, market and people parts—and how failure to integrate them might lead to unanticipated competitive, technical or people problems. Therefore, the organization ought to find some framework—probably the open sociotechnical system framework—which the various special functions might accept as a way of integrating their various contributions, and which might develop as a new form of total system diagnosis, leading to action which will effect great improvememnts in the way the organization goes about its tasks.

However much they have been persuaded by reasoned argument or by fear of missing something, senior managers will still tend to see the project as a little woolly. It will be regarded as something to watch in case it gets out of hand and something that can be easily stopped if, for example, cash gets short or if it looks as though the unions are going to try to muscle in. They will almost certainly want to feel that they must appoint someone to take the responsibility for seeing that they get value for money from the exercise, or at least some credit for being bold or experimental; but close surveillance in terms of conventional criteria of success could inhibit the development of a working interdisciplinary team and lead to the fulfilment of all the gloomy prophecies of failure. How much better to play it safe through the formal machinery of management consultation, bargaining and personnel administration, and hold on to managerial prerogative and one's image of oneself, even at the cost of tolerating mediocrity.

REFERENCES

1. For a summary of this work see: Tom Lupton, (1971) *Management and the Social Sciences* Penguin Books, London
2. For a description of what is meant by an open socio-technical system see, for example, A. K. Rice (1963) *The Enterprise and its Environment*, Tavistock Institute, London

8 MANAGING STRATEGIC CHANGE
James Brian Quinn

Previous articles have tried to demonstrate why executives managing strategic change in large organizations should not—and do not—follow highly formalized textbook approaches in long-range planning, goal-generation and strategy formulation. Instead, they artfully blend formal analysis, behavioural techniques and power politics to bring about cohesive, step-by-step movement towards ends which initially are broadly conceived, but which are then constantly refined and reshaped as new information appears. Their integrating methodology can best be described as 'logical incrementalism'.

But is this truly a process in itself, capable of being managed? Or does it simply amount to applied intuition? Are there some conceptual structures, principles or paradigms that are generally useful? Wrapp, Normann, Braybrooke, Lindblom and Bennis provide some macrostructures incorporating many important elements they have observed in strategic change situations. These studies offer important insights into the management of change in large organizations. But my data suggest that top managers in such enterprises develop their major strategies through processes which neither these studies nor more formal approaches to planning adequately explain. Managers *consciously* and *proactively* move forward *incrementally*:

To improve the quality of information utilized in corporate strategic decisions

To cope with the varying lead times, pacing parameters and sequencing needs of the 'subsystems' through which such decisions tend to be made

To deal with the personal resistance and political pressures any important strategic change encounters

To build the organizational awareness, understanding and psychological commitment needed for effective implementation

To decrease the uncertainty surrounding such decisions by allowing for

Quinn, J. B. (1980) Managing strategic change. Reprinted by permission of *Sloan Management Review* Summer Vol. 21 No. 4 pp 3–20 interactive learning between the enterprise and its various impinging environments

To improve the quality of the strategic decisions themselves by: systematically involving those with most specific knowledge; obtaining the participation of those who must carry out the decisions; and avoiding premature momenta or closure which could lead the decision in improper directions

How does one manage the complex incremental processes which can achieve these goals? The following is perhaps the most articulate short statement on how executives proactively manage incrementalism in the development of corporate strategies:

> Typically you start with general concerns, vaguely felt. Next you roll an issue around in your mind till you think you have a conclusion that makes sense for the company. You then go out and sort of post the idea without being too wedded to its details. You then start hearing the arguments pro and con, and some very good refinements of the idea usually emerge. Then you pull the idea in and put some resources together to study it so it can be put forward as more of a formal presentation. You wait for 'stimuli occurrences' or 'crises', and launch pieces of the idea to help in these situations. But they lead toward your ultimate aim. You know where you want to get. You'd like to get there in six months. But it may take three years, or you may not get there. And when you do get there, you don't know whether it was originally your own idea—or somebody else had reached the same conclusion before you and just got you on board for it. You never know. The president would follow the same basic process, but he could drive it much faster than an executive lower in the organization.[1]

Because of differences in organizational form, management style or the content of individual decisions, no single paradigm can hold for all strategic decisions. However, very complex strategic decisions in my sample of large organizations tended to evoke certain kinds of broad process steps. These are briefly outlined. While these process steps occur generally in the order presented, stages are by no means orderly or discrete. Executives do consciously manage individual steps proactively, but it is doubtful that any one person guides a major strategic change sequentially through all the steps. Developing most strategies requires numerous loops back to earlier stages as unexpected issues or new data dictate. Or decision times can become compressed and require short-circuiting leaps forward as crises occur. Nevertheless, certain patterns are clearly dominant in the successful management of strategic change in large organizations.

CREATING AWARENESS AND COMMITMENT— INCREMENTALLY

Although many of the sample companies had elaborate formal environmental scanning procedures, most major strategic issues first emerged in vague or undefined terms, such as 'organizational overlap', 'product proliferation', 'excessive exposure in one market' or 'lack of focus and motivation'. Some appeared as 'inconsistencies' in internal action patterns of 'anomalies' between the enterprise's current posture and some perception of its future environment. Early signals may come from anywhere and may be difficult to distinguish from the background 'noise' or ordinary communications. Crises, of course, announce themselves with strident urgency in operations-control systems. But, if organizations wait until signals reach amplitudes high enough to be sensed by formal measurement systems, smooth, efficient transitions may be impossible.

Need-sensing: Leading the Formal Information System

Effective change managers actively develop informal networks to get objective information—from other staff and line executives, workers, customers, board members, suppliers, politicians, technologists, educators, outside professionals, government groups and so on—to sense possible needs for change. They purposely use these networks to short-circuit all the careful screens their organizations build up to 'tell the top only what it wants to hear'. For example:

> Peter McColough, chairman and CEO of Xerox, was active in many high-level political and charitable activities—from treasurer of the Democratic National Committee to chairman of the Urban League. In addition, he said, 'I've tried to decentralize decision-making. If something bothers me, I don't rely on reports or what other executives may want to tell me. I'll go down very deep into the organization, to certain issues and people, so I'll have a feeling for what they think.' He refused to le this life be run by letters and memos. 'Because I came up by that route, I know what a salesman can say. I also know that before I see . . . [memos] they go through fifteen hands, and I know what that can do to them.[2]

To avoid undercutting intermediate managers, such bypassing has to be limited to information-gathering, with no implication that orders or approvals are given to lower levels. Properly handled, this practice actually improves formal communications and motivational systems as well. Line managers are less tempted to screen information and lower levels are flattered to be able 'to talk about the very top'. Since people sift signals about threats and opportunities through perceptual screens defined by their own values, careful executives make sure their sensing networks include people who look at the world very differently than do those in the enterprise's dominating culture. Effective executives consciously seek options and threat signals beyond the *status quo*. 'If I'm not two to three years ahead of my organization, I'm not doing my job' was a common comment of such executives in the sample.

Amplifying Understanding and Awareness

In some cases executives quickly perceive the broad dimensions of needed change. But they still may seek amplifying data, wider executive understanding of issues or greater organizational support before initiating action. Far from accepting the first satisfactory (satisfying) solution—as some have suggested they do—successful managers seem consciously to generate and consider a broad array of alternatives. Why? They want to stimulate and choose from the most creative solutions offered by the best minds in their organizations. They wish to have colleagues knowledgeable enough about issues to help them think through all the ramifications. They seek data and arguments sufficiently strong to dislodge preconceived ideas or blindly followed past practices. They do not want to be the prime supporters of losing ideas or to have their organizations slavishly adopt 'the boss's solution'. Nor do they want—through announcing decisions too early—to threaten prematurely existing power centres which could kill any changes aborning.

Even when executives do not have in mind specific solutions to emerging problems, they can still proactively guide actions in intuitively desired directions—by defining what issues staffs should investigate, by selecting principal investigators and by controlling reporting processes. They can selectively 'tap the collective wit' of their organizations, generating more awareness of critical issues and forcing initial thinking down to lower levels to achieve greater involvement. Yet they can also avoid irreconcilable opposition, emotional overcommitment or organizational momenta beyond their control by regarding all proposals as 'strictly advisory' at this early stage.

As issues are clarified and options are narrowed, executives may systematically alert ever wider audiences. They may first 'shop' key ideas among trusted colleagues to test reponses. Then they may commission a few studies to illuminate emerging alternatives, contingencies or opportunities. But key players might still not be ready to change their past action patterns or even be able to investigate options creatively. Only when persuasive data are in hand and enough people are alerted and 'on board' to make a particular solution work, might key executives finally commit themselves to it. Building awareness, concern and interest to attention-getting levels is often a vital—and slowly achieved—step in the process of managing basic changes. For example:

In the early 1970s there was still a glut in world oil supplies. Nevertheless, analysts in the General Motors Chief Economists's Office began to project a developing US dependency on foreign oil and the likelihood of higher future oil prices. These concerns led the board in 1972 to create an ad hoc energy task force headed by David C. Collier, then treasurer, later head of GM of Canada and then of the Buick Division. Collier's group included people from manufacturing, research, design, finance, industry-government relations, and the economics staff. After six months of research, in May of 1973 the task force went to the board with three conclusions: (1) there was a developing energy problem, (2) the government had no particular plan to deal with it, (3) energy costs would have a profound effect on GM's business. Collier's report created a good deal of discussion around the company in the ensuing months. 'We were trying to get other people to think about the issue,' said Richard C. Gerstenberg, then chairman of GM.[3]

Changing Symbols: Building Credibility

As awareness of the need for change grows, managers often want to signal the organization that certain types of change are coming, even if specific solutions are not in hand. Knowing they cannot communicate directly with the thousands who could carry out the strategy, some executives purposely undertake highly visible actions which wordlessly convey complex messages that could never be communicated as well—or as credibly—in verbal terms. Some use symbolic moves to preview or verify intended changes in direction. At other times, such moves confirm the intention of top management to back a thrust already partially begun—as Mr. McColough's relocation of Xerox headquarters to Connecticut (away from the company's Rochester reprographics base) underscored that company's developing commitment to product diversification, organizational decentralization and international operations. Organizations often need such symbolic moves—or decisions they regard as symbolic—to build credibility behind a new strategy. Without such actions even forceful verbiage might be interpreted as mere rhetoric. For example:

> In GM's downsizing engineers said that one of top management's early decisions affected the credibility of the whole weight-reduction program. 'Initially, we proposed a program using a lot of aluminum and substitute materials to meet the new "mass" targets. But this would have meant a very high cost, and would have strained the suppliers' aluminum capacity. However, when we presented this program to management, they said, "Okay, if necessary, we'll do it." They didn't back down. We began to understand then that they were dead serious. Feeling that the company would spend the money was critical to the success of the entire mass reduction effort.'

Legitimizing New Viewpoints

Often before reaching specific strategic decisions, it is necessary to legitimize new options which have been acknowledged as possibilities, but which still entail an undue aura of uncertainty or concern. Because of their familiarity, older options are usually perceived as having lower risks (or potential costs) than newer alternatives. Therefore, top managers seeking change often consciously create forums and allow slack time for their organizations to talk through threatening issues, work out the implications of new solutions, or gain an improved information base that will permit new options to be evaluated objectively in comparison with more familiar alternatives. In many cases, strategic concepts which are at first strongly resisted gain acceptance and support simply by the passage of time, if executives do not exacerbate hostility by pushing them too fast from the top. For example:

> When Joe Wilson thought Haloid Corporation should change its name to include Xerox, he first submitted a memorandum asking colleagues what they thought of the idea. They rejected it. Wilson then explained his concerns more fully, and his executives rejected the idea again. Finally Wilson formed a com-

mittee headed by Sol Linowitz, who had thought a separate Xerox subsidiary might be the best solution. As this committee deliberated, negotiations were under way with the Rank Organizations and the term Rank-Xerox was commonly heard and Haloid-Xerox no longer seemed so strange. 'And so,' according to John Dessauer, 'a six-month delay having diluted most opposition, we of the committee agreed that the change to Haloid-Xerox might in the long run produce sound advantages.'[4]

Many top executives consciously plan for such 'gestation periods' and often find that the strategic concept itself is made more effective by the resulting feedback.

Tactical Shifts and Partial Solutions

At this stage in the process, guiding executives might share a fairly clear vision of the general directions for movement. But rarely does a total, new corporate posture emerge full-grown—like Minerva from the brow of Jupiter—from any one source. Instead, early resolutions are likely to be partial, tentative or experimental. Beginning moves often appear as mere tactical adjustments in the enterprise's existing posture. As such, they encounter little opposition, yet each partial solution adds momentum in new directions. Guiding executives try carefully to maintain the enterprise's ongoing strengths while shifting its total posture incrementally—at the margin—towards new needs. Such executives themselves might not yet perceive the full nature of the strategic shifts they have begun. They can still experiment with partial, new approaches and learn without risking the viability of the total enterprise. Their broad early steps can still legitimately lead to a variety of different success scenarios. Yet logic might dictate that they wait before committing themselves to a total new strategy. As events unfurl, solutions to several interrelated problems might well flow together in a not-yet-perceived synthesis. For example:

In the early 1970s at General Motors there was a distinct awareness of a developing fuel economy ethic. General Motors executives said, 'Our conclusions were really at the conversational level—that the big car trend was at an end. But we were not at all sure sufficient numbers of large car buyers were ready to move to dramatically lighter cars.' Nevertheless, GM did start concept studies that resulted in the Cadillac Seville.

When the oil crisis hit in fall 1973, the company responded in further increments, at first merely increasing production of its existing small-car lines. Then as the crisis deepened, it added another partial solution, the subcompact 'T car'—the Chevette—and accelerated the Seville's development cycle. Next, as fuel economy appeared more saleable, executives set an initial target of removing 400 pounds from B-C bodies by 1977. As fuel economy pressures persisted and engineering feasibilities offered greater confidence, this target was increased to 800–1000 pounds (three mpg). No step by itself shifted the company's total strategic posture until the full downsizing of all lines was announced. But each partial solution built confidence and commitment toward a new direction.[5]

Broadening Political Support

Often these broad, emerging, strategic thrusts need expanded political support and understanding to achieve sufficient momentum to survive. Committees, task forces and retreats tend to be favoured mechanisms for accomplishing this. If carefully managed, these do not become the 'garbage cans' of emerging ideas, as some observers have noted. By selecting the committee's chairman, membership, timing and agenda, guiding executives can largely influence and predict a desired outcome, and can force other executives towards a consensus. Such groups can be balanced to educate, evaluate, neutralize or overwhelm opponents. They can be used to legitimize new options or to generate broad cohesion among diverse thrusts, or they can be narrowly focused to build momentum. Guiding executives can constantly maintain complete control over these 'advisory processes' through their various influences and veto potentials. For example:

IBM's Chairman Watson and Executive Vice President Learson had become concerned over what to do about: third generation computer technology, a proliferation of designs from various divisions, increasing costs of developing software, internal competition among their lines, and the needed breadth of line for the new computer applications they began to foresee. Step by step, they oversaw the killing of the company's huge Stretch computer line (uneconomic), a proposed 8000 series of computers (incompatible software), and the prototype English Scamp Computer (duplicative). They then initiated a series of 'strategic dialogues' with divisional executives to define a new strategy. But none came into place because of the parochial nature of divisional viewpoints.

Learson, therefore, set up the SPREAD Committee, representing every major segment of the company. Its twelve members included the most likely opponent of an integrated line (Haanstra), the people who had earlier suggested the 8000 and Scamp designs, and Learson's handpicked lieutenant (Evans). When progress became 'hellishly slow', Haanstra was removed as chairman and Evans took over. Eventually the committee came forth with an integrating proposal for a single, compatible line of computers to blanket and open up the market for both scientific and business applications, with 'standard interface' for peripheral equipment. At an all-day meeting of the fifty top executives of the company, the report was not received with enthusiasm, but there were no compelling objections. So Learson blessed the silence as consensus saying, 'OK, we'll do it—i.e., go ahead with a major development program.'[6]

In addition to facilitating smooth implementation, many managers reported that interactive consensus building processes also improve the quality of the strategic decisions themselves and help achieve positive and innovative assistance when things otherwise could go wrong.

Overcoming Opposition: 'Zones of Indifference' and 'No Lose' Situations

Executives of basically healthy companies in the sample realized that any attempt to introduce a new strategy would have to deal with the support its predecessor had. Barring a major crisis, a frontal attack on an old strategy could be regarded as an attack on those who espoused it—perhaps properly—and brought the enterprise to its present levels of success. There often exists a variety of legitimate views on what could and should be done in the new circumstances that a company faces. And wise executives do not want to alienate people who would otherwise be supporters. Consequently, they try to get key people behind their concepts whenever possible, to coopt or neutralize serious opposition, if necessary, or to find 'zones of indifference' where the propositions would not be disastrously opposed.[7] Most of all they seek 'no lose' situations which will motivate all the important players toward a common goal. For example:

> When James McFarland took over at General Mills from his power base in the Grocery Products Divison, another serious contender for the top spot had been Louis B. 'Bo' Polk, a very bright, aggressive young man who headed the corporation's acquisition-diversification program. Both traditional lines and acquisitions groups wanted support for their activities and had high-level supporters. McFarland's corporate-wide 'goodness to greatness' conferences . . . first obtained broad agreement on growth goals and criteria for all areas.
>
> Out of this and the related acquisition proposal process came two thrusts: (1) to expand—internally and through acquisitions—in food-related sectors and (2) to acquire new growth centers based on General Mills' marketing skills. Although there was no formal statement, there was a strong feeling that the majority of resources should be used in food-related areas. But neither group was foreclosed, and no one could suggest the new management was vindictive. As it turned out, over the next five years about $450 million was invested in new businesses, and the majority were not closely related to foods.

But such tactics do not always work. Successful executives surveyed tended to honour legitimate differences in viewpoints and noted that initial opponents often shaped new strategies in more effective directions and became supporters as new information became available. But strong-minded executives sometimes disagreed to the point where they had to be moved or stimulated to leave; timing could dictate very firm top-level decisions at key junctions. Barring crises, however, disciplinary steps usually occurred incrementally as individual executives' attitudes and competencies emerged vis-à-vis a new strategy.

Structuring Flexibility: Buffers, Slacks and Activists

Typically there are too many uncertainties in the total environment for managers to programme or control all the events involved in effecting a major change in strategic direction. Logic dictates, therefore, that managers purposely design flexibility into their organizations and have resources ready to deploy incrementally as events demand. Planned flexibility requires: proactive horizon scanning to identify the general nature and potential impact of opportunities and threats the firm is most likely to encounter; creating sufficient resource buffers—or slacks—to respond effectively as events actually unfurl; developing and positioning 'credible activists' with a psychological commitment to move quickly and flexibly to exploit specific opportunities as they occur; and shortening decision lines from such people (and key operating managers) to the top for the most rapid system response. These—rather than precapsuled (and shelved) programmes to respond to stimuli which never quite occur as expected—are the keys to real contingency planning.

The concept of resource buffers requires special amplification. Quick access to resources is needed to cushion the impact of random events, to offset opponents' sudden attacks, or to build momentum for new strategic shifts. Some examples will indicate the form these buffers may take.

> For critical purchased items, General Motors maintained at least three suppliers, each with sufficient capacity to expand production should one of the others encounter a catastrophe. Thus, the company had expandable capacity with no fixed investment. Exxon set up its Exploration Group to purposely undertake the higher risks and longer-term investments necessary to search for oil in new areas, and thus to reduce the potential impact on Exxon if there were sudden unpredictable changes in the availability of Middle East oil. Instead of hoarding cash, Pillsbury and General Mills sold off unprofitable businesses and cleaned up their financial statements to improve their access to external capital sources for acquisitions. Such access in essence provided the protection of a cash buffer without its investment. IBM's large R&D facility and its project team approach to development assured that it had a pool of people it could quickly shift among various projects to exploit interesting new technologies.[8]

When such flexible response patterns are designd into the enterprise's strategy, it is proactively ready to move on those thrusts—acquisitions, innovations or resource explorations—which require incrementalism.

Systematic Waiting and Trial Concepts

The prepared strategist may have to wait for events, as Roosevelt awaited a trauma like Pearl Harbor. The availability of desired acquisitions or real estate might depend on a death, divorce, fiscal crisis, management change or an erratic stock market break. Technological advances may have to await new knowledge, inventions or lucky accidents. Despite otherwise complete preparations, a planned market entry might not be wise until new legislation, trade agreements, or competitive shake-outs occur. Organizational moves have to be timed to retirements, promotions, management failures and so on. Very often the specific strategy adopted depends on the timing or sequence of such random events. For example:

Although Continental Group's top executives had thoroughly discussed and investigated energy, natural resources, and insurance as possible 'fourth legs' for the company, the major acquisition possibilities were so different that the strategic choice depended on the fit of particular candidates—e.g., Peabody Coal or Richmond Insurance—within these possible industries. The choice of one industry would have precluded the others. The sequence in which firms became available affected the final choice, and that choice itself greatly influenced the whole strategic posture of the company.

In many of the cases studied, strategists proactively launched trial concepts— Mr McColough's 'architecture of information' (Xerox), Mr Spoor's 'Super Box' (Pillsbury)—in order to generate options and concrete proposals. Usually these 'trial balloons' were phrased in very broad terms. Without making a commitment to any specific solution, the executive can activate the organization's creative abilities. This approach keeps the manager's own options open until substantive alternatives can be evaluated against each other and against concrete current realities. It prevents practical line managers from rejecting a strategic shift, as they might if forced to compare a 'paper option' against well-defined current needs. Such trial concepts give cohesion to the new strategy while enabling the company to take maximum advantage of the psychological and informational benefits of incrementalism.

SOLIDIFYING PROGRESS—INCREMENTALLY

As events move forward, executives can more clearly perceive the specific directions in which their organizations should—and realistically can—move. They can seek more aggressive movement and commitment to their new perceptions, without undermining important ongoing activities or creating unnecessary reactions to their purposes. Until this point, new strategic goals might remain broad, relatively unrefined, or even unstated except as philosophic concepts. More specific dimensions might be incrementally announced as key pieces of information fall into place, specific unanswered issues approach resolution, or significant resources have to be formally committed.

Creating Pockets of Commitment

Early in this stage, guiding executives may need actively to implant support in the organization for new thrusts. They may encourage an array of exploratory projects for each of several possible options. Initial projects can be kept small, partial or ad hoc, neither forming a comprehensive programme nor seeming to be integrated into a cohesive strategy. Executives often provide stimulating goals, a proper climate for imaginative proposals and flexible resource support, rather than being personally identified with specific projects. In this way they can achieve organizational involvement and early commitment without focusing attention on any one solution too soon or losing personal credibility if it fails.

Once under way, project teams on the more successful programme in the sample became ever more committed to their particular areas of exploration. They became pockets of support for new strategies deep within the organization. Yet, if necessary, top managers could delay until the last moment their final decisions blending individual projects into a total strategy. Thus, they were able to obtain the best possible match among the company's technical abilities, its psychological commitments, and its changing market needs. By making final choices more effectively—as late as possible with better data, more conscientiously investigated options and the expert critiques competitive projects allowed—those executives actually increased technical and market efficiencies of their enterprises, despite the apparent added costs of parallel efforts.

In order to maintain their own objectivity and future flexibility, some executives choose to keep their own political profiles low as they build a new consensus. If they seem committed to a strategy too soon, they might discourage others from pursuing key issues which should be raised. By stimulating detailed investigations several levels down, top executives can seem detached yet still shape both progress and ultimate outcomes—by reviewing interim results and specifying the timing, format and forums for the release of data. When reports come forward, these executives can stand above the battle and review proposals objectively, without being personally on the defensive for having committed themselves to a particular solution too soon. From this position they can more easily orchestrate a high-level consensus on a new strategic thrust. As an added benefit, negative decisions on proposals often come from a group consensus that top executives can simply confirm to lower levels, thereby preserving their personal veto for more crucial moments. In many well-made decisions people at all levels contribute to the generation, amplification and interpretation of options and information to the extent that it is often difficult to say who really makes the decision.

Focusing the Organization

In spite of their apparent detachment, top executives do focus their organizations on developing strategies at critical points in the process. While adhering to the rhetoric of specific goal-setting, most executives are careful *not* to state new goals in concrete terms before they have built a consensus among key players. They fear that they will prematurely centralize the organization, pre-empt interesting options, provide a common focus for otherwise fragmented opposition or cause the organization to act prematurely to carry out a specified commitment. Guiding executives may quietly shape the many alternatives flowing upward by using what Wrapp refers to as 'a hidden hand'. Through their information networks they can encourage concepts they favour, let weakly supported options die through inaction and establish hurdles or tests for strongly supported ideas with which they do not agree but which they do not wish to oppose openly.

Since opportunities for such focusing generally develop unexpectedly, the timing of key moves is often unpredictable. A crisis, a rash of reassignments, a reorganization or a key appointment may allow an executive to focus attention on particular thrusts, add momentum to some and, perhaps, quietly phase out others. Most managers surveyed seemed well aware of the notion that 'if there are no other options, mine wins'. Without being Machiavellian, they did not want misdirected options to gain strong political momentum and later have to be terminated in an open bloodbath. They also did not want to send false signals that stimulated other segments of their organizations to make proposals in undesirable directions. They sensed very clearly that the patterns in which proposals are approved or denied will inevitably be perceived by lower echelons as precedents for developing future goals or policies.

Managing Coalitions

Power interactions among key players are important at this stage of solidifying progress. Each player has a different level of power determined by his or her information base, organizational position and personal credibilty. Executives legitimately perceive problems or opportunities differently because of their particular values, experiences and vantage points. They will promote the solutions they perceive as the best compromise for the total enterprise, for themselves, and for their particular units. In an organization with dispersed power, the key figure is the one who can manage coalitions. Since no one player has all the power, regardless of that individual's skill or position, the action that occurs over time might differ greatly from the intentions of any of the players. Top executives try to sense whether support exists among important parties for specific aspects of an issue and try to get partial decisions and momenta going for those aspects. As 'comfort levels' or political pressures within the top group rise in favour of specific decisions, the guiding executive might, within his or her concept of a more complete solution, seek—among the various features of different proposals—a balance that the most influential and credible parties can actively support. The result tends to be a stream of partial decisions on limited strategic issues made by constantly changing coalitions of the critical power centres. These decisions steadily evolve toward a broader consensus, acceptable to both the top executive and some 'dominant coalition' among these centres.

As a partial consensus emerges, top executives might crystallize issues by stating some broad goals in more specific terms for internal consumption. Finally, when sufficient general acceptance exists and the timing is right, the goals may begin to appear in more public announcements. For example:

> As General Mills divested several of its major divisions in the early 1960s, its annual reports began to refer to these as deliberate moves 'to concentrate on the company's strengths' and 'to intensify General Mills' efforts in the convenience foods field'. Such statements could not have been made until many of the actual divestitures were completed, and a sufficient consensus existed among the top executives to support the new corporate concept.

Formalizing Commitment by Empowering Champions

As each major strategic thrust comes into focus, top executives try to ensure that some individual or group feels responsible for its goals. If the thrust will project the enterprise in entirely new directions, executives often want more than mere accountability for its success—they want real commitment. A significantly new major thrust, concept, product or problem solution frequently needs the nurturing hand of someone who genuinely identifies with it and whose future depends on its success. For example:

> Once the divestiture program at General Mills was sufficiently under way, General Rawlings selected young 'Bo' Polk to head up an acquisition program to use the cash generated. In this role Polk had nothing to lose. With strong senior management in the remaining consumer products divisions, the ambitious Polk would have had a long road to the top there. In acquisitions, he provided a small political target, only a $50 000 budget in a $500 million company. Yet he had high visibility and could build his own power base, if he were successful. With direct access to and the support of Rawlings, he would be protected through his early ventures. All he had to do was make sure his first few acquisitions were successful. As subsequent acquisitions succeeded, his power base could feed on itself—satisfying both Polk's ego needs and the company's strategic goals.

In some cases, top executives have to wait for champions to appear before committing resources to risky new strategies. They may immediately assign accountability for less dramatic plans by converting them into new missions for ongoing groups.

From this point on, the strategy-process is familiar. The organization's formal structure has to be adjusted to support the strategy. Commitment to the most important new thrusts has to be confirmed in formal plans. Detailed budgets, programmes, controls and reward-systems have to reflect all planned strategic thrusts. Finally, the guiding executive has to see that recruiting and staffing plans are aligned with the new goals and that—when the situation permits—supporters and persistent opponents of intended new thrusts are assigned to appropriate positions.

Continuing the Dynamics by Eroding Consensus

The major strategic changes studied tended to take many years to accomplish. The process was continuous, often without any clear beginning or end. The decision-process constantly moulded and modified management's concerns and concepts. Radical crusades became the new conventional wisdom and over time totally new issues emerged. Participants or observers were often not aware of exactly when a particular decision had been made or when a subsequent consensus was created to supersede or modify it; the process of strategic change was continuous and dynamic. Several GM executives described the frequently imperceptible way in which many strategic decisions evolved:

> We use an iterative process to make a series of tentative decisions on the way we think the market will go. As we get more data we modify these continuously. It is often difficult to say who decided something and when—or even who originated a decision. . . . Strategy really evolves as a series of incremental steps. . . . I frequently don't know when a decision is made in General

Motors. I don't remember being in a committee meeting when things came to a vote. Usually someone will simply summarize a developing position. Everyone else either nods or states his particular terms of consensus.

A major strategic change in Xerox was characterized this way:

How was the overall organization decision made? I've often heard it said that after talking with a lot of people and having trouble with a number of decisions which were pending, Archie McCardell really reached his own conclusion and got Peter McColough's backing on it. But it really didn't happen quite that way. It was an absolutely evolutionary approach. It was a growing feeling. A number of people felt we ought to be moving toward some kind of matrix organization. We have always been a pretty democratic type of organization. In our culture you can't come down with mandates or ultimatums from the top on major changes like this. You almost have to work these things through and let them grow and evolve, keep them on the table so people are thinking about them and talking about them.

Once the organization arrives at its new consensus, the guiding executive has to move immediately to ensure that this new position does not become inflexible. In trying to build commitment to a new concept, individual executives often surround themselves with people who see the world in the same way. Such people can rapidly become systematic screens against other views. Effective executives therefore purposely continue the change process, constantly introducing new faces and stimuli at the top. They consciously begin to erode the very strategic thrusts they may have just created—a very difficult, but essential, psychological task.

INTEGRATION OF PROCESSES AND OF INTERESTS

In the large enterprises observed, strategy formulation was a continuously evolving analytical-political consensus process with neither a finite beginning nor a definite end. It generally followed the sequence described. Yet the total process was anything but linear. It was a grouping, cyclical process that often circled back on itself, with frequent interruptions and delays. Pfiffner aptly describes the process of strategy formation as being 'like fermentation in biochemistry, rather than an industrial assembly line'.[9]

Such incremental management processes are not abrogations of good management practice. Nor are they Machiavellian or consciously manipulative manoeuvres. Instead, they represent an adaptation to the practical psychological and informational problems of getting a constantly changing group of people with diverse talents and interests to move together effectively in a continually dynamic environment. Much of the impelling force behind logical incrementalism comes from a desire to tap the talents and psychological drives of the whole organization, to create cohesion and to generate identity with the emerging strategy. The remainder of that force results from the interactive nature of the random factors and lead times affecting the independent subsystems that compose any total strategy.

An Incremental—not Piecemeal—Process

The total pattern of action, though highly incremental, is not piecemeal in well-managed organizations. It requires constant, conscious reassessment of the total organization, its capacities and its needs as related to surrounding environments. It requires continual attempts by top managers to integrate these actions into an understandable, cohesive whole. How do top managers themselves describe the process? Mr Estes, president of General Motors, said:

> We try to give them the broad concepts we are trying to achieve. We operate through questioning and fact gathering. Strategy is a state of mind you go through. When you think about a little problem, your mind begins to think how it will affect all the different elements in the total situation. Once you have had all the jobs you need to qualify for this position, you can see the problem from a variety of viewpoints. But you don't try to ram your conclusions down people's throats. You try to persuade people what has to be done and provide confidence and leadership for them.

Formal-analytical Techniques

At each stage of strategy development, effective executives constantly try to visualize the new patterns that might exist among the emerging strategies of various subsystems. As each subsystem strategy becomes more apparent, both its executive team and top-level groups try to project its implications for the total enterprise and to stimulate queries, support and feedback from those involved in related strategies. Perceptive top executives see that the various teams generating subsystem strategies have overlapping members. They require periodic updates and reviews before higher echelon groups that can bring a total corporate view to bear. They use formal planning processes to interrelate and evaluate the resources required, benefits sought, and risks undertaken vis-à-vis other elements of the enterprise's overall strategy. Some use scenario-techniques to help visualize potential impacts and relationships. Others utilize complex forecasting models to understand better the basic interactions among subsystems, the total enterprise and the environment. Still others use specialized staffs, 'devil's advocates', or 'contention teams' to make sure that all important aspects of their strategies receive a thorough evaluation.

Power-behavioural Aspects: Coalition Management

All of the formal methodologies help, but the real integration of all the components in an enterprise's total strategy eventually takes place only in the minds of high-level executives. Each executive may legitimately perceive the intended balance of goals and thrusts differently. Some of these differences may be openly expressed as issues to be resolved when new information becomes available. Some differences may remain unstated—hidden agenda to emerge at later dates. Others may be masked by accepting so broad a statement of intention that many different views are included in a seeming consensus, when a more specific statement might be divisive. Nevertheless, effective strategies do achieve a level of understanding and consensus sufficient to focus action.

Top executives deliberately manage the incremental processes within each subsystem to create the basis for consensus. They also manage the coalitions that lie at the heart of most controlled strategy developments.[10] They recognize that they are at the confluence of innumerable pressures—from stockholders, environmentalists, government bodies, customers, suppliers, distributors, producing units, marketing groups, technologists, unions, special issue activists, individual employees, ambitious executives and so on—and that knowledgeable people of good will can easily disagree on proper actions. In response to changing pressures and coalitions among these groups, the top management team constantly forms and reforms its own coalitions on various decisions.[11]

Most major strategic moves tend to assist some interests—and executives' careers—at the expense of others. Consequently, each set of interests serves as a check on the others and thus helps maintain the breadth and balance of strategy.[12] To avoid significant errors some managers try to ensure that all important groups have representation at or access to the top.[13] The guiding executive group may continuously adjust the number, power or proximity of such access points in order to maintain a desired balance and focus.[14] These delicate adjustments require constant negotiations and implied bargains within the leadership group. Balancing the focuses that different interests exert on key decisions is perhaps the ultimate control top executives have in guiding and coordinating the formulation of their companies' strategies.[15]

Establishing, Measuring and Rewarding Key Thrusts

Few executives or management teams can keep all the dimensions of a complex evolving strategy in mind as they deal with the continuous flux of urgent issues. Consequently, effective strategic managers seek to identify a few central themes that can help to draw diverse efforts together in a common cause.[16] Once identified, these themes help to maintain focus and consistency in the strategy. They make it easier to discuss and monitor proposed strategic thrusts. Ideally, these themes can be developed into a matrix of pogrammes and goals, cutting across formal divisional lines and dominating the selection and ranking of projects within divisions. This matrix can, in turn, serve as the basis for performance measurement, control and reward systems that ensure the intended strategy is properly implemented.

Unfortunately, few companies in the sample were able to implement such a complex planning and control system without creating undue rigidities. But all did utilize logical incrementalism to bring cohesion to the formal-analytical and power-behavioural processes needed to create effective strategies. Most used some approximation of the process sequence previously described to form their strategies at both subsystem and overall corporate levels. A final summary example demonstrates how deliberate incrementalism can integrate the key elements in more traditional approaches to strategy formulation.

In the late 1970s a major nation's largest bank named as its new president and

CEO a man with a long and successful career, largely in domestic operating positions. The bank's chairman had been a familiar figure on the international stage and was due to retire in three to five years. The new CEO, with the help of a few trusted colleagues, his chief planner, and a consultant, first tried to answer the questions: 'If I look ahead seven to eight years to my retirement as CEO, what should I like to leave behind as the hallmarks of my leadership? What accomplishments would define my era as having been successful?' He chose the following goals:

1. To be the country's number one bank in profitability and size without sacrificing the quality of its assets or liabilities
2. To be recognized as a major international bank
3. To improve substantially the public image and employee perceptions of the bank
4. To maintain progressive policies that prevent unionization
5. To be viewed as a professional, well-managed bank with strong, planned management continuity
6. To be clearly identified as the country's most professional corporate finance bank, with a strong base within the country but with foreign and domestic operations growing in balance
7. To have women in top management and to achieve full utilization of the bank's female employees
8. To have a tighter, smaller headquarters and a more rationalized, decentralized corporate structure

The CEO brought back to the corporate offices the head of his overseas divisions to be COO and to be a member of the executive committee, which ran the company's affairs. The CEO discussed his personal views concerning the bank's future with this committee and also with several of his group VPs. Then, to arrive at a cohesive set of corporate goals, the executive committee investigated the bank's existing strengths and weaknesses (again with the assistance of consultants) and extrapolated its existing growth trends seven to eight years into the future. According to the results of this exercise, the bank's foreseeable growth would require that:

1. The bank's whole structure be reoriented to make it a much stronger force in international banking
2. The bank decentralize operations much more than it ever had
3. The bank find or develop at least 100 new top-level specialists and general managers within a few years
4. The bank reorganize around a 'four-bank' principle (international, commercial, investment and retail banks) with entirely new linkages forged among these units
5. These linkages and much of the bank's new international thrust be built on its expertise in certain industries, which were the primary basis of its parent country's international trade
6. The bank's profitability be improved across the board, especially in its diverse retail banking units

To develop more detailed data for specific actions and to further develop consensus around needed moves, the CEO commissioned two consulting studies: one on the future of the bank's home country and the other on changing trade patterns and relationships worldwide. As these studies became available, the CEO allowed an ever wider circle of top executives to do a critique on the studies' findings and to share their insights. Finally, the CEO and the executive committee were willing to draw up and agree to a statement of 10 broad goals (parallel to the CEO's original goals but enriched in flavour and detail). By then, some steps were already under way to implement specific goals (for example, the four-bank concept). But the CEO wanted further participation of his line officers in the formulation of the goals and in the strategic thrusts they represented across the whole bank. By now 18 months had gone by, but there was widespread consensus within the top management group on major goals and directions.

The CEO then organized an international conference of some 40 top officers of the bank and had a background document prepared for this meeting containing: the broad goals agreed upon; the 10 major thrusts that the executive committee thought were necessary to meet these goals; the key elements needed to back up each thrust; and a summary of the national and economic analyses the thrusts were based upon. The 40 executives had two full days to do a critique, question, improve and clarify the ideas in this document. Small work groups of line executives reported their findings and concerns directly to the executive committee. At the end of the meeting, the executive committee tabled one of the major thrusts for further study, agreed to refined wording for some of the bank's broad goals and modified details of the major thrusts in line with expressed concerns.

The CEO announced that within three months each line officer would be expected to submit his/her own statement of how his/her unit would contribute to the major goals and thrusts agreed on. Once these unit goals were discussed and negotiated with the appropriate top executive group, the line officers would develop specific budgetary and nonbudgetary programmes showing precisely how their units would carry out each of the major thrusts in the strategy. The CEO was asked to develop measures both for all key elements of each unit's fiscal performance and for performance against each agreed upon strategic thrust within each unit. As these plans came into place, it became clear that the old organization had to be aligned behind these new thrusts. The CEO had to substantially redefine the CEO's job, deal with some crucial internal political pressures, and place the next generation of top managers in the line positions supporting each major thrust. The total process from concept formulation to implementation of the control system was to span three to four years, with new goals and thrusts emerging flexibly as external events and opportunities developed.

CONCLUSIONS

In recent years, there has been an increasingly loud chorus of discontent about corporate strategic planning. Many managers are concerned that despite elaborate strategic planning systems, costly staffs for planning and major commitments of their own time, their most elaborately analyzed strategies never get implemented. These executives and their companies generally have fallen into the trap of thinking about strategy formulation and implementation as separate, sequential processes. They rely on the awesome rationality of their formally derived strategies and the inherent power of their positions to cause their organizations to respond. When this does not occur, they become bewildered, if not frustrated and angry. Instead, successful managers in the companies observed acted logically and incrementally to improve the quality of information used in key decisions; to overcome the personal and political pressures resisting change; to deal with the varying lead times and sequencing problems in critical decisions; and to build the organizational awareness, understanding and psychological commitment essential to effective strategies. By the time the strategies began to crystallize, pieces of them were already being implemented. Through the very processes they used to formulate their strategies, these executives had built sufficient organizational momentum and identity with the strategies to make them flow toward flexible and successful implementation.

REFERENCES

1. See J. B. Quinn (1979) Xerox Corporation (B) (copyrighted case, Amos Tuck School of Business Administration, Dartmouth College, Hanover, NH)
2. Quinn (1979) *op. cit.*
3. See J. B. Quinn (1978) General Motors Corporation: the downsizing decision (copyrighted case, Amos Tuck School of Business Administration, Dartmouth College, Hanover, NH)
4. See J. H. Dessauer (1971) *My Years with Xerox: the billions nobody wanted,* Doubleday, Garden City, NY
5. Quinn (1979) *op. cit.*
6. See T.A. Wise (1966) I.B.M.'s $5 billion gamble, *Fortune*, September, pp 118–24; T. A. Wise (1966), The rocky road to the marketplace (Part II: I.B.M.'s $5 billion gamble), *Fortune*, October, pp 138–52
7. For an excellent overview of the processes of co-optation and neutralization, see Sayles (1964). For perhaps the first reference to the concept of the "zone of indifference," see C. I. Barnard (1938) *The Functions of the Executive*, Harvard University Press, Cambridge, MA. The following two sources note the need of executives for coalition behaviour to reduce the organizational conflict resulting from differing interests and goal preferences in large organizations: Cyert and March (1963); J. G. March (1964) *Business Decision Making*, In H. J. Leavitt and L. R. Pondy (Eds) Readings in Managerial Psychology, University of Chicago Press, Chicago
8. Quinn (1979) *op. cit.*
9. See J.M. Pfiffner (1960) Administrative rationality, *Public Administration Review*, Summer, pp 125–32
10. See R. James (1978) *Corporate Strategy and Change—the management of people,* monograph, The University of Chicago. The author does an excellent job of pulling together the threads of coalition management at top organizational levels
11. See Cyert and March (1963), p 115
12. Lindblom (Spring 1959) notes that every interest has a 'watchdog' and that purposely allowing these watchdogs to participate in and influence decisions creates consensus decisions that all can live with. Similar conscious access to the top for different interests can now be found in corporate structures
13. See Zaleznik (May–June 1970)

14. For an excellent view of the bargaining processes involved in coalition management, see Sayles (1964), pp 207–17
15. For suggestions on why the central power figure in decentralized organizations must be the person who manages its dominant coalition, the size of which will depend on the issues involved, and the number of areas in which the organizations must rely on judgemental decisions, see Thompson (1967)
16. Wrapp (September–October 1967) notes the futility of a top manager trying to push a full package of goals

9 COPING WITH CHANGE
Derek Taylor

Every thoughtful manager knows how rapidly the environment within which he/ she works is changing. What he/she is less certain about is how to deal with the changes in an organized and systematic manner. But one textile company can now make the claim that it is, in fact, able to view its environment in a much more comprehensive and meaningful way; to recognize that it is no longer a single business but a multiplicity of businesses, each at a different stage of development and each with its own individual needs; to identify more effectively the barriers to further profitable growth in each business and develop new strategies and plans for overcoming them and making more money; to use existing resources more effectively in pursuing growth and profit objectives; to identify more quickly the needs for additional resources and other organizational changes; and to implement revised strategies faster.

One of the principal instruments for bringing about the necessary changes in behaviour has been development of a fact-finding and planning process which involves directly the people who must put into effect the plans which they themselves recommend. This has a number of implications for a company's planning process. The textile company concerned is a medium-sized firm engaged in manufacturing and marketing textile products. Before the project began, it had a turnover of about £6 million and was losing money. The company had ambitions to grow—over the past few years manufacturing capacity has more than doubled. The man who was the chief executive when the project began is a keen innovator and has strong leanings towards a participative system of management. The management team is composed of young and enthusiastic executives who are committed to making a success of the business.

When the study began the company had a conventional organization structure, with sales, production, development and finance as the main functions. The marketing director, however, was beginning to introduce the concept of product management and had appointed two former sales representatives to manage two

Taylor, D. (1977) Coping with change, *Management Today*, Oct pp 81–83 key product market sectors. The planned increase in manufacturing capacity began to come on stream coincidentally with a major downturn in demand from the company's traditional markets. Consequently, the company tried to increase sales volume at a time when there was excess capacity in the industry and profit margins were under pressure. Inflation was also having an adverse effect on profits, and in the state of the market the company was unable to recover its increased costs.

The company had made the decision to get involved in a number of new products and markets; one such situation looked particularly promising. However, the company was dissipating its energies by attempting to exploit too many different market segments, some of which were unprofitable. There was a lack of knowledge and understanding about many of the markets being served. This meant that a number of areas with considerable potential were being neglected because of a lack of resources. Management was uncertain about which problems needed to be solved in order to achieve an adequate level of profits. It was recognized that effort had to be focused more precisely, but management was not sure how. The management team was prepared to accept an external change agent and cooperate with him to gain a better understanding of the company's real situation; it was also anxious to explore any possible options.

Three groups of factors were studied:

1.   *The company's environment*—represented by the needs, demands and values of the individuals, groups, organizations and other parts of society with an interest in the company
2.   *The company norms*—in other words, the beliefs, ideas, values and goals embodied in the company, particularly those held by the people in positions of power. (It must be recognized that there may be a number of power groups at different levels within a company.) These norms include, for example, ideas and beliefs about such things as what business(es) the company is engaged in; what is important for success in the industry concerned; and how to make money
3.   *The organization itself*, which includes factors such as resources—people, skills, product/services, plant and machinery, money and the like—the organization structure, management processes, the exchange process (the conversion of one type of resource into another), control processes, company or departmental strategies and plans and the like.

In terms of this approach, suggested by Dr Richard Normann of Lund, Sweden, a company is successful when it is in tune with its environment. In other words, there should be congruence among the three groups noted. If there are any mismatches among the three, the company will not be as successful as it might be. Consequently, as the environment changes the company's performance will deteriorate, unless a process of adjustment brings the three groups of factors back into tune.

A central aspect of strategic planning is to develop an understanding of a company's situation in relation to its environment. Another key task is to identify and generate solutions for the problems created by mismatches between the environment and the company's norms and organization. Absolute congruence between these elements is not necessary; in fact, such a state would be impossible to maintain for long, because the environment and the organization are themselves changing constantly. The aim is for the company to be more capable than its competitors at identifying and correcting mismatches which will affect significantly its future viability. It should also be realized that mismatches will often provide alert managers with opportunities for profitable growth. It is not only mismatches among each of the three groups of factors which may affect adversely the performance of a company. Mismatches between the factors contained within one group may similarly impede performance.

Many examples of mismatches between the organization and the environment can be cited. One company began to lose business and to incur losses when its methods of manufacture became much less cost-effective than those of its competitors. Another company devoted resources to the development of a product group for which demand was static and which failed to expand even with product modifications. A third company allocated sales resources to a market which was declining and neglected the opportunities presented by an expanding market in which it was also engaged.

There can be mismatches between what a company should be doing to exploit its environment and ideas (which are no longer valid) held by members of the main power groups about what is required for success. For example, the textile company described was devoting considerable resources to traditional markets with which members of the leading power group were familiar, but which were no longer profitable. At the same time, they were paying less attention to a newer business area from which the company was making much of its money and which had greater profit potential, in both short and medium term.

THE NEW MD CAUSED A MISMATCH

In another mature and successful company a common type of mismatch occurred following the appointment of a new managing director. His ambitions for profitable growth led him to set goals which were far higher than those of his predecessor. This imposed demands for change on the company's level of activities, its organization and the markets it was attempting to exploit; and this in turn created great difficulties.

An example of a mismatch within one factor group occurred in a company with a functional organization structure. The production and sales departments had objectives which led to major conflicts. These were pursued relentlessly, often at the expense of the business as a whole. The production director was concerned with manufacturing as small a range of products as possible, in order to keep his costs to a minimum; the sales director was keen to offer a wider range of products to the marketplace, to assist him to achieve his budgeted level of turnover. This inadequately controlled situation resulted in a reduction in profitability and, at the same time, placed the long-term survival of the company at hazard.

In another company, two key members in the leading power group held conflicting beliefs about what the company needed to do to make money. Their ideas were based on differing perceptions of the company's situation in its environment. This led to a schizophrenic type of behaviour on the part of the company, which had a disturbing effect on its relationship with its customers.

CHANGES IMPOSED ON OTHER PEOPLE

Conflicts often occur when changes are imposed on part of an organization as a result of decisions made by the leading power group without reference to the people who will be affected by the changes. Typical examples of such problems are: a lack of commitment to changes of strategy at middle and other levels of management, inadequate support for newly introduced systems and procedures and new investments in plant and equipment which do not achieve expected increases in productivity.

There are many reasons why mismatches can occur between a company and its environment. Among them are:

1. A limited knowledge of the environment in which it is operating
2. Not having identified the market segments which provide opportunities for growth
3. Not having assessed the strength of competition
4. Having no competitive advantages in those market segments where it wishes to succeed and make money
5. A lack of awareness of important trends in the environment, which either represent threats to its future well-being or alternatively present opportunities for increasing profits
6. Insufficient financial resources to make necessary changes
7. Inadequate resources for exploiting existing product/market segments
8. A lack of the resources and skills needed to develop effective and imaginative strategies
9. Interdepartmental or interfunctional barriers which inhibit communications or which prevent the kind of feedback which is essential if a company is to learn how to contend with new problems.

Many significant mismatches can result from conflicts among different systems of ideas, beliefs, values and goals within a company. Some of the norms of the company may be divorced from present realities because members of a significant power group cannot be convinced that their firmly held ideas are inappropriate. In one company a key man had an emotional attachment to his belief about how the company made money; this was based on past successes, but was no longer true. He was not prepared to support an internal change which ran counter to this belief—a change which was essential for the company's success.

Success in pursuing a new business strategy involves change in people's behaviour. This in turn depends on modifying the ideas, beliefs, values and goals of these people. It is well-known, however, that information on its own is rarely sufficient to change firmly held beliefs or attitudes. There is no easy solution to this problem. Experience suggests, however, that changes in an existing strategy can be facilitated by involving those people who are responsible for implementing the changes in the processes of fact-finding and problem-solving which lead to the choice of a new course of action. This is one of the most telling arguments for encouraging greater participation in decision-making by those who must implement the decisions.

There are other reasons why a greater number of people at all levels in the organization should participate in decision-making—particularly so where decisions which involve changing past practices are concerned. Environmental changes create more problems of 'strategy' or 'transition' than can be handled unaided by the specialized resources which many companies allocate to deal with them. All too often such problems are left to an already overloaded top manager and his/her immediate advisers. If not resolved, the problems will go by default, until the pressures they generate become too great to ignore. A company which arranges for these problems of transition to be handled by people at lower levels in the organization, those who will have to implement the consequent changes, can often gain competitive advantages from the situation.

Often it is the wrong people who are learning. In one company, a strategic planner developed an answer to a particular problem, but was unable to carry conviction with those responsible for taking action. In another company, the conclusions formed about the company's future activities were not soundly based; this was partly because of the limited intellectual calibre of the person making the decision, and partly because of the limitations of the tools he was using. These examples underline the importance of having the right kind of learning taking place in a company. The right people must also be involved. This is an essential part of the process of changing their ideas, beliefs, values and goals. It will also improve the knowledge and skills of those who are enabled to participate more fully in decision-making.

WHO SHOULD LEARN WHAT?

Who should learn what is far too important an issue for a company to leave to chance. It should become an explicit process and be managed accordingly. Moreover, the learning should be structured, in order to involve those whose attitudes have a large influence on the organization's ability to deal with the problems arising from change. The learning process should also enable participants to become familiar with the theories and techniques which can assist in developing a business. An example of such a theory is that associated with the Boston Consulting Group, which relates market share to the scope for making money in a product/market segment.

If it is to be fully effective, planning should be seen as a process both of learning and of change. Moreover, it is a process which cannot be confined to a professional planner and the immediate staff, but should involve the managers and others at various levels in the organization who must ultimately implement any changes of strategies or plans. Ideally, the planning of future strategies should start from where a company is at the time of the review. It should seek to modify the existing course of action as a result of studying:

(a)   Relevant changes in the environment

(b)   The company's situation in the environment, particularly with respect to how it is making money

(c)   What the company is doing internally to ensure that its activities in the market place are adequately supported

(d)   Short- and long-term objectives

(e)   The mismatches which exist and other barriers to further profitable growth, which will be revealed by a careful appraisal of product/market relationships, technology, administration, organization structure and the use of finance

The planning process should involve identifying the different businesses in which the company is engaged. Most companies are engaged in more than one business, although this is often not appreciated by management. This will enable responsibility for business planning to be shared with middle managers and staff, who in many companies are not involved in this activity. This approach to developing the different businesses in which a company can be engaged has a number of advantages. The first is that it is possible to plan individual strategies for each separate and distinct business. This is generally more effective than attempting to develop an across-the-board strategy which attempts to satisfy a number of different businesses.

BASIS FOR ENTREPRENEURIAL DEVELOPMENT

The second advantage is that it allows a number of profit centres to be created. These can form the basis of further entrepreneurial development. It also provides more opportunities for people to learn the requirements of general management, as distinct from purely functional skills. A further advantage of this approach is that it will tend to diminish interdepartmental barriers, as functional specialists are given the opportunity to develop a better understanding of the contribution that they, and others, make to the business.

These ideas are currently being put into practice by the textile company in the case. The business activities of the company were divided into three sectors. Each of these was allocated to a different group of executives who were drawn mainly from the ranks of middle and junior managers. The groups were set the task of establishing the character of the different businesses in each sector. They were then asked to identify any mismatches between the different businesses and their internal and external environments. The fact-finding was conducted in such a way as to avoid any participant feeling threatened by the findings of his group.

The next stage of the process was to develop plans for rectifying the mismatches, in order to achieve profitable growth. The original groups were reconstituted at this point, to ensure that the planning and problem-solving was being done by those who would implement the solutions. A significant feature of the process is that participants have been encouraged to question their activities in relation to the profits which they generate. They are also seeking ways to increase profitability.

From being a functional organization engaged in the business of producing and marketing textile products, the company is now consciously developing a number of different businesses. Furthermore, each of these is handled by its own task group, which includes the functional specialists needed to develop the business. It is still too early to assess fully the effectiveness of these changes. However, they are creating a more flexible organization in which the responsibility for making profits is now widely distributed throughout the management team. It is no longer just left to the chief executive, as in the past. Moreover, people welcome the responsibility—and they are generating the positive action plans for improving the profit position on which the company's future depends.

10 THE POVERTY OF PROBLEM-SOLVING
Geoffrey Vickers

THE PROPER ROLE OF SYSTEMS ANALYSIS

Most of the papers presented to this meeting* seem to me to disclose one or more
of three misconceptions about what systems analysis should be and might be.
These, I shall suggest, sometimes exaggerate, sometimes restrict and always distort what should be regarded as the proper contribution to policy-making to be
expected of the profession of the systems analyst—an important profession,
though not a new one, except for the new technique which is now at its
disposal.

The first of these misconceptions is the idea that systems analysis is primarily a
technique for solving problems. It should rather, I suggest, be regarded as a
means of understanding situations. Understanding may or may not be followed
by the hope that something can be done to make the situation better or to stop it
getting worse. And if so, a second and different round of analysis will follow. The
analyst is then required to analyze over some future time-span the hypothetical
situation which would be created if the hypothetical action were taken. He/she
may even be required to compare the probable outcomes of more than one
hypothetical response or himself/herself to suggest and explore the effect of one
or more possible responses. And at this stage he/she may regard himself/herself,
if not as a problem solver, at least as one concerned with exploring the possibility
of a solution. But a 'second round' by no means always follows. Once the situation is understood it is often apparent without further analysis both what if anything can be done and what needs to be done. The luxury of choosing between
alternatives is by no means always open. In any case to focus on problem-solving
is to divert attention from the far more important function of problem definition
and to confuse the continuing process of system regulation with the episodic

Vickers, G. (1981) The poverty of problem-solving, *Journal of Applied Systems Analysis*, Vol. 8, pp 15–
21 © Jeanne Vickers

*This chapter is an extended version of a paper and subsequent talk given to a meeting on systems
analysis in urban policy-making organized through the Systems Science Programme of NATO. It
took place at New College Oxford in September 1980. The proceedings of the meeting were published
by Plenum Press.

activity of seeking specific goals and the much more frequent and radically different activity of averting specific threats.

Of course people do not seek to deepen their understanding of a situation unless it is causing them some concern, but this of itself does not necessarily create a problem, still less a soluble one.

Concerns may be of two kinds—perception of some present state which awakens anxiety or of some imaginable future state which awakens aspiration. But it does not follow that concerned persons can do anything either to abate their anxiety or to realize their hope. Through most of human history most human ills have been regarded not as problems but as part of the human condition. Some still are; others should be. It is important to know the difference.

Nor does government or management consist primarily in solving problems. It consists in regulating systems. Systems analysis means to me the analysis of a system. And the system to be analyzed has first to be defined by reference to the concern which makes it of interest to the policy maker.

This defining of the situation to be analyzed is a crucial preliminary task of the systems analysts. They must include all those factors, which are so important in the context of that concern, that none can be omitted without making nonsense of the others. (Water pollution, for example, is not a very important factor to someone planning a system of water-borne transport but it is vital if his/her concern is a trout hatchery or the distribution of drinking water). Some concerns relate to situations which are much simpler to analyze than others. Some relate to situations which are impossible to analyze because we do not know the crucial factors involved, or because we do not agree about them. Some relate to situations which we can analyze but not model in any quantitative way. The systems analyst should know these differences better than anyone; and the client senses them and is influenced by them in deciding what analyses to commission. It is no accident that these papers are almost wholly about transportation problems. None is concerned with crime or unemployment or housing policy or (with one partial exception) with education or with the treatment of cultural minorities. Yet these are major concerns of city governments and threaten dangers at least as great as overcrowded roads and subways.

I do not criticize these omissions. They acknowledge the limitations of systems analysis or at least of its current concepts of 'modelling', which are limited as well as enlarged by concern with quantitative computerized models so obsessive as almost to extinguish belief in the unaided powers of human judgement on which human governance has relied, not always unsuccessfully, for many millenia before the present generation. It is this obsession, as Dr Archibald has pointed out[1], which has virtually confined the phrase 'systems analysis' to 'systems modellers' and brought into use the wider phrase 'policy analysis' to cover all analyses made by whatever means to help the policy maker.

I do, however, criticize the paradoxical eclipse of the concept of system itself. Contributors always use the adjective systematic rather than systemic. One paper defines systems analysis as 'any rational procedure for understanding urban problems and predicting and prescribing possible solutions' and further defines these as 'systematic procedures which are at least partly explicit'. The terms *rational* and *systematic* remain undefined except that the procedures which they involve must be 'at least partly explicit'. There is scarcely any indication that *systems* (open systems for our purposes) are a specific kind of phenomenon, a broad class indeed but one which has important characteristics in common and that the study of them has greatly clarified and modified our conception of the nature and purpose of government and to a lesser extent of business management.

SYSTEMS AND THEIR REGULATION

Open systems have four characteristics which I wish to stress, familiar though they are, because they profoundly affect the nature of government and hence the objects of systems analysis.

First, an open system is a form more enduring than its constituents. The old philosopher who insisted that we cannot step twice into the same river seems to me to have been wilfully perverse. For he doubtless knew as well as we that the name of a river is the name of a form, not the name of a particular collection of water which happens to be flowing through it at any moment of time. The first concern of any systems analyst is to identify the factors which are preserving this form and to determine whether they are equal to their task. For these forms can change or oscillate between extremes or even dissolve. The dimension of stability-instability is inseparable from the concept of form. The form of a river is largely given by external factors, chiefly the contours of its catchment area. The form of an organism is largely given by internal factors, some of which are set to follow a course of most complex development, whilst others, such as those which preserve the internal temperature of so-called warm-blooded animals (and countless other internal relations, chemical and physical) are set to preserve internal stasis despite external change. The form of a society is determined partly by external pressures and opportunities and partly by internal cultural structures ranging from explicit laws to the countless subtle conventions which deter or control the spread of deviance.

Systems, then, are bundles of interacting relations, internal and external. The internal ones enable each to maintain coherence even through change. The external ones regulate the system's relation as a whole with its milieu including all the other systems of which it forms part. This is as true of a city government as of a cat. A city government contains departments, most of which are responsible for maintaining some set of relations within acceptable or at least viable limits—the relation of sewers to sewerage, schools to schoolchildren, roads to traffic and a dozen others. Other departments are concerned with the relations of the government as a whole with its surround, notably the relation of its revenue to its expenditure. All these departments compete with each other for scarce resources and some involve sometimes inconsistent activities. And each set of relations has a limit beyond which its breakdown will have sudden, acute and possibly irreversible repercussions on all the others. (How few city activities can continue if the sewers stop working!) The primary task of government is to keep all these relations, internal and external, within their permissible ranges—and hence to detect and correct instabilities before they become overwhelming. Its secondary task is to alter some or all of these relationships, if and when it can, in a way which is regarded by all who cannot be ignored as being on the whole more acceptable to them.

All this was true of times far more stable than our own. Today we see everywhere evidence of instability approaching breakdown. Inflation, unemployment, multiplying populations, increasing cost of energy and raw materials, degeneration of the biosphere, famine and endemic war all signal the breakdown of systems necessary to the survival of the race or at least of most of the major political systems by which human life is at present sustained on the planet. A systems view is necessary and it is useful even when it can be neither computerized nor quantified.

Everyone knows, for example, that if Britain continues to increase the populations of its prisons which are already grossly overcrowded even by the nineteenth-century standards to which many of them were built, something will pass a critical point and the system will break down. Perhaps all the prison governors will resign. Perhaps all the warders will walk out. Perhaps the felons will burn the places down. Perhaps. . . . No-one can predict precisely when the system will break down or what will trigger the breakdown or what form it will take. But the event is sufficiently certain to set a host of different 'problems' at different levels of the hierarchy—to prison governors regulating as best they may the relations of felons to prisons and especially to their warders and to each other; to the police in deciding what prosecutions to bring; to judges deciding what prison sentences to award; to the Home Office considering the organization of the service, the building of new prisons and alternative forms of custodial and noncustodial care; and to sociologists and others seeking to understand the generation of crime. All require analysis of many situations. Probably none would be aided by a computerized model. Yet I see no reason to suppose that any of them are beyond the understanding of a human mind.

Whether such understanding would be attained by a wholly rational process depends on the meaning given to that term but almost any currently accepted meaning would be obviously inadequate for at least four familiar reasons. First the judgements made by men about men are inescapably affected by the human experience of those who make the judgements and are usually affected for the better. Most of our vocabulary concerning human experience would have no meaning if it were not enlightened by experience of our own. Second these judgements involve appreciations of value as well as fact; for if no human value were involved there would be no concern and no analysis. Third human experience and action takes place in specific contexts and is radically affected by them. There is no means of formulating laws appropriate to each of an indefinite number of contexts or laws of any substantial use which are so general as to be indifferent to context. Fourth the situation as validly analyzed by each actor in a situation is different from the analysis made by all the others, even though each actor is aware of those others and takes account of them. For example, the situation posed by the collapse in demand for steel looks different and is different for a steel worker, a plant manager, a steel marketeer and a general manager, even though each succeeds by an effort of imagination in understanding what the appreciations of others mean to them and incorporating as much of it as is relevant to them. Concerns are highly personal and unless the essential parts of the analysis made by each are common to all, no concerted action is to be expected. The technologist of pre-1914, turning one physical state into another to the general delight and amazement of others and as indifferent to its systemic effects as they were, is the most unsuitable of all imaginable soils in which to grow the systems analyst of today.

REGULATION AS RESPONSE TO CHANGE

My experience of what I understand by systems analysis has not been primarily in the area of urban government but I will summarize it briefly to make the point. It begins on 12 November 1918—long before anyone was talking systems language, but not before competent policy makers were thinking systemically. On that day—the morning after the armistice which ended the First World War—the general commanding the division in which I was serving in France called together his battalion commanders and addressed them in substance as follows

Gentlemen, have you considered how you are going to manage without the Germans? Reflect on the changed situation in which this armistice has left you.

For more than four years everything we have done has been dictated by the German army as everything it has done has been dictated by the Allies. And our efforts to destabilize each other have produced a situation not merely stable but self-stabilizing. Until these last few months every attack by one side has petered out from inability to sustain its own momentum, at least as much as from the resistance of the other side. And now after only a few months of mobile warfare the inherent weaknesses have broken surface, political agreement has stopped the war—and where are we?

For more than four years France has been divided into an occupied zone—occupied by the Germans—and a free zone, defended by us. Now all the Germans will be gone in a few weeks but we shall be here for months. For the policy is to demobilize our army individually from here. Meantime we shall be the 'occupiers'. The French who were behind the German lines will be free to get their working life back into its familiar pattern. The French on our side will still have hundreds of thousands of idle, armed, alien men in their barns and houses. Think what that will be like for them.

And this demobilization policy. Men who have been out here for years may wait for months before the factories where they have been promised their old jobs can be turned round for civilian work again. But boys who have been out less than a year may be the first to go home to places in universities which are empty and waiting for them. All good logical sense. But think what it will be like for the old timers?

And how will they pass their time? Toughening up for a next battle that isn't going to be fought? Learning skills to win a war that has already been won?

They can't play football all day. Yet your continually shrinking force will be here all through a Normandy winter.

The conclusions are obvious. The external relations that matter to you now are no longer with the Germans or even with me but with the French civilian population and with the demobilization authorities at home. The first must be fostered as never before. The second must be trusted and endured. Neither will happen unless your men understand and respond to the changes I am describing. Please see that they do. Internally you have to find ways for them to spend their time bearably, if possible, enjoyably, even usefully. You are sure to find lots of internal resources if you look for them—skills which people have and will gladly teach: skills which others will be glad to learn. Present the situation to your men as a problem and engage them in solving it. And please start today. Today everyone is just listening to the silence. Tomorrow they will begin asking questions about what happens next. I want them to come up with the answers I'm giving you. This is a transient situation but it will last for months, and a lot can go wrong in a few months. Start now.

Across more than 60 years I remember that man with respect and admiration. He told his hearers nothing they did not know but he sent them away with an understanding of the situation and what it demanded of them which none, I think, had when he arrived. He did not weigh alternatives. The policy was clear once the situation was understood.

Did he act rationally? Certainly not irrationally, and yet what he said was not derived simply by logical deduction from proved or assumed postulates. It was primarily an exercise in empathy. He had never been a French farmer or a conscripted toolmaker but his experience of being human, though gained in the restricted context of a British pre-First-World-War regular soldier, was sufficient for him to see the situation not only as it was for him but as it would be seen by people whose position and experience was remote from his own. This is an important element in human judgement. Has it any bearing on the analysis of urban problems? What about those high-rise, low-rent apartment blocks of which at least two have had to be demolished by explosives within 30 years of their construction because no-one would live in them? Presumably those who decided on them and planned them calculated the costs and benefits in terms of site economy, increased traffic density, containment of urban sprawl, relative cost of erection and maintenance and other such quantifiable features. But it remains an essential criterion of success of any policy that it should be acceptable to those for whose benefit it is designed. The insights of General Campbell would perhaps have averted one of the most dramatic boobs in the history of urban planning.

My experience of systems analysis seems always to have been gained in the context of some sudden instability. But so have yours. Even transport problems become urgent only when the demand for mobility passes or is seen to be about to pass the facilities for mobility to an extent sufficiently acute to be deemed unacceptable by those affected. This threshold of the unacceptable is highly subjective but no less important for that. And it tends to be reached suddenly. For worsening relations tend to escalate and the threshold between the bearable and the unbearable is hard to anticipate until it is crossed. I recall the European glut of coke in the depression between the wars when the collapse in the demand for steel left the makers of the 'hard' coke used in blast furnaces with the alternatives of extinguishing their ovens or throwing their production on to the domestic market, already served in those days by the coke produced as a by-product by the gas industry. Their consumers, like the German army in 1918, had suddenly gone away. The only overriding certainty was that some agreement between the stranded coke producers of five countries would be less disastrous for them than a 'free for all' battle. I recall the even more elusive problems of the short-term money market when, following the first bank failures, confidence evaporated— confidence of banks in each other, confidence of industrial clients in banks, confidence of everyone in the banking system. Of all the constituents in any system of relations, confidence is the most basic and the hardest to renew.

This is no place to tell the resultant stories. They had a common theme—the restoration of stable relationships and of the trust by which all relationships are sustained. They had a common factor—shared understanding of what had destabilized those relations and what were the limits within which self-sustaining balance could be again restored. They had a common outcome—shared revision, usually downwards of the threshold of the acceptable.

They also shared some element of encouragement; for they showed that the self-regulating capacity of these complex systems was very great. This lesson was to be intensified for me a few years later when I found myself concerned with economic intelligence during the Second World War. It had been expected that the increased interdependence of the world for technological skills and materials would make economic limitations far more important and economic targets far more vulnerable. Again it was found that politico-economic systems are far more adaptive than had been expected—provided always that the will to sustain them remained unimpaired.

When in the years after the war I read some of the founding fathers of cybernetics and systems theory—Wiener, Bertalanffy, Ross Ashby—I felt much as I had felt 30 years before when that general analyzed what the armistice 'meant' for us. I remember still the intellectual excitement of acquiring a conceptual framework which made sense of much that I already knew and promised better understanding of whatever I might learn thereafter. Far more important, it seemed to promise a basis for common understanding of a manifestly unstable world and hence hope for common action and acceptance of action on a scale which would manifestly be needed but had not previously been in sight. Another 30 years on that hope is heavily clouded.

Two landmarks taken almost at random will make the point. In the early 1950s the State of California commissioned several 'systems analyses' of different fields of governmental activity. I write from memories I cannot now confirm and hope that I do not understate the vision behind those enquiries. But if I recall the affair aright, one inquiry concerned the disposal of 'trash'—but not the generation of trash. I was shocked. Could a systemic view take the generation of trash as given and concern itself only with disposing of a nuisance which was expanding exponentially? Apparently it could. I could think of many reasons why the inquiry's terms of reference should be thus truncated but none of them was encouraging.

A decade later the British report of Traffic in Towns[2] was more encouraging. This report (the Buchanan report) began by gently rewriting its terms of reference which were to consider the 'problem' of vehicular traffic in towns. This, said the committee, was no problem—only a symptom of the fact that modern towns generated more vehicular traffic than their often mediaeval layout could contain. They could be redesigned in four dimensions (including the allocation of temporal time bands) so as to accommodate more traffic. The report illustrated a host of unfamiliar innovations. Equally their activities could be regulated so as to generate less traffic. But urban design and urban activities, not merely roads and traffic were the minimal factors for inclusion in the situation to be analyzed. And the criteria for assessing any hypothetical action for improving the situation were equally widened, for any change would surely affect not only the flow of traffic but also pedestrian access, pedestrian safety, amenity, parking and the whole quality of urban life.

I was encouraged. This was no mere technical report. It was education in the art of governing and of being governed. I would like to see it a textbook in all secondary schools.

For there is no more important element in education today than the understanding of the systems which we form and by which we are both sustained and constrained. And these systems are formed not wholly or even chiefly of roads and buildings but of the standards of expectation entertained by ordinary men and women. These standards especially in the West are today, as I believe, exaggerated and conflicting to an unparalleled degree. Technological euphoria comparable in its potency and unreality to a Polynesian cargo cult is combined with eclipse and confusion of ethical standards and even of the relevance of ethical standards to a degree which seems to me wholly inconsistent with the demands made on every individual and every society by living in an overcrowded world of limited resources. My view may be unduly dark but even if it is, there must remain in my view a radical inconsistency between the traditional attitude of technology and the realities of government.

'The difficult we do at once. The impossible takes a little longer.' So boasted the technologist in his finest hour. None but the craziest autocrat has ever claimed such power in the field of government, least of all in the government of peoples among whom even small minorities today have powers of veto and destruction of which even majorities did not dream in days gone by. And on the other hand is the field of *knowledge* (obscure and ambiguous word!) which the technologist claims today is curiously limited. For it is increasingly confined to processes which can be transferred to a computer, still usually defined as 'logical processes which can be fully described' and therefore programmed) whereas even such confused epistemology as we have credits us with far wider mental capacities than this.

THE MEANING OF RATIONALITY

Thus I return to a topic on which I have already touched, the meaning of rationality. Almost all the papers at this conference declare their allegiance to the god of rationality but its meaning seems to vary as much as those of most gods to their various worshippers. For all it has a strong negative connotation—the reverse of what is irrational or, worse still, antirational. But can there be mental activities which are neither rational nor irrational? For many the proposition seems to be regarded as a contradiction in terms. Yet it was not always so and it is less so today than it was a hundred years ago.

This is no place for an essay on epistemology but it should be possible to make four points without fear of serious contradiction and it may be useful to do so.

First, the power to reason deductively by logical steps from known premises or from hypotheses to their necessary or probable results is a useful and distinctive property of the human mind for which the word *rationality* might well be reserved, as in fact it often is.

Brain scientists distinguish a separate mental capacity, involving the manipulation of form and context, figure and ground; it is sensitive to context rather than to cause and effect. They identify this as the source of creativity, including the origination of those scientific hypotheses which are subsequently tested by deductive processes. They thus legitimize what for many is a fact of direct experience, that thinking involves a dialogue between at least two mental faculties of which one is tacit, though its activities can be recognized. Since most brain scientists are neurophysiologists, much interest has attached to the location of these two faculties in different hemispheres of the brain. Recent work suggests that either location can in time learn to perform at least some of the functions of the other if the other is wholly removed. For the epistemologist these questions of location and of adaptation are unimportant. What matters is the confirmation that we possess at least two 'cognitive styles'[3] which supplement each other.

Third, nothing we yet know 'scientifically' about the working of the brain accounts adequately for the 'mental maps' which we all build up from experience and reflection (including the experience of communication with other human beings) and which we constantly use for three not always consistent purposes—to guide effective action; to sustain successful communication with each other; and to make meaningful and bearable all incoming experience, including our memory of past experience. It would none the less be more than perverse to try to ignore such maps since without them we could not carry on any of these three essential activities. Nor should we try to exclude their contents from the corpus of our knowledge, even though we know that they are fragmentary and not necessarily shared by others. Nor should we ignore our ability to understand or imagine the mental maps of others. For though such understanding is bound to be partial, sometimes wrong and often misleading it immensely exceeds anything we could construct without it.

Fourth, what I have called *concern* (which includes the whole field of what is commonly called values) is essential to the accumulation, use and revision of knowledge and can be neither kept in a separate compartment nor reduced to conditioned or unconditioned responses or to purposeful sequences which leave the origin of the purpose unexplained. The most important impact of control theory on our understanding of the higher levels of human motivation may well be that it legitimizes the concept of internal standards capable of generating signals of match and mismatch which in turn give coherence and quality to human behaviour.[4] Shared standards of this kind have always been necessary to the coherence of human societies. They are the prime sources of both commitment and constraint and their decay is the most sinister feature of the current human predicament, especially in the West.

They are not, of course, solely a personal artifact. Human beings are both social and acculturable creatures and such regularities as their societies show are intersubjective artifacts. Most philosophers of science today would, I think, agree that even the immense system of natural science is fundamentally only an intersubjective artifact. It may be hoped then that the nineteenth-century concept of knowledge as either subjective or objective (the first illusory, the second real) is at last widening to make room for the intersubjective dimension. Policy makers have never been able to avoid it. Their advisers should not try to do so.

The domain of the intersubjective can no longer be ignored, even though it may mislead. It conditions and enables all our understanding, scientific as well as political and ethical and aesthetic, our understanding of ourselves and each other even more than our understanding of the natural world. The analysts with their computer have as much right in that world as anyone else but at the moment have perhaps more influence. We do not want them to make it wholly in their own image.

REFERENCES

1. Archibald, A. (1979) Policy analysis and social science, *Proceedings of the Annual Meeting of the Association for Canadian Studies* (July)
2. *Traffic in Towns* (1963) HMSO, London
3. Gahn, D. (1974) Implications for psychiatry of left and right hemisphere specialisation, *Archives of General Psychiatry*, Vol. 31 (October)
4. I have developed this idea in (1973) Motivation theory—a cybernetic contribution, *Behavioral Science*, Vol. 18 (July). Reprinted in G. Vickers (1980) *Responsibility: its Sources and Limits*, Intersystems Publications. Seaside, CA

11   A BIAS FOR ACTION
T. J. Peters and R. H. Waterman

Eighty per cent of success is showing up.

                —Woody Allen

But above all try something.

                —Franklin Delano Roosevelt

Ready. Fire. Aim.

                —Executive at Cadbury's

There's an excitement about being in the game parks of East Africa that's impossible to describe. The books do not do it. The slides and movies do not do it. The trophies most of all do not do it. When you are there, you feel it. People who have been there can hold one another in rapt conversation for hours about it; people who have not been there cannot quite imagine it.

We experience some of the same helplessness in describing an excellent company attribute that seems to underpin the rest: action orientation, a bias for getting things done. For example, we were trying to depict to an executive responsible for project management coordination how it might be possible radically to simplify the forms, procedures, paperwork and interlocking directorates of committees that had overrun his system. We said, quite off-handedly, 'Well, at 3M and TI they don't seem to have these problems. People simply talk to each other on a regular basis.' He looked at us blankly. Our words hardly sounded like exotic advice—or even helpful advice. So we said, 'You're not competing with 3M. Let's go to St Paul for a day and take a look. You'll be surprised.'

Our friends at 3M were tolerant of the excursion, and we observed all sorts of strange goings-on. There were a score or more casual meetings in progress with salespeople, marketing people, manufacturing people, engineering people, R & D people—even accounting people—sitting around, chattering about new-product problems. We happened in on a session where a 3M customer had come to talk informally with about 15 people from four divisions on how better to serve his company. None of it seemed rehearsed. We did not see a single structured presentation. It went on all day—people meeting in a seemingly random way to get things done. By the end of the day our friend agreed that our description had been fairly accurate. Now *his* problem was the same as ours: he did not know how to describe the situation to anyone else.

It's very difficult to be articulate about an action bias, but it's very important to try, because it is a complex world. Most of the institutions that we spend time with are ensnared in massive reports that have been 'massaged' by various staffs and sometimes, quite literally, hundreds of staffers. All the life is pressed out of the ideas; only an iota of personal accountability remains. Big companies seem to foster huge laboratory operations that produce papers and patents by the ton, but rarely new products. These companies are besieged by vast interlocking sets of committees and task forces that drive out creativity and block action. Work is governed by an absence of realism, spawned by staffs of people who have not made or sold, tried, tasted or sometimes even seen the product, but instead have learned about it from reading dry reports produced by other staffers.

However, life in most of the excellent companies is dramatically different. Yes, they too have task forces, for example. But one is more apt to see a swarm of task forces that lasts five days, has a few members and results in line operators doing something differently rather than the 35-person task force that lasts 18 months and produces a 500-page report.

The problem we are addressing in this chapter is the all-too-reasonable and rational response to complexity in big companies: coordinate things, study them, form committees, ask for more data (or new information systems). Indeed, when the world is complex, as it is in big companies, a complex system often does seem in order. But this process is usually greatly overdone. Complexity causes the lethargy and inertia that make too many companies unresponsive.

The important lesson from the excellent companies is that life does not have to be that way. The excellent companies seem to abound in distinctly individual techniques that counter the normal tendency toward conformity and inertia. Their mechanism comprises a wide range of action devices, especially in the area of management systems, organizational fluidity, and experiments—devices that simplify their systems and foster a restless organizational stance by clarifying which numbers really count or arbitrarily limiting the length of the goal list.

ORGANIZATIONAL FLUIDITY: MBWA

Both Warren Bennis in *The Temporary Society* and Alvin Toffler in *Future Shock* identified the need for the 'adhocracy' as a way of corporate life. In rapidly changing times, they argued, the bureaucracy is not enough. By 'the bureaucracy', they mean the formal organization structure that has been established to deal with the routine, day-in, day-out items of business—sales, manufacturing and so on. By 'the adhocracy', they mean organizational mechanisms that deal with all the new issues that either fall between bureaucratic cracks or span so many levels in the bureaucracy that it's not clear who should do what; consequently, nobody does anything.

The concept of organizational fluidity, therefore, is not new. What *is* new is that the excellent companies seem to know how to make good use of it. Whether it's their rich ways of communicating informally or their special ways of using ad hoc devices, such as task forces, the excellent companies get quick action just because their organizations are fluid.

The nature and uses of communication in the excellent companies are remarkably different from those of their nonexcellent peers. The excellent companies are a vast network of informal, open communications. The patterns and intensity cultivate the right people's getting into contact with each other, regularly, and the chaotic/anarchic properties of the system are kept well under control simply because of the regularity of contact and its nature (for example, peer versus peer in quasi-competitive situations).

The intensity of communications is unmistakable in the excellent companies. It usually starts with an insistence on informality. At Walt Disney Productions, for instance, everyone from the president on down wears a name tag with only his or her first name on it. HP is equally emphatic about first names. Then come the open door policies. IBM devotes a tremendous amount of time and energy to them. The open door was a vital part of the original Watson philosophy, and it remains in force today—with 350 000 employees. The chairman continues to answer all complaints that come in to him from any employee. Open-door use is pervasive at Delta Airlines as well; at Levi Strauss it means so much that they call the open door the 'fifth freedom'.

Getting management out of the office is another contributor to informal exchanges. At United Airlines, Ed Carlson labelled it 'Visible Management' and 'MBWA—Management By Walking About'. HP treats MBWA ('Management by Wandering Around' in this instance) as a major tenet of the all-important 'HP Way'.

Another vital spur to informal communication is the deployment of simple physical configurations. Corning Glass installed escalators (rather than elevators) in its new engineering building to increase the chance of face-to-face contact. And, 3M sponsors clubs for any groups of a dozen or so employees for the sole purpose of increasing the probability of stray problem-solving sessions at lunchtime and in general. A Citibank officer noted that in one department the 'age-old operations versus lending-officer' split was solved when all in the group moved to the same floor with their desks intermingled.

What does it add up to? Lots of communication. All of HP's golden rules have to do with communicating more. Even the social and physical settings at HP foster it: you cannot wander around long in the Palo Alto facilities without seeing lots of people sitting together in rooms with blackboards, working casually on problems. Any one of those ad hoc meetings is likely to include people from R & D, manufacturing, engineering, marketing, and sales. That's in marked contrast to most large companies we have worked with, where the managers and analysts never meet or talk to customers, never meet or talk to salesmen, and never look at or touch the product (and the word *never* is not chosen lightly). A friend at HP, talking about that company's central lab organization, adds: 'We aren't really sure what structure is best. All we know for certain is that we start with a remarkably high degree of informal communication, which is the key. We have to preserve that at all costs.' The 3M beliefs are similar, which led one of its executives to say, 'There's only one thing wrong with your excellent company analysis. You need a ninth principle—communications. We just plain talk to each other a lot without a lot of paper or formal rigmarole.' All of these examples add up to a virtual *technology of keeping in touch*, keeping in constant informal contact.

In general, we observe the tremendous power of the regular, positive peer review. A simple tale comes from Tupperware. Tupperware makes about $200 million in pretax earnings on about $800 million in sales of simple plastic bowls. The key management task is motivating the more than 80 000 salespeople, and a prime ingredient is 'Rally'. Every Monday night all the saleswomen attend a rally for their distributorship. At Rally, everyone marches up on stage—in the reverse order of last week's sales—during a process known as Count Up (while their peers celebrate them by joining in All Rise). Almost everyone, if she has done anything at all, receives a pin or badge—or several pins and badges. Then they repeat the entire process with small units marching up. On the one hand, this is a fairly punishing drill—straight head-on-head competition that cannot be avoided. On the other hand, it is cast with a positive tone: everybody wins; applause and hoopla surround the entire event; and the evaluation technique is informal rather than paper-laden. In fact, the entire Tupperware system is aimed at generating good news opportunities and celebration. Every week there is an array of new contests. Take any three moribund distributorships: management will give a prize to whichever one has the best sales increase in the next eight weeks. Then there are the 30 days of Jubilee each year in which *15 000* are feted (3000 at a time in week-long events) with awards, prizes and ceremonies of all kinds. The entire environment is one that utilizes, in the extreme, positive reinforcement.

Above all, when we look at HP, Tupperware and others, we see a very conscious management effort to do two things: honour with all sorts of positive reinforcement any valuable, completed action by people at the top and more especially way down the line; and seek out a high volume of opportunities for good news swapping.

We should note that when we were doing the first round of survey interviews, the three principal interviewers gathered together after about six weeks. When we tried to summarize what seemed most important (and different) to us, we unanimously agreed that it was the marvellously informal environments of the excellent companies. We have not changed our view since. The name of the successful game is rich, informal communication. The astonishing by-product is the ability to have your cake and eat it, too; that is, rich informal communication leads to more action, more experiments, more learning and simultaneously to the ability to stay better in touch and on top of things.

Now consider this. 'The Chase senior executive's voice was tinged with reluctant admiration,' reports *Euromoney*. 'If they don't like it at Citibank, they change it—not gradually, like we would, but immediately, even if they have to turn the bank upside down to do it.' And this: one IBM executive commented, 'It is said that back in the 1960s, IBM set an objective of being able to mount a major reorganization in just a few weeks.' IBM's values remain constant, and the attendant stability permits it structurally to shift major hunks of resources to attack a particular problem. At the smaller end of the spectrum, the CEO of successful TRAK, a $35-million, sporting-goods company, noted that in order to keep his stars turned on he had to move to a flexible organization: 'You've got to keep coming up with new projects to hang on to valuable people . . . . [Our approach] is flexible reorganization and task teams. We're making it a permanent part of our organizing scheme.'

Again, Harris Corporation has done the virtually impossible: it has largely licked the problem of diffusing research funded by the government into areas that are commercially viable. Many others have tried, and almost all have failed. The prime ingredient in Harris's success is that the management regularly shifts chunks of engineers (25 to 50) out of government projects and moves them, as a group, into new commercial venture divisions. Similar moves have been crucial to Boeing's success. One officer notes: 'We can do it [create a big new unit] in two weeks. We couldn't do it in two years at International Harvester.'

There are scores of variations on this theme in the excellent companies, but they all come down to a refreshing willingness readily to shift resources: chunks of engineers, chunks of marketers, products among divisions and the like.

Chunking

We vividly recall walking into the office of a top-flight line officer who was now a 'product group coordinator'. He was a tough old nut who had won his spurs solving labour negotiation problems. Now his desk was bare, and he thumbed idly through a *Harvard Business Review* collection of human relations articles. When we talked about what he was up to, he produced a list of committees that he chaired. This illustration adds up, de facto, to the matrix; it adds up to an environment of fragmented responsibilities. It does not add up to what we found in the excellent companies.

The line officer who has headed one of Exxon's Asian affiliates for the last 10 years made a presentation on 'strategy' at a recent top management meeting. He reported a remarkable tale of improvement. Was it a tale of shrewd foresight and bold strategic moves? Not in our view. It was a story, instead, of a series of pragmatic actions. In almost every one of the 10 years, some single problem had been knocked off. One year a blitzkrieg group came through from regional headquarters and helped him get receivables under control. Another year, the attack was aimed at closing down some unprofitable segments. In another year, a further blitz effort helped work out a novel arrangement with distributors. It was a classic example of what we have come to call the 'theory of chunks'. We have come to believe that the key success factor in business is simply getting one's arms around almost any practical problem and knocking it off – now. Exxon in Japan simply executed (to near perfection) a series of practical manoeuvres. They made each problem manageable. Then they blitzed it. The time associated with each programme was fairly short. That it was the *real* number one priority for that short period of time was unquestioned. It sounded like strategic foresight, but we would argue that it was a much more remarkable trait: they had just gotten a string of practical tasks done correctly.

There is an underlying principle here, an important trait of the action orientation that we call chunking. That simply means breaking things up to facilitate organizational fluidity and to encourage action. The action-oriented bits and pieces come under many labels—champions, teams, task forces, czars, project centres, skunk works and quality circles—but they have one thing in common. They never show up on the formal organization chart and seldom in the corporate phone directory. They are nevertheless the most visible part of the adhocracy that keeps the company fluid.

The small group is the most visible of the chunking devices. Small groups are, quite simply, the basic organizational building blocks of excellent companies. Usually when we think of organizational building blocks, we focus on higher levels of agglomeration—departments, divisions or strategic business units. Those are the ones that appear on the organization charts. But in our minds, the small group is critical to effective organizational functioning. In this sense (as well as many others) the excellent companies look very Japanese. In *Japan As Number One*, Ezra Vogel says that the entire business and social structure of Japanese companies is built around the Kacho (section head) and the 8-to-10-person group that typically comprises a section:

> The essential building block of a company is not a man with a particular role assignment and his secretary and assistants. The essential building block of the organization is the section . . . The lowly section, within its sphere, does not await executive orders but takes the initiatives . . . . For this system to work effectively leading section personnel need to know and to identify with company purposes to a higher degree than persons in an American firm. They achieve this through long experience and years of discussion with others at all levels.

Apparently the small group as a building block works in the United States as well, although not as so natural a part of the national culture as it does in Japan. In the new-product area, 3M has several hundred 4-to-10-person venture teams running about. Or recall TI's 9000 teams zipping about looking for small productivity improvements. In Australia, one of the few large companies with an excellent labour record is ICI. Among the programmes that managing director Dirk Ziedler implemented in the early 1970s was a series of interlocking teams that look very much like the Japanese section.

The true power of the small group lies in its flexibility. New product teams are formed anywhere at 3M and nobody worries very much about whether or not they fit exactly into division boundaries. Appropriately, TI chairman Mark Shepherd calls his company 'a fluid, project-oriented environment'. The good news from the well-run companies is that what ought to work does work.

It's also quite remarkable how effective team use in the excellent companies meets, to a tee, the best academic findings about the make-up of effective small groups. For instance, the effective productivity or new product teams in the excellent companies usually range from 5 to 10 in size. The academic evidence is clear on this: optimal group size, in most studies, is about 7. Other findings are supportive. Teams that consist of *volunteers*, are of *limited duration* and *set their own goals* are usually found to be much more productive than those with the obverse traits.

The Ad-hoc Task Force

The task force can be the epitome of effective chunking. Unfortunately, it can also become the quintessence of hopeless bureaucracy. How well we remember the analysis! The client was a $600 million sector of a several-billion-dollar company. We inventoried the task forces and there were 325 of them formally in existence. So far, not much news. What really floored us, and the company in turn, was that not a single task force had completed its charge in the last three years. Not a single one had been disbanded either. In a similar situation with another client we randomly picked task-force reports and found that the typical length was well over 100 pages; sign-offs ran from 20 on up to nearly 50.

Let's quickly review recent history to understand the current love affair with task forces. Although they undoubtedly existed previously in many unlabelled forms, NASA and the Polaris programme gave them a good name. NASA invented the ad-hoc team structure and in early programmes delivered the goods. The Polaris submarine programme worked even better. The task-force notion then diffused to industry and was used for everything. By 1970, it had become incorporated so pervasively in many large companies that it had become just one additional part of the rigid system it was meant to fix.

In hindsight, several things went wrong. Like any other tool adopted within a bureaucratic context, it eventually became an end in itself. Paper-pushing and coordination took the place of task-directed activity. Stodgy, formal, paper-bound, rule-driven institutions layered the task force on a maze that lay beneath, rather than using it as a separable, action-inducing chunk. Task forces became nothing more than coordinating committees—with a different name. Like other management tools adopted in the wrong context, the task force made things worse, not better.

That's the bad news. The goods news is that in organizations in which the context is right—ready acceptance of fluidity and adhocracy—the task force has become a remarkably effective problem-solving tool. In effect, it is the number one defence against formal matrix structures. It acknowledges the need for multifunctional problem-solving and implementation efforts, but not through the establishment of permanent devices.

A story helps to illustrate our point. In the midst of this survey, one of us walked into Digital headquarters in Maynard, Massachusetts, on a blustery February day. After we had finished the formal part of the interview, we asked one executive to describe some of the actual stuff he would be working on for the next few days. We wanted to get a flavour for the way things really work at Digital.

He said that he and six other people from the company were about to reorganize the national sales force. Each of the seven is a senior line manager. Each has full authority to sign off on the change for his group. We were talking to this fellow on a Thursday. He and the group would be leaving for Vail, Colorado (they are not fools at Digital), that evening. He said, 'We'll be back by Monday night, and I expect we'll announce the changes in the sales force on Tuesday. The front end of the implementation should be well in place a week or so later.'

As we did more interviewing, we repeatedly heard variations on this theme. The hallmarks of task-force work that we found at such disparate companies as Digital, 3M, HP, TI, McDonald's, Dana, Emerson Electric and Exxon were strikingly different from the bureaucratic model we had come to expect from so many other situations. At the excellent companies, task forces were working the way they are supposed to work.

There are not many members on these task forces, usually 10 or less. They really are the incarnation of the small group properties we talked about earlier. The unfortunate contrasting tendency in the bureaucratic model is to involve everyone who might have an interest. Task-force membership typically balloons to the twenties, and we have even seen a few with as many as 75 members. The point is to limit active task-force participation to the principal actors. That would not work in many companies, because it requires trust on the part of those left out that they will be represented well.

The task force reporting level, and the seniority of its members, are proportional to the importance of the problem. If the problem is a big one, virtually all members are senior people and the task force reports to the chief executive. It is essential that the people have the charter to make stick whatever they recommend. A Digital executive said, 'We want senior members only, no substitutes. The kinds of people we want are busy people whose main objective is to get off the damned task force and get back to work.' We call this the 'busy member theorem'.

The duration of the typical task force is very limited. This is a compelling characteristic. At TI, it's rare if any task force lasts more than four months. Among the exemplary companies, the idea that any task force could last more than six months is repugnant.

Membership is usually voluntary. This was explained to us best at 3M: 'Look, if Mike asks me to serve on a task force, I will. That's the way we do things. But it had better be a real problem. There'd better be some results. If there aren't, I'm damned if I'm going to waste my time helping Mike again. If it's my task force, I'll try to make sure that those who spend time on it get real value from it.'

The task force is pulled together rapidly, when needed, and usually not accompanied by a formal chartering process. Since task-force work is the primary means of problem-solving in complex, multifunctional environments, the survey companies, fortunately, are able to pull them together at the drop of a hat and with little fanfare. By contrast, in the bureaucracy of 325 task forces described earlier, formal written charters (often lengthy) accompanied each task force.

Follow-up is swift. TI is exemplary in this regard. We are told that three months after a task force is formed, senior management wants to know what happened as a result. 'Nothing; we're still working on a report,' is not a satisfactory answer.

No staff are assigned. About half of the 325 task forces mentioned earlier had permanent staff assigned to them: paper shufflers associated with a paper-shuffling group. In *no* instance at TI, HP, 3M, Digital or Emerson was there a report of a 'staff' person permanently assigned to a task force as an executive director, an 'assistant to' or a full-time report writer.

Documentation is informal at most, and often scant. As one executive told us, 'Task forces around here are not in the business of producing paper. They are in the business of producing solutions.'

Finally, we must reiterate the importance of context, of climate. The necessity of open communications was underscored by IBM's Frederick Brooks in his discussion of the System 360 development, for which he was a principal architect. Although this was a giant project team and much larger in scope than what is typically meant by a task force, the structure was fluid. According to Brooks, reorganizations took place with great regularity. Contact among members was intense; all principal players met in conference for a half day each week to review progress and decide on changes. Minutes were published within less than 12 *hours*. Everyone on the project had access to all the information needed: every programmer, for instance, saw all the material coming from every group on the project. Nobody who attended the weekly meetings came in an advisory (staff) role. 'Everyone had the authority to make binding commitments,' says Brooks. The System 360 group had annual 'supreme court' sessions, which typically lasted two full weeks. Any problems not solved elsewhere were resolved in this intensive two-week interchange. Most companies we observed could not conceive of sending 20 key players off for two weeks; or of meeting together for a half day each week. Nor could they conceive of widespread information sharing or meetings at which all participants had the authority to making binding commitments.

The difference between this and the way so many other organizations do business is so striking that one more example from the nonexcellent side seems a fitting close to this section. We were recently asked to review why a computer-based management information system project was not working. This project crossed many organizational boundaries and had been organized as a task force. We pieced together a case history of its activities over the previous year, and found that, although it was following most of the rules of good task-force management, the computer people and the division people were almost never in face-to-face communication, except at formal meetings. They could, for example, have moved into a common facility; a small group, they could even have worked in the same room. But neither was willing to do so. On trips to the field, they could have stayed in the same hotel, but they never did. One side claimed it was staying in less expensive hotels; the other countered that it was staying closer to the plants. They could have at least dined together after hours on field trips, but one side liked to play tennis and the other did not. It all sounds pretty silly, and client executives did not believe us, initially. But when we finally got all the people in the same room, they reluctantly agreed that we were right on every score. It would be nice to report that it got better after that, but it never did. The project, sound in all respects from a business standpoint, was eventually scrubbed.

Project Teams and Project Centres

The analysis of the task force is a favourite. Everyone does it, yet the excellent companies use this mundane tool quite differently from the rest. The task force is an exciting, fluid, ad-hoc device in the excellent companies. It is virtually *the* way of solving and managing thorny problems, and an unparalleled spur to practical action.

IBM organized for the System 360 project by using the very large task-force or project team, another form of adhocracy. People say that the project moved forward with lots of fits and starts, but the System 360's organization, particularly in its later years, clearly attracted the institution's top talent and set it to work on the monumental task—with no distractions. Companies like Boeing, Bechtel and Fluor use massive project teams like this all the time. Indeed, it is fundamental to their way of doing business as so much of their business is project work. They have an impressive ability to shift rapidly between structures—their routine structure for day-to-day affairs and their project-team structure. What is perhaps even more impressive, though, is to see a big company that *does* not routinely use project teams shifting into this mode with the ease of an experienced driver shifting gears. That seemed to be the case with IBM and the System 360, and we are impressed.

General Motors provides another particularly striking example of use of the temporary structure. The automotive industry is under attack. Virtually everything American automotive management does seems to be a day late and a dollar short. Yet we are impressed by any $60-billion institution that can beat its principal domestic competitors by almost three years on an implementation task, which is exactly what GM did with its down-sizing project. The principal vehicle was the project centre, a classic temporary organization. GM's project centre took 1200 key people out of the historically autonomous GM divisions—including the division's most important people, such as the chief engineers—and put them in the project centre. The centre lasted for four years. It had a clear task: to get the down-sizing job fully specified, under way and passed back to the divisions for final implementation. The real magic to the story is that when the task was accomplished, the project centre for down-sizing disappeared in 1978. GM, in fact, was so pleased with the down-sizing success that it has chosen to adopt project centres as a prime mode of organizing for the 80s. Eight project centres now exist in a special project-centre building. Two of these are currently working on the electric car and overall engine computerization; another is working on labour issues.

Most organizations, when confronted with an overwhelming strategic problem, either give it to planning staffs or tack it on to the objectives of numerous otherwise busy line managers. If staff is supposed to solve the problem, commitment never develops. If the usual line organization is supposed to solve it, momentum never develops. IBM's System 360 or GM's down-sizing project are dramatic, promising examples of the way in which problems like this can be successfully attacked.

The Japanese use this form of organization with frightening alacrity. To build a world-competitive position in, say, robotics or microcomputing, the Japanese pull key people from various companies into project centres to do the basics in development research. When the key technological problems have been solved, the key people go back to their own companies and compete vigorously with one another. Products are then ready for the world—after they have been honed by tough competition within Japan.

Honda's CVCC programme is an example. Key people were pulled off all other tasks and put on the CVCC project for several years. Canon did the same thing in developing its Canon AE-1; the company bundled 200 of its senior engineers together in 'Task Force X' for two and a half years until the AE-1 was developed, implemented and successfully launched in the market place.

There are numerous other examples of chunking, discussed in our book, *In Search of Excellence*. Here, however, there are four main messages that we want to get across about chunking. First, ideas about cost efficiency and economies of scale are leading us into building big bureaucracies that simply cannot act. Second, the excellent companies have found numerous ways (not just a few) to break things up in order to make their organizations fluid, and to put the right resources against problems. Third, all the chunking and other devices will not work unless the context is right. Attitudes, climate and culture must treat ad-hoc behaviour as more normal than bureaucratic behaviour. Finally, the free-wheeling environments in which ad-hoc behaviour flourishes are only superficially unstructured and chaotic. Underlying the absence of formality lie shared purposes, as well as an internal tension and a competitiveness that make these cultures as tough as nails.

EXPERIMENTING ORGANIZATIONS

'Do it, fix it, try it,' is our favourite axiom. Karl Weick adds that 'chaotic action is preferable to orderly inaction'. 'Don't just stand there, do something,' is of the same ilk. Getting on with it, especially in the face of complexity, does simply come down to trying something. Learning and progress accrue only when there is *something* to learn from, and the something, the stuff of learning and progress, is any completed action. The process of managing this can best be thought of in terms of the experiment and, on a more pervasive basis, the experimenting process.

The most important and visible outcropping of the action bias in the excellent companies is their willingness to try things out, to experiment. There is absolutely no magic in the experiment. It is simply a tiny completed action, a manageable test that helps you learn something, just as in high-school chemistry. But our experience has been that most big institutions have forgotten how to test and learn. They seem to prefer analysis and debate to trying something out, and they are paralyzed by fear of failure, however small.

The problem was accurately described recently in *Science*. NASA 'invented' a technique called Success Oriented Management (SOM) to control space-shuttle development. It assumes that everything will go right. As one official put it, 'It means you design everything to cost and then pray.' The intention was to eliminate parallel and possibly redundant development in test hardware, in response to the current cost pressures facing the agency. But as *Science*—and others—noted, the programme has led to wholesale deferrals of difficult work, embarrassing accidents, expensive redesigns, erratic staffing and the illusion that everything is running well. 'The net effect of this management approach,' says *Science*, 'has been an absence of realistic plans, inadequate understanding of the status of the program, and the accumulation of schedule and cost deficits without visibility.'

Nowhere has the problem been more obvious than in the development of the space shuttle's three main engines. *Science* reports, 'Rather than test each engine component separately, NASA's main contractor simply bolted it all together, and—with fingers crossed—turned on the power. At least five major fires resulted.' Under the influence of SOM, NASA officials began to confuse prediction with reality (in fairness, this was probably forced on them by political reality). NASA suffered from 'technological hubris', says a Senate analyst. 'Managers become overconfident that technological breakthroughs would materialize to save the situation.' This is certainly not the NASA of old, where redundancy was purposeful, testing took place regularly and programmes were on time—and worked.

The similarity and abundance of such tales is frightening, and they add up to nothing less than common management practice. For example, a giant bank prepared to introduce travellers' cheques into a highly competitive market. A task force laboured 18 months and produced a cabinetful of market analyses. As the nationwide launch date approached, we asked the head of the project what he had done in the way of hard market testing. He answered that he had talked to two banker friends in Atlanta about carrying the cheques. 'Two?' was our incredulous reaction. 'Two,' he affirmed. 'We weren't sure the project would be approved. We didn't want to tip our hand.'

We hear feeble excuses like this day in and day out. On the other hand, we were impressed by an incisive comment made by a friend at Crown Zellerbach, a competitor of P & G in some paper product markets. 'P & G tests and tests and tests. You can see them coming for months, often years. But you know that when they get there, it is probably time for you to move to another niche, not to be in their way. They leave no stone unturned, no variable untested.' P & G is apparently not afraid of testing and therefore telegraphing its moves. Why? Because, we suspect, the value added from learning before the nationwide launch so far exceeds the costs of lost surprise.

Getting on with it marks P & G and most of the excellent companies. Charles Phipps, of Texas Instruments, describes the company's early success, its willingness to be bold and daring. He captures the spirit of the experiment—TI's ability to learn quickly, to get something (almost anything) out in the field. 'They surprised themselves: as a very small company, $20 million, with very limited resources, they found they could outmanouevre large laboratories like Bell Labs, RCA and GE in the semiconductor area, because they'd just go out and try to *do* something with it, rather than keep it in the lab.'

Example after example reflected the same experimenting mentality. At Bechtel, senior engineers talk about their guiding credo, maintaining a 'fine feel for the do-able'. At Fluor, the principal success factor may be what they call 'taking an idea and making metal out of it'. At Activision, the watchword for video-game design is 'build a game as quickly as you can. Get something to play with. Get your peers fooling with it right away. Good ideas don't count around here. We've got to see something.' At a successful $25-million designer-household-goods operation, Taylor & Ng in San Francisco, owner Win Ng describes his philosophy: 'Developing a prototype early is the number one goal for our designers, or anyone else who has an idea, for that matter. We don't trust it until we can see it and feel it.'

At HP, it's a tradition that product-design engineers leave whatever they are working on out on top of their desk so that anyone can play with it. Walking around is the heart of their philosophy for all employees, and the trust level is so high that people feel free to tinker with the things their colleagues are inventing. One young engineer says: 'You quickly learn that you ought to have something for people to play with. You are told probably on the first day that the fellow walking around playing with your gadget is likely to be a corporate executive, maybe even Hewlett or Packard.' HP also talks about the 'next bench syndrome'. The idea is that you look around you to people working at the next bench and think of things that you might invent to make it easier for them to do their jobs.

Robert Adams, head of R & D at 3M, puts it this way: 'Our approach is to make a little, sell a little, make a little more.' McDonald's has more experimental menu items, store formats and pricing plans than any of its competitors. In the course of our first three hours of interviewing at Dana, we heard mention of more than 60 different productivity experiments that were going on at one plant or another. P & G is, as we have said, especially well known for what one analyst calls its 'testing fetish'. Other examples from well-managed companies pour in daily. According to one analyst, 'Bloomie's [Bloomingdale's] is the only large-volume retailer that experiments storewide.' In fact, in response to that observation, an employee from Levi Strauss who was attending a recent seminar piped up and said, 'You know that's where Levi got the faded jeans idea. Bloomie's was buying our jeans and bleaching them.' Holiday Inns is said to have 200 test-hotel sites in operation where they are continually experimenting with rooms, pricing and restaurant menus. At the very successful Ore-Ida company, market tests, taste tests, pricing tests and consumer panels are under way continuously, and the chief executive is as familiar with these tests and their results as he is with the 'financials'.

The critical factor is an environment and a set of attitudes that encourage experimentation. This comment, by the man who invented the transistor, catches the quintessence of the experiment:

I lean more to being a believer of low cunning and expediency . . . . How do you go about starting a job? You have the people who read everything; they don't get anywhere. And the people who read nothing—they don't get anywhere either. The people who go around asking everybody, and the people who ask nobody. I say to my own people, 'I don't know how to start a project. Why don't you step out and do an experiment?' You see, there is one principle here. You don't first start on something which is going to take six man-months before you get to the answer. You can always find something in which, in a few hours of effort, you will have made some little steps.

David Ogilvy likewise says there is no more important word than *test*:

The most important word in the vocabulary of advertising is TEST. If you pre-test your product with consumers, and pretest your advertising, you will do well in the marketplace. Twenty-four out of twenty-five new products never get out of test markets. Manufacturers who *don't* test-market their products incur the colossal cost (and disgrace) of having their products fail on a national scale, instead of dying inconspicuously and economically in test markets. Test your promise. Test your media. Test your headlines and your illustrations. Test your level of expenditure. Test your commercials. Never stop testing and your advertising will never stop improving . . . . Most young men in big corporations behave as if profit were not a function of time. When Jerry Lambert scored his first breakthrough with Listerine, he speeded up the whole process of marketing by dividing time into *months*. Instead of locking himself into *annual* plans, Lambert reviewed his advertising and his profits every month. The result was that he made $25 000 000 in eight years, where it takes most people twelve times as long. In Jerry Lambert's day, the Lambert Pharmacal Company lived by the month, instead of by the year. I commend that course to all advertisers.

Peter Peterson (now chairman of Lehman Brothers), speaking of the days when he was president of Bell & Howell, provides a lovely, concrete example of an experiment:

Have you heard of zoom lenses? One of the great advantages of being new in a company is that you are thoroughly unaware of what cannot be done. I thought a zoom camera was something that you used for football games. That was my image—an extraordinarily expensive object. One day I was in the lab, and there was a zoom lens. I have never seen one in my life, and I put it up to my eyes, and—well, it is a very dramatic thing. They explained to me that this was not applicable to consumer products, because it would cost a fair amount of money and so on. I asked, 'What would it cost to make a camera for me—just one with a zoom lens on it?' They said, 'Just one? Do you mean a crude modification? I think we would probably spend $500 on it.' I said, 'Well, suppose we do that; because my rates come pretty high, it will cost at least $500 for us to continue this discussion for another hour or two, so let's just do this.' I took this camera home. At a dinner party that night, I put this zoom lens on the piano, and I asked everybody coming in if they wouldn't participate in a very sophisticated piece of market research; namely, to put the camera to their eye. To the man, the reaction was extraordinarily enthusiastic: 'My, this is marvellous; I've never seen anything like this in my life.' We did this for about $500 .... If more industry would try out new ideas on a low-cost basis, perhaps their expectations of what the market will bear would go up.

Peterson's story contains several important messages about the experimenting mentality in business. The obvious one is the cost effectiveness of trying something as an alternative to analyzing everything. Less obvious is the ability of people to think more creatively—and at the same time concretely—with prototype in hand.

In his classic work *Language in Thought and Action*, S. I. Hayakawa captures the essence of the phenomenon when he points out that a cow is not a cow. Bessie the cow is not Janie the cow. He is talking about the importance of being able to leap from one level of abstraction to another—from cow to Bessie and Janie—in order to think clearly or communicate effectively.

For instance, one of us recently spent a pleasant weekend afternoon concocting homemade soap. The task is not too complex. The manual we used was clearly, even, at times, beautifully written. Yet we did a host of things wrong, we learned a score or more little tricks that will help next time around—all in just two or three hours. For example, exact alignment of temperatures between the lye mixture and the dissolved fats mixture is critical. The manual is clear on this and provides lots of tips. But still we had problems; one pan was metal, shallow and had a large surface area; the other container was glass, tall and narrow. Shape and material differences, among other things, led to substantially different cooling rates at the critical moment. Only 'feel' can help one to confront such complex phenomena quickly. The richness of the experience (in mathematical parlance, the number of variables surfaced and manipulated) that occurs *solely* when one is exposed tangibly to a subject, material or process is unmatchable in the abstract, via paper analysis or description.

Thus, when 'touch it', 'taste it', 'smell it' become the watchwords, the results are most often extraordinary. Equally extraordinary are the lengths to which people will go to avoid the test-it experience. Fred Hooven, protégé or Orville Wright, holder of 38 major patents, and senior engineering faculty member at Dartmouth, describes a ludicrous, yet all too typical, case:

> I can think of three instances in my career in which my client was making no progress on a complicated mechanical problem, and I insisted that the engineers and the technicians [model builders] be put in the same room. In each case the solution came rapidly. *One objection I remember being offered was that if we put the engineers in the same room with the shop it would get the drawings dirty.*

Hooven adds, in support of the overall point,

The engineer must have immediate and informal access to whatever facilities he needs to put his ideas into practice .... It costs more to make drawings of a piece than to make the piece, and the drawing is only one-way communication, so that when the engineer gets his piece back he has probably forgotten why he wanted it, and will find out that it doesn't work because he made a mistake in the drawings, or that it needs a small change in some respect, which too often takes another four months to make right.

So, via experimentation, it is much easier for people (for example, designers, marketers, presidents, salesmen, customers) to think creatively about a product or be creative about product uses, if a prototype, which is to say a low level of abstraction, is in hand. Thus, no amount of market research would have predicted the phenomenal success of the Apple II computer. We think it was the combination of a high-quality product and the emergence of an astonishing network of user groups, all playing with the machines and contributing new software almost daily, that made it such a success. No market research would have predicted that a woman we know would be the single biggest user of the Apple in her family; she, least of all, would have predicted that. It was starting her own business, based in her home, and having the Apple there, where she could try it and play with it at leisure, that made all the difference. Beforehand, had you told her about the wonders of word-processing, she would have predicted (in fact, did predict) that she would not use it. The concept was too abstract. Having the machine to play with, though, made her a convert.

That is why HP puts such emphasis on having its engineers leave their new experimental prototypes out where others can fool around with them. That is why Peterson's dinner-party market research on the zoom lens was, in fact, the most sophisticated marketing research imaginable.

Speed and Numbers

Alacrity and sheer numbers of experiments are critical ingredients to success through experimentation. Several years ago, we studied the successful versus the less successful wildcatters in the oil business. We concluded that if you had the best geologists, the latest in geophysical technique, the most sophisticated equipment and so on, the success rate in wildcat-drilling in established fields would amount to about 15 per cent. Without all these plusses, the success ratio dips to around 13 per cent. That finding suggests that the denominator—the number of tries—counts for a great deal. Indeed, an analysis of Amoco, recently revitalized to become the top US domestic oil finder, suggests just one success factor: *Amoco simply drills more wells.* The company's head of production, George Galloway, says, 'Most favorable results were unforeseen by us or anybody else .... That happens *if* you drill a lot of wells.' We found the same phenomenon in minerals exploration. The critical difference between the unsuccessful exploration companies is a dramatic difference in the amount of diamond (bit) drilling that they do. Although diamond drilling *looks* expensive, it is the only way to find out what's really down there. The rest is all speculation, however well-informed, by the geologists and geophysicists.

A former Cadbury's senior manager likewise underscores the value of speed and numbers. He recalls Cadbury's appointment of a new product-development executive. The fellow looked at what was lying fallow in the development pipeline and blithely announced that there would be six new product rollouts in the next 12 months, and six in the 12 months thereafter. Almost everything he planned to roll out had been in various states of limbo for two to seven years. He met his schedule, and three of the products are still big winners today. A veteran of the event commented, 'You can cut the time to launch *at will*, if you just want to. He went through twelve in just twenty-four months. We wouldn't have done an iota better if we had taken five years to launch the same volume.'

Peterson explains the rationale behind the Cadbury phenomenon. An experiment, because it is a simple action, can be subjected to unreasonably tight deadlines. Under deadline pressure—*and* with manageable acts to perform—the impossible occurs regularly, it seems. Peterson comments:

> It has been my observation that people often work on something for years and then some urgent situation comes up . . . and it suddenly comes through. Now, in one case we had an 8 mm electric eye movie camera in development, and we anticipated it would take about three years to complete. Then one day the marketing vice president decided to try a different technique. He took something down to the engineers and said, 'I just got an announcement that our competitors have an 8 millimeter electric eye camera!' Within 24 hours they had a completely different approach. I wonder just what is the role of urgency?

Speed means 'quick in' (try it now) *and* also 'quick out'. Storage Technology President Jesse Aweida's penchant for making decisions keeps the whole company in a state of constant experimentation. *Fortune* reports:

> A disc drive . . . cost $1500 more to make than it sold for. With characteristic dispatch, Aweida raised the price 50%, and when that didn't work, killed off the product, despite having invested $7 million in it . . . . He loathes inaction. As he told STC's national sales meeting last January, 'I often believe that making a decision, even a bad decision, is better than making no decision at all.' His ability to change course quickly has rescued the company from some of its bad decisions. Fortunately for STC, Aweida's vaulting ambition is balanced by his knack for quick correction.

There is a quality in experimentation as a corporate mind set that resembles nothing so much as a game of stud poker. With each card the stakes get higher, and with each card you know more, but you never really know enough until the last card has been played. The most important ability in the game is knowing when to fold.

With most projects or experiments, no matter how many milestones you set or PERT charts you draw, all you are really buying with the money invested is more information. You never know for sure until after the fact whether it has all been worthwhile or not. Moreover, as the project or experiment gets rolling, each major step becomes much more expensive than the last one—and harder to stop because of sunk costs and, especially, ego commitments. The crucial management decision is whether to fold. The best project management and experimenting management systems we have seen treat these activities more or less like poker. They break them up into manageable chunks; review quickly; and don't overmanage in the interim. Making it work simply means treating major projects as nothing more than experiments, which is indeed what all of them are, and having the poker player's mental toughness to fold one hand and immediately start another whenever the current hand stops looking promising.

Cheap Learning: Invisibility and Leaky Systems

Experimentation acts as a form of cheap learning for most of the excellent companies, usually proving less costly—and more useful—than sophisticated market research or careful staff planning. Again, talking of his days at Bell & Howell, Peterson is quite clear about this:

> Before we let an idea get emasculated, and before we let any thoroughly rational appraisal of the idea convince us that it will not work, we ask ourselves another question. Is there any way that we can experiment with this idea at low cost? The experiment is the most powerful tool for getting innovation into action and probably is not as widely used as it should be in American Industry .... The point I am trying to make is that if we can get the concept of the experiment built into our thinking and thereby get evidence on a lot of these 'cans', 'won'ts', 'shouldn'ts' etc., more good ideas will be translated into action .... Let me give you ... [an] example. Because we are not a large company we cannot afford to take massive risks in spending millions of dollars promoting something without knowing whether it will be effective or not. One day someone walked in with an idea that, on the surface, was 'preposterous'. Those who have read the Harvard marketing casebooks will know every reason why this will not work: why not sell a $150 movie camera [this was 1956] by direct mail? ... Rather than say, 'Gentlemen, this idea is preposterous,' we tried to build in this notion: 'Let's examine some reasons it might work.' Then we asked the key question: 'What would it cost us to try out the idea?' The cost was only about $10 000. The point is that we could have spent $100 000 worth of time over-intellectualizing this problem .... Nine out of ten experts will tell you this idea just will not work. Yet it did and is now a basis of an important and profitable new business for us. It is possible for us all to get a little pompous about the power of an intellectual, rational approach to an idea that is often extremely complex.

Another important property of the experiment is its relative invisibility. At GE, one term for experimenting is *bootlegging*. (The parallel term at 3M is *scrounging*.) There the tradition of squirreling away a little bit of money, a little bit of manpower, and working outside the mainstream of the organization is time-honoured. Huge GE successes, such as those mentioned earlier in engineered plastics and aircraft engines, have resulted directly from bootlegging. The process has been essential to GE. In fact, a recent analysis suggested that virtually every major GE breakthrough in the past couple of decades had its origins in some form of bootlegging. Several observers have said the same thing about IBM.

One former colleague of the senior Mr Watson goes so far as to suggest that a company's innovative health can best be measured by the amount of surreptitious bootlegging going on. Tait Elder, who headed 3M's New Business Ventures Division (NBVD), comments that planning, budgeting and even control systems should be specifically designed to be 'a little leaky'. Lots of people need a way to scrounge money and play at the margin with budgets in order to pursue maverick programmes.

Finally, and most important, is *the user connection*. The customer, especially the sophisticated customer, is a key participant in most successful experimenting processes. We have treated this at length in our book; here we will simply say that much of the excellent companies' experimentation occurs in conjunction with a lead user. Digital has more inexpensive experiments going on than any of its competitors. (HP and Wang are close on Digital's heels.) Each is *with* a user, *on* a user's premises.

The McDonald's experiments, obviously, are all done in conjunction with users—the customers. Many companies, on the other hand, wait until the perfect widget is designed and built before subjecting it—late in the game and often after millions of dollars have been spent—to customer scrutiny. The Digital, McDonald's, HP, 3M magic is to let the user see it, test it and reshape it—very early.

The Experimenting Context

Just as we said that the ad-hoc devices, such as task forces, will not work unless the environment supports fluidity and informality, experimenting will not work if the context is wrong. Management has to be tolerant of leaky systems; it has to accept mistakes, support bootlegging, roll with unexpected changes and encourage champions. Isadore Barmash, in *For the Good of the Company*, presents a fascinating chain reaction whereby just one person, Sam Neaman, triggered an extravagantly successful experimenting process that, in the 60s, added millions of dollars to the bottom line for McCrory's stores. It is such a superb description of how a successful experimenting process gets going that we will quote Neaman—then executive without portfolio, later chief executive—at length:

> I had no authority . . . but here was an opportunity. Here was a store that had lost so much money. I wanted to know what it took to make a good store. So I said to John [a store manager], 'Look, we are going to bring into this store a group of people, a team, and you'll be the quarterback. You and they will go and visit all the competition in town and write up what you find. You'll check our merchandise and write it up. Every evening you'll hold classes with a blackboard and will have a consultation with everyone . . . . In addition, I'm gonna bring in the regional manager, merchandisers, buyers, and other store managers. I want to know the sum total of our know-how by taking a sampling of a group of people dedicated to finding out what they can do thinking together.' For weeks they studied the store. They had a tough time agreeing with each other, but they did. The spirit was sky-high; excitement was beyond

description. Why? For the first time they were given a chance to express themselves as individuals and as a group, each one giving the best that he knew . . . . Not a nickel was spent. Every change was made from what we had in the store. Floors were changed, aisles widened, walls painted. It was a new store, a pleasure to the eye.

What put that store across? They knew they had to visit all the competition and then look at our store with a cold eye. They applied what they learned. Up till then, they had to look at the eyeballs of the boss and guess what it was he wanted. All I did was ask them to use their senses and their heads, and I got a damn good store. Over the next two years, it reduced its losses and then started making money. After all the hustle-bustle, the whole company became aware of it. The chairman and his entourage came running to see what was happening. Now everybody jumped on the bandwagon. Now everybody wanted a district—every vice president, the executive vice president, even the chairman.

Show the people a way. That's what I did. I even had a place to send everyone. Indianapolis. 'Go to Indianapolis in Indiana,' I told them. 'Go there, look at the store, and learn. It was put together by people like you, using spit and polish and only their own normal talents.' A little while later, in the home office, I changed the pattern. To a variety chain vice president who was in charge of buying, I said, 'All right, Joe, you don't have to go to the Midwest. Do me an Indianapolis right here in New York. You have seen what can be done. So go do an Indianapolis in Flushing. But I don't want you to copy it. We'll keep Indianapolis as a sort of school.' I told him to give me his version of a good variety store in Flushing.

Well, several weeks later he invited me to the store and I found one of the most beautiful retail stores I have ever seen. I immediately invited a few others to see it. You never would have believed that this horrible store would be the attraction of the neighborhood and the jewel of the company. Sales began rising right away, and the store became our best in New York. But what it also did was to challenge the other home-office executives to go out and 'Do an Indianapolis.'

As the parent company began to brag more and more, I expanded the variations. I used the idea of the Indianapolis store as a visual aid. This meant devising a system of selecting one unit for improvement, getting the people to bring it into shape, then bringing others to see what they did so they could learn from it. This became a substitute for writing memos or giving instructions on the phone. Instead, I said, 'Come look and see. This is the new company— nothing else is—this is it!' I instructed every district (10 to 15 stores) that it must have its own model store. Every district manager would have to reflect all his knowledge in one store and from that 'Indianapolis' improve all the stores in his district. It would be his model, his manager's model, and the model for everyone who would look at it. The idea caught on like wildfire. They did it evenings, Sundays, holidays. The Sundays became big shindigs with beer and food provided by the store's restaurant manager. They had the year of their life getting the chain in shape, all 47 districts.

Neaman's description is more than just a story of lots of people experimenting; it's also a story of people allowed to stick out a little bit, people who start to feel like winners. Most important here, it's a story of the context that allows—indeed, actually encourages—people to try things. Beyond what we have already talked about, there seem to be two important contextual aspects to the process of experimenting in companies.

The first is slightly forced but mostly natural diffusion, diffusion that builds on itself. The heart of the diffusion process is how one starts. 'Beginnings are such delicate times,' one sage commented. He is right. You start with the easy stuff, the things that are easy to change, and the places where your support base within the company is clear. We saw Neaman doing just that. Indianapolis was neither the biggest nor most visible store. But it was, under Neaman's tutelage, a store that was ripe to try something. A friend, Julian Fairfield, had as an early management job the problem of turning around a wire and cable plant that was performing miserably. 'Everything was wrong,' he said. 'I didn't know where to start. So I started with housekeeping. It was the one thing everyone could agree on, and it was easy to fix. I figured if I became a fanatic on housekeeping, which was easy to improve, they would naturally begin to buy in to some other changes.' They did.

Chase Manhattan Bank recently finished a major, successful adjustment of its retail (consumer) operation. The story was virtually the same. Management started with the regional manager who was most excited about doing something. Hers was not the biggest, the worst or the best region. It was simply one that was ripe for change. That regional manager tried things out, tested things, scored some visible wins. The saga diffused from one volunteer to the next. Only at the end did the most recalcitrant come on board. Similarly, McDonald's introduction of the breakfast menu started in the boondocks. A few franchisees picked it up and it then spread, over a two-year period, like wildfire. It now accounts for 35 to 40 per cent of McDonald's revenues. At Bloomingdale's, the experimental process started much the same way: the easiest possible department to do over was the chairman's favourite, imported foods. That's where it started. Then came furniture. High fashion, which has gotten most of the subsequent attention but was the hardest to change, came last.

The process of building momentum by accumulating small successes is nicely described by consultant Robert Schaffer:

> The essential idea is to focus immediately on tangible results—rather than programs, preparations and problem-solving—as the first step in launching performance improvement thrusts . . . . It is almost always possible to identify one or two specific short-term bottom line goals for which the ingredients for success are in place. . . . The *results-first* approach changes the whole psychology of performance improvement . . . . People must ask different kinds of questions . . . . Not, 'What is standing in the way?' but rather, 'What are some things we can accomplish in the next little while?' . . . Instead of trying to overcome resistance to what people are *not* ready to do, find out what they *are* ready to do . . . . Almost inevitably, when the managers successfully complete a project. they have many ideas about how to organize subsequent steps.

Schaffer describes, à la Neaman in Indianapolis, how to pick a manageable task. He suggests honing and honing until the do-able emerges.

Select *one* branch whose manager seems *interested* in innovation and progress. Work with a team of sales people to increase sales on a *few* selected lines, perhaps in only some *selected* market sectors, by a *specific* percent in a matter of a *month* or six weeks. As they see tangible results, they are to . . . recommend how to expand the test [italics ours].

Schaffer, like Neaman, Fairfield, Chase Manhattan and Bloomingdale's, unearths a large bunch of variables. The experimenting process is almost revolutionary. It values action above planning, doing above thinking, the concrete above the abstract. It suggests, in a very Zen-like fashion, going with the flow: do-able tasks, starting with the easiest and most ready targets, looking for malleable champions rather than recalcitrant naysayers. The image of a host of modest risk takers at Bloomingdale's, 3M, TI, Dana, McDonald's, GE, HP or IBM comes to mind. The whole notion of risk-taking is set on its ear. It becomes risky in the excellent companies not to take a little risk, not to 'step out and do a little something'. The management task becomes one of nurturing good tries, allowing modest failures, labelling experiments after the fact as successes, leading the cheers and quietly guiding the diffusion process. The experiment is at the very heart of a new approach to managing, even in the midst of the most staggering complexity at a GE or IBM.

SIMPLIFYING SYSTEMS

Fluidity, chunking and experimenting are interestingly abetted by the character of the excellent companies' formal systems. For instance, a junior colleague recently gave one of us a reading assignment in preparation for an interview with a client. He had put together a set of accumulated proposals that had come up to our client's division president. The shortest ran to 57 pages. That's not the way it is at Procter & Gamble.

P & G systems are small in number and simple in construction, in harmony with the institution's no-nonsense approach to execution. Managers talk about 'the grooves being deep and clear'. Their systems are well-oiled, well-understood, to the point. At P & G the language of action—the language of the systems—is the fabled *one-page memorandum.*

We recently had breakfast with a P & G brand manager and asked if the one-page memorandum legend was really true. 'It waxes and wanes,'* he said, 'but I just submitted a set of recommendations to make a few changes to my brand's strategy. It ran a page and a quarter and got kicked back. It was too long.' The tradition goes back to Richard Deupree, past president:

Deupree strongly disliked any memorandum more than one typewritten page in length. He often would return a long memo with an injunction: 'Boil it down

*For example, Chairman Neil McElroy's historic memorandum of 13 May 1931, recommending brand versus brand competition, 'bravely ran to three pages'.

to something I can grasp.' If the memo involved a complex situation, he some-times would add, 'I don't understand complicated problems. I only understand simple ones.' When an interviewer once queried him about this, he explained, 'Part of my job is to train people to break down an involved question into a series of simple matters. Then we can all act intelligently.'

Ed Harness, P & G's recently retired chairman, echoes the tradition: 'A brief written presentation that winnows fact from opinion is the basis for decision-making around here.'

The proliferation of MIS and forecasting models, the endless battles between numerous staffs—and the attendant 'politicalization' of the problem-solving process—are among the reasons for growing unreliability. A one-page memo helps a lot. In the first place, there are simply fewer numbers to debate, and the ability to cross-check and validate 20 on one page, say, is easier than 20 times 100. It focuses the mind. Moreover, one stands on display. You cannot reasonably hold someone responsible for getting a number wrong deep in Appendix 14. If there are only 20 numbers, on the other hand, accountability goes up automatically—and breeds reliability. Sloppiness is simply inconsistent with the one-page memo.

B. Charles Ames, past president of Reliance Electric and now president of Acme-Cleveland, makes a related point. 'I can get a division manager to cough up a 70-page proposal overnight,' he says. 'What I don't seem to be able to do is get a one-page analysis, a graph, say, that shows the trend and projection, and then says, "Here are the three reasons it might be better; here are the three things that might make it worse." '

John Steinbeck once said that the first step toward writing a novel is to write a one-page statement of purpose. If you cannot get the one page clear, it is not likely you will get far with the novel. We are told that that is fairly conventional wisdom in the writing trade, but it apparently eludes most businessmen. It's little wonder that key assumptions get lost in a 100-page investment proposal. The logic probably is loose. The writing most likely is padded. The thinking is almost by definition shoddy. And, worse, the ensuing debate about the proposal among senior executives and reviewers is apt to be similarly unfocused.

A financial analyst once said of P & G, 'They are so thorough it's boring.' Another added, 'They are a very deliberate, exacting company.' Outsiders wonder how they can be all *that* thorough, deliberate and exacting if reports are only a page long. Part of the answer lies in the struggle to get it all on that one page. Tradition has it that the typical first memo by an assistant brand manager or young brand manager requires at least 15 drafts. Another part of the answer is that they have plenty of back-up analysis available, just like everyone else. The difference at P & G is that they do not inflict all those pages on one another. Still another compelling feature of the one-page cult is: less paper!

The power of the one-page memo is that its real impact goes much deeper than this partial list of traits. Apropos of curbing the paper chase and favouring action, Jorge Diaz Serrano, chairman of Pemex, the Mexican oil company, reports that he quit responding in writing to all written material and started using the phone;

he aimed to establish a model of communication for the company. And Harry Gray, chairman of United Technologies, says:

> I am known as a man who hates paper. When I first took over the job as chief executive, I called all the principal officers together in a room and told them of this insane dislike of paper. I have a phobia about it. I also told them that I had been burdened for one year in reading all of their carbon copies of what they considered to be important correspondence. I directed them to cease and desist and not to send me another piece of paper except for one-page memos.

Charles Ames, talking about his earlier experience at Reliance, speaks of the love affair with complex systems that often hides an inability to manage the basics:

> We had planning systems of every sort from very long-term strategic systems to short-terms ones. But we couldn't predict what we were going to sell next *month*. I dismantled the five-year planning system, and went to a one-year planning system, and next to a quarterly system. We ended up running the company on a thirty-day system for a year or so. Only then did we learn to get the numbers right. Eventually we built back up to a long-term system, though never back to the epic proportions of the one we'd had originally.

Contrary to Ames's initial experience, Emerson Electric, Dana, TI and other companies foster quick response through focus on *one or two closely watched numbers*. For example, a *New York Times* report on Emerson Electric notes:

> Division presidents and their top lieutenants are put under the microscope at headquarters every month by their group vice president. The focus is more on the present than the future. Three items—inventories, profits, and sales—form a crucible for managers. They are told that what they've got to do is make sure the profit is delivered each month, each quarter, and—ultimately—the full year.

Similarly, a *Management Today* article on Dana states:

> Although head office does not require much in the way of written reports, it does need a certain minimum of information. The most important item is the revenue figure. In the old days it used to come up, along with much else, in an actual-against-budget tabulation by the 20th of the following month. Under the current system, the divisions transmit to head office, by phone or telex, their invoice total, and approximate profit earned, at the end of each working day.

Virtually any system can be cleaned up and made simple. Some watchwords at TI are: 'More than two objectives is no objectives,' and 'We got over the scoring phase in the early Seventies.' Yes, TI is a systems-driven company; Haggerty, ex-chairman, spent a decade instilling what he calls the 'language' of the Objectives, Strategies and Tactics system. But the principal OST thrust is on fostering informal communications and personal accountability—and there's no better window on TI's techniques than the seemingly mundane two-objectives point. Most MBO systems we have run across include up to 30 annual objectives for a single manager. It's obvious that no-one gets more than a handful of activities done every few months. TI simply recognizes this fact: 'We've been through it all. Each manager used to have a bunch of objectives. But gradually we trimmed and trimmed and trimmed. Now each PCC manager [Product Customer Center, the TI equivalent of a division] has *one* milestone a quarter. That's it. You *can*—and we do—expect someone to get one thing done.'

Others have instituted similar routines. Chairman John Hanley of Monsanto (P & G-trained, interestingly) says: 'Three to five objectives [a year] is a maximum.' HP's John Young echoes Hanley: 'In our strategic reviews, the critical point is the division general manager's three to five objectives [for the year]. We really don't need the financials. The only reason that I use them is to keep the division managers happy. If they get those objectives right, the financials will follow.' The nature of the HP objectives is important to action too—and, again, so different from those in the nonexcellent companies. Objectives at HP are *activities*, not abstract financials over which the manager has little control; for instance: 'Get the plant in Eugene, Oregon, up to 75 per cent capacity by 15 March' or 'Get the sales force in the Western Region spending 50 per cent of their time calling on customers of type X rather than type Y by 31 October.'

While one-page memos, honest numbers and focused objectives are the systems traits of the excellent companies, the context is equally important. The trouble is that the context can be observed only as the sum of scores of seemingly mundane traits. Plenty of companies have tried all the traits and the systems—brief communications, fact-based decision-making, management by objectives. But they try, do not succeed initially and then give up; another gimmick down the drain. Few persist with systems design until they have the trade-off between simplicity and complexity right. P & G has been deepening the grooves of its one-page communications system for 40 years.

THE ACTION ORIENTATION

There is no more important trait among the excellent companies than an action orientation. It seems almost trivial: experiments, ad-hoc tasks forces, small groups, temporary structures. Whether it's the introduction of IBM's System 360 (a seminal event in American business history) or a three-day ad-hoc task force at Digital, these companies, despite their vast size, are seldom stymied by overcomplexity. They do not give in and create permanent committees or task forces that last for years. They do not indulge in long reports. Nor do they install formal matrices. They live in accord with the basic human limitations we described earlier: people can only handle a little bit of information at one time, and they thrive if they perceive themselves as even somewhat autonomous (for example, experimenting modestly).

The major complaint about organizations is that they have become more complex than is necessary. Refreshingly, the excellent companies are responding by saying: If you have a major problem, bring the right people together and expect them to solve it. The 'right people' very often means senior people who 'do not have the time'. But they do, somehow, have the time at Digital, TI, HP, 3M, IBM, Dana, Fluor, Emerson, Bechtel, McDonald's, Citibank, Boeing, Delta and the others. They have the time in those institutions because those companies are not transfixed with organization charts or job descriptions or that authority exactly matches responsibility. Ready. Fire. Aim. Learn from your tries. That's enough.

PART 3
STRATEGIES

The six chapters in this part provide advice in the requirements of viable intervention strategy for managing change. The first one, by Wendy Pritchard, gives a review of Organizational Development (OD) and explains some of the recent advances in this field. She writes from the viewpoint of a manager in a large multinational, as a consumer and user of OD. In contrast Derek Pugh is writing as a practitioner and academic. He presents a simple summary of the essential features of successful strategies.

The overlap between Systems Thinking and OD emerges in Pugh's article and in the Tudor Rickards chapter 'Making New Things Happen'. Both approaches have a great deal in common, and it appears that the two fields are converging. Each has built on the action-research model of development through practise, and both approaches emphasize the importance of process in intervention. The mechanical application of these strategies is likely to make any change-problem worse because of alienation and suspicion. Managing change in a complex setting is a process which must take account of external changes taking place alongside the intervention. In addition there is the splash and ripple of the intervention itself. These are unpredictable, requiring that a change strategy has self-regulating loops to ensure that these are accommodated and not ignored.

Blackler and Brown look back at changes within Shell and abstract lessons from the experience which are then presented as a philosophy of management. In contrast Kotter and Schlesinger raise the point of choosing strategies which overcome common problems of resistance to change. Their work is based on American examples and must be translated into a UK context.

'People and Systems' dates from the mid-Sixties but is a comprehensive introduction to the role of systems thinking in this field. It is an important reading in this collection and although a little longer than the others here deserves careful attention. In the later parts of this chapter some predictions and claims for new developments are made. These are worth examining down the telescope of 20 years, for they provide a unique perspective on change-problems which are still with us today.

12 WHAT'S NEW IN ORGANIZATIONAL DEVELOPMENT
Wendy Pritchard

Organization development (OD) is a label representing a developing number of interrelated fields. At its broadest it is concerned with boundaries and relationships at a number of different levels between enterprises, their stakeholders and society, and the way in which these relationships could change or improve over time.

Other labels which I would see as related to or sometimes included within organization development are the 'quality of working life' (QWL), sociotechnical approaches, productivity and quality improvement, organization effectiveness, organization change, quality circles and even industrial democracy. For a very readable review of the field I recommend the article by Faucheux, Amado and Laurent in the *Annual Review of Psychology* which includes reviews of recent books and research and comparisons of US and European orientations.[1] They feel that the label OD may be no longer adequate to describe the developments in the past few years, and hope for the development of a unified theoretical base. Typically, people who specialize in these fields carry out a role variously described as adviser, consultant, facilitator, change agent, occupational psychologist, third party, behavioural scientist and probably other titles too. For convenience here I will use the title OD practitioner.

'OPEN-SYSTEMS' APPROACH

OD practitioners are using 'open systems' as a basis for their thinking about organizations and how they work in practice. Open-systems planning was developed by Clarke, Krone and McWhinney and has been described by Jayaram and also by Krone.[2] Their model goes some way towards integrating some of the disparate aspects of OD and considers organizations, or any part of an organization, as sitting in and relating to its (changing) environment. Within the organization a number of interdependent parts can be identified. For example:

Pritchard, W. (1984) What's new in organizational development? *Personnel Management*, July pp 30–33

(a)   at the hub, goals and strategies
(b)   the task and technology
(c)   the structure, systems and procedures
(d)   the people, skills, experience, attitudes
(e)   the processes—communication, planning, problem-solving, decision-making, evaluating
(f)   the culture and style.

   The model suggests that for organizations to be healthy and to survive and/or grow in their changing environments, there needs to be equilibrium or balance across the various boundaries. By a process of diagnosis using appropriate data collection and analysis techniques (for example, structured questionnaires, interviews, observation, group discussions), conflicts and imbalances can be detected and action plans developed to move towards balance. A good example of a diagnosis of this sort is described by Donald Mungall in his article on organizational change on a North Sea project.[3] He describes how he used a simplified systems framework to help analyze problems which were being experienced by the project team manifesting themselves in delays and cost escalation. He used this framework as a basis for categorizing the information he collected and for feeding it back for discussion with the project organization in order to validate the diagnosis and use it as a basis for joint action planning. A number of practical actions were then implemented relating to the project organization structure, working and staffing. Donald describes the OD contribution in the following way:

   The OD contribution took various forms, most of them not obvious to, or seen by, many of the project personnel. The most obvious contribution took the form of the organisation diagnosis.
   Other contributions included:
      Acting as consultant to the project manager on the design principles, implementation and review of the reorganisation.
      Acting as consultant to individual managers within the project on problems facing them, planning for action, and exploring different 'ways of doing' and their consequences on behaviour, on systems and on structures.
      Process consulting at numerous project meetings.
      Organising and running an intergroup workshop between onshore and offshore staff to determine better ways of communicating between the 'beach' and the platform through improved use of technology, procedures and face-to-face meetings.
      Preparing the ground for co-operative working between individuals, between groups and within groups. This mainly occurred on the boundaries between planning and construction, between offshore and onshore managements and on the interface between the three task groups.
      Jointly working with managers in helping them manage their 'boun-

daries', including the boundary between the project and their parent organisations.

Bringing issues into focus before they reached crisis point.

Acting as a 'catalyst', for example, in providing opportunities for project staff to raise and tackle 'real' but difficult issues.

In summary, the OD contribution was geared to help technically dominated and high task-centred project personnel to increase their awareness and their ability to manage the interaction and inter-dependencies between the technical and the social systems which made up their project, and to effectively manage both the people and the task together.

This example illustrates well for me a shift I perceive in OD practitioners towards a more integrated approach away from just dealing with one or two elements of organizations improvement alone (for example, team-building). Donald Mungall's work and other (largely Shell) case studies are described in a book published in 1985.

STRATEGIC PLANNING AND CHANGE

Systems-thinking, whilst simple in itself, has, I believe, become more sophisticated in its application. In the last few years OD work has become more closely linked with strategic planning in helping organizations not just to examine their present state, but to look at their future possible environments, choices about future likely goals in these environments and the capacities and steps needed to be taken to move from the present state towards the possible future states. This approach reflects a shift away from problem-centred OD to more future-centred. Colin Sheppard describes this in a paper presented at a BIM seminar.[4]

Beckhard's and Harris's book *Organisational Transitions: Managing Complex Change* was ahead of its time in 1977 in presenting an illustrated model for organizational diagnosis, and particularly in describing clear, practical ways of working through the steps of looking at the possible future states of an organization, at its present state and at the changes and mechanisms needed for moving from the present state to the desired state.[5] This process is used by organizations both to look at how they can develop as well as how they need to react to externally induced change. OD practitioners can help to set up and design the steps involved that are appropriate for particular organizations and then to work through them. In some organizations OD practitioners are increasingly working more closely with planning staff.

The steps an organization takes in making its plans can be thought of as a learning process. The organization takes note of possible events in its future environment and makes plans to adapt itself accordingly and then to review the effect of this adaptation. The way in which these plans are produced can be as important as the plans themselves. This process of planning is an opportunity deliberately to set up a learning process for appropriate people in the organization. So, for example, the whole management team could take part in a workshop; cross-departmental teams could take part in elements of the planning process. Whilst this takes time, people who have taken part in this sort of approach regard it as an investment with payoffs over and above the production of plans. These include improvements in working relationships with peers; conflicts about future direction dealt with more openly; the addition of the future business context to today's decision-making in individuals' jobs; greater commitment to and understanding of the plans themselves.

Considering planning as a learning process and possible ways of developing this within organizations is discussed by R. Ackoff in his book, *Creating the Corporate Future*.[6]

CULTURE AND STYLE

Another illustration of a 'systems' approach to organizational thinking and the need to manage 'soft' and 'hard' aspects of organizations in an integrated manner can be found in Peters' and Waterman's bestselling book *In Search of Excellence*. Their study of excellent companies has led them to develop a framework of seven 'S's: superordinate goals, style, systems, staff, skills, strategy, structure and they envisage—rather as with a systems framework—goals being central and the six other 'S's as being interdependent. They say:

> It suggests the wisdom of taking seriously the variables in organizing that have been considered soft, informal or beneath the purview of top management interest. We believe that style, systems, skills, superordinate goals can be observed directly, even measured—if only they are taken seriously. We think that these variables can be at least as important as strategy and structure in orchestrating major change; indeed, that they are almost critical for achieving necessary, or desirable, change. A shift in systems, a major retraining program for staff, or the generation of top-to-bottom enthusiasm around a new superordinate goal could take years. Changes in strategy and structure, on the surface, may happen more quickly. But the pace of real change is geared to all seven 'S's.[7]

This move into exploring the 'softer' areas of organization such as style or culture, and regarding them as important mediators of organizational effectiveness, is of course a current debate with many of the traditionally 'harder' oriented management consultants, and there have been numerous writings on the subject. One book which helps to look at this in a practical way is Deal and Kennedy's *Corporate Cultures—The Rites and Rituals of Corporate Life* which includes chapters on diagnosing and changing cultures.[8]

Another writer who has looked both conceptually and practically at managing strategic change is Noel Tichy.[9] He examines the interdependence of political, cultural and technical aspects of diagnosing, planning, implementing and evaluating strategic changes. His book contains concepts, models, practical tools and case illustrations, which are helpful for OD practitioners, planners and managers alike.

SOCIOTECHNICAL APPROACHES

Whilst some of the earliest work was done many years ago at the Tavistock Institute of Human Relations and in Norway, more widespread work is now going on using 'sociotechnical' approaches to design and redesign of machines and plant. These are design approaches which attempt to optimize jointly the technical, human and organizational aspects around it. Typically, this involves engineers, designers, those involved in operating the design and union representatives working with OD practitioners from an early stage.

Working this way does produce differences in technical design or layout to a traditional technical design approach, as is illustrated in some of the following examples. Typically, the design team includes an increasing proportion of operating staff as time goes on, so that not only do they contribute operator thinking to the design but, in learning about operating this particular design, they can help to anticipate problems. These design principles apply particularly well to green-field sites, but they have also been used in plant update or redesign. They, of course, include work and job design.

The history, both of concepts and industrial applications, and the practice of these approaches is well and simply summarized by Trist in an excellent monograph. He details the steps and principles involved in work design and the principles involved in employing this thinking at an organizational level. A succinct account of more detailed steps involved in these approaches appears in an article by James Taylor.[10]

One example of the application of sociotechnical principles is the design of Shell Canada's Sarnia Chemical Plant. This green-field site plant was designed using sociotechnical principles and is particularly interesting in that social issues were given much greater weight vis-à-vis technical issues and much earlier consideration than is usual in traditional plants. An unusually simple union agreement was established, and the plant design was based on a philosophy statement, which included criteria for the work design such as:

Employees are capable of making proper decisions given the necessary training and information.

Advancement and growth are achieved to the individual's fullest potential and capability.

Compensation is awarded on the basis of demonstrated knowledge and skill.

Information flow is directed to those in positions to most quickly act upon it.

'Whole jobs' are designed to provide maximum individual involvement.

Maximum amount of self-regulation and discretion is required.

Artificial, traditional or functional barriers are eliminated.

Work schedules should minimize time spent on shift.

Errors are reviewed from 'what can we learn' point of view.

Status differentials should be minimized.

Considerations arising from human factors at the plant had far-reaching effects on technical decisions. It was decided, following considerable debate and analysis, to eliminate traditional jurisdictional boundaries and operate the whole plant virtually as a single department, staffed by self-regulating teams with multiple skills. Supervision would be reduced, and operating decisions would be made in future at the lowest possible levels, with team members having direct access to computer control data that they would need for their work.

The effects on the physical and technical aspects of the design of the plant were dramatic. The polypropylene and isopropyl-alcohol production systems were combined, which meant combining the process-control centres and moving the laboratory inside the complex. The various key offices and buildings were rearranged as far as possible to bring people close together.

The plant was staffed by six 18-person multiskilled shift-operating teams, who do all their own control testing and much of the maintenance engineering work. There are only 14 specialist engineering maintenance staff, formed into a craft team, and two full-time lab staff, together with a management group much smaller than the one originally proposed.

Separate process operating skills have been identified and grouped in 'job knowledge clusters', and speciality skills have been divided into modules. By acquiring combination of skills team-members have open to them a large variety of routes from lower to higher rates of pay.

The work force at Sarnia was recruited with special care and has been much more highly trained than is usual in such plants. The training ended with the total staff agreeing and recording 'norms' of behaviour thought to be consistent with the philosophy statement. This in turn led to the establishment of an important site committee called the 'team norm review board', which plays a major part in the handling of disputes.

A much more detailed account of this fascinating project is given by Norman Halpern, who was the OD practitioner working throughout the design and development of the plant, in *People and Organisations Interacting*.[3]

Another example of the successful application of work design principles can be seen in Volvo's group working approach to organization which it believes has made substantial contributions to quality and efficiency as well as increasing job satisfaction and responsibility. In a recent article H. G. Jones describes the basic idea of group working:

> To expand the work content for an individual operator by making a group of between, say, four and 20 people responsible as a team for a recognizable sub-assembly, instead of each undertaking a series of repetitive tasks. The work content of the subassembly might take, say, 20 minutes, compared with two minutes for the repetitive task. Alternatively, in a continuous process such as a chemical plant, the group could take on responsibility for a whole section, including maintenance and the forward planning of raw materials, as well as day-to-day operations.[11]

Volvo found that groups develop at different paces in terms of the activities they take on. Jones describes this:

> A discovery confirmed over several years is that, in a suitable environment, many of the people engaged in group-working progressively expand their job

capacity. At first, they limit themselves to learning how to work as a group on the fairly obvious tasks directly concerned with the physical aspects of the job. The next stage is often for the group members to enlarge the scope of their job by undertaking various adjustments of the equipment that previously might have needed the attention of a different operator or even a skilled one.

One of the objectives has always been for the group to develop autonomy in doing its job: increasingly, this has been regarded as an important feature of industrial democracy. Once a degree of autonomy has been achieved, it is a natural step for some groups to have ambitions in the direction of planning. However, experience indicates that, at any point in time, working groups are not all at the same level of performance. At Olofström, five different levels of performance have been defined: they build up as a number of specified activities are carried out.

Volvo groups at Olofström have now become self-regulating in that the workers themselves determine when further groups are needed and when the groups should progress through the different levels of performance.

QUALITY AND PRODUCTIVITY

This link between systems-approaches to work design and quality and productivity improvement, illustrated by Volvo and others, is one on which many OD practitioners are engaged in various forms. Productivity and quality improvement are increasingly being seen as interconnected with, for example, work design, style of organization, strategy, business objectives. A good illustration of this integrated approach is given by Ben Scribner's account of Bethlehem Steel in the USA.[12] Bethlehem Steel was under pressure from poor financial performance and productivity, coupled with demand from customers for improved quality. In examining their steel operations, they found there was no possibility of their 'spending their way back to prosperity', and concluded that there were substantial changes needed in the way their human resources were used. They initiated a cultural change process to introduce a more participative management style and involve employees as stakeholders of the enterprise.

One element of their participative management strategy was joint union and management establishment of group problem-solving activities (rather similar to quality circles). Teams were established on the different work sites and are seen as an important part of the participative management effort. The overall strategy for implementing participative management included five main elements:

1. Develop internal resources through training and experience to assist with the changes required
2. Provide for simultaneous broad coverage of people and areas of application
3. Develop vehicles for change including problem-solving teams, quality improvement projects within the problem-solving teams, office automation and a more participative plant-planning process whereby plants developed their own plans and targets for implementation.

4. Assure plant and department autonomy whilst managing own change processes. This coincided with some structural and procedural changes whereby plants become more accountable financially
5. Base the effort on a common collaborative group problem-solving model, in which people were trained throughout the organization.

Whilst at the time of writing the paper Ben Scribner felt it was too early to evaluate the 'bottom line' effect, he says: 'What is of major importance to Bethlehem is that there is ample objective evidence that the new culture is changing. The people who have been impacted directly by the new management style feel it is worthwhile and long overdue.'

Bethlehem Steel had some internal OD consultants, developed an internal network of resources and used two groups of external GWL/OD practitioners. This example, I feel, illustrates well a strategic and pragmatic approach to integrated change in different aspects of an organization.

ARRIVING AT A STRATEGY

I believe that organization development is part of personnel management which plays an integral role in the strategic management and organization effectiveness of an enterprise.

What strategy should personnel managers use in keeping their organizations appropriately equipped with these skills? The answer in practice seems to be to buy or to grow or a combination of these two. Some personnel managers have these skills themselves. A few employ OD practitioners as part of their career development within personnel; some employ OD practitioners on short-term contracts; some hire external consultants for short projects, or on a regular basis over a number of years. Some external consultants offer a 'developmental' approach, that is, that part of the agreement with external consultants is that they help to develop skills in internal resources so that the organization develops its own capabilities over time. There is, of course, no 'right' strategy. Different combinations are likely to suit different companies' needs.

REFERENCES

1. Faucheux C, Amado G, Laurent A. (1982) Organisation development and change, *Annual Review of Psychology*, Vol. 33, pp 343–70
2. Jayaram G. K. (1976) *Open systems planning* in Bennis W. G, Benne K. A, Chin R. and Corey K. (Eds) *The Planning of Change* (3rd edition), Holt Reinehart and Winston, New York. Krone C. Open systems redesign in Adams J. B. (Ed) *Theory & Method in Organisational Development: an evolutionary process*, NTL Institute for Applied Behavioural Science, Arlington, VA
3. Mungall D. K. (1982) Organisational change on a North Sea Project, *Personnel Management Review* (May), (Shell journal available from PNRL/5, Shell International Petroleum, Shell Centre, London SE1 7NA). Brakel A. (1985) *Organisations and Interacting*, John Wiley & Sons
4. Sheppard C. (1984) Balancing directions and capability for results and the management of conflict (paper presented May 1984 at BIM seminar on the management of conflict)
5. Beckhard R. and Harris R. T. (1977) *Organisational Transitions: managing complex change*, Addison Wesley, London

6. Ackoff R. (1981) *Creating the Corporate Future*, John Wiley, New York
7. Waterman R. H. and Peters T. J. (1982) *In Search of Excellence*, Harper and Row. See also Waterman R. H, Peters T. J. and Phillips, J. R. (1980) Structure is not organisation, *Business Horizons* (June)
8. Deal T. E. & Kennedy A. A. (1982) *Corporate Cultures – The Rites and Rituals of Corporate Life*, Addison-Wesley, London
9. Tichy N. (1983) *Managing Strategic Change – technical, political and cultural dynamics*, John Wiley, New York
10. Trist E. (1981) *The evolution of socio-technical systems – a conceptual framework and an action research program*, Occasional Paper No. 2, June 1981, Ontario QWL Centre, 400 University Ave, Toronto, Ontario, M7A 1T7. Taylor J. C. (1975) The human side of work: the socio-technical approach to work system design, *Personnel Review* Summer
11. Jones H. G. (1983) Regrouped success at Volvo, *Management Today*, February (also included in this volume)
12. Scribner B. (1983) *Participative management implementation strategy at Bethlehem Steel Corporation*, Procedures of OD Network National Conference USA (1101 Park Avenue, Plainfield, New Jersey 07060, USA)

13 UNDERSTANDING AND MANAGING ORGANIZATIONAL CHANGE
Derek Pugh

It is a paradox of organizational life that situations and problems which cry out most strongly for change are often the very ones which resist change most stubbornly.

On *logical* grounds, this is most difficult to understand. If, in economic terms, firms are rational, resource-allocating mechanisms for optional performance, then proposals for increasing output or efficiency by changing methods, procedures or organization should be easily discussed and adopted. And this should be particularly so in situations where performance is far from optimal.

Yet, as anyone who has tried it knows, this does not happen. The most likely response to a change proposal is a series of outraged objections, some relevant (for no proposer of change can have thought out all the implications) some irrelevant (just waiting for an opportunity to surface and using this one).

The most likely results are: nothing happens; if the proposer has sufficient persuasiveness, there is a cosmetic change but the underlying situation remains unaltered or soon reverts to what it was before; if the proposer has sufficient power, the change is pushed through but at the cost of conflict, resentment and reduced motivation which results in negative consequences which were not intended and which may be greater than the benefits.

As a behavioural scientist, I get involved in situations, for example, where a traditional administrative consultant's 'rationalization' has been railroaded through by top management, and where the indignations and resentments still fester among the management and staff affected, two or three years after the event.

On *psychological* grounds, which are not necessarily the same as logical ones, these results are easier to understand. Most individuals react to threats and unknown dangers by going rigid (which is why the 007s of this world have to undertake considerable and rigorous training to maintain their flexibility in conditions of danger).

Pugh, D.S. (1978) Understanding and managing organizational change, *London Business School Journal*, Vol. 3, No. 2, pp 29–34

The most usual reaction of a manager or department which is failing or under pressure is to go for 'more of the same'; to carry on doing harder what was done before, even if this is manifestly seen—by others—to be inadequate. As the frustration increases so the people will become aggressive—but aggressively rigid. Try suggesting a change in this situation, but be ready to duck, since in the extreme the aggression will not be limited to words. Clearly this is not the time for a rational discussion of change.

On *organizational* grounds too, resistance to change can be understood when it is realized that from the behavioural point of view, organizations are coalitions of interest groups in tension. Management vs workers, productions vs sales, accounting vs R and D, Union A vs Union B, Head Office vs production location, the groupings and the accompanying tensions are legion. The resultant organization is a particular balance of forces which had been hammered out over a period of time and which is continually subject to minor modifications through hierarchically initiated adjustments and cross-group negotiations.

A real change proposal, that will amost inevitably change the current balance, is thus likely to encounter resistance. And when this is compounded by psychological resistance from rigid people under threat, it is not surprising that managing change is difficult.

It is for this reason that one of the most basic characteristics of organizations is that they are what is called *ultrastable*. They find it difficult to change, not because of inertia but because they run like mad to stay in the same place. It is not that unusual for me to be told by directors, managers and shop stewards in a firm that personally they would like to see change made, but it cannot be done.

So real organizational change often comes about: much too late, in situations of considerable failure (orders lost, profits down, budgets out of control, morale low, resentment high); with little time for thought and only scant consideration of alternatives because of the need to cope with the emergency; and paying the price of considerable frustration, conflict and dislocation in order to live to fight another day.

An effective manager, on the other hand: *anticipates* the need for change as opposed to reacting after the event to the emergency; *diagnoses* the nature of the change that is required and carefully considers a number of alternatives that might improve organizational functioning, as opposed to taking the fastest way to escape the problem; and *manages* the change process over a period of time so that it is effective and accepted as opposed to lurching from crisis to crisis.

Here are four principles for understanding organizational change.

Principle One: Organizations are organisms. They are not mechanisms which can be taken apart and reassembled differently as required. They can be changed, but the change must be approached carefully with the implications for the various groupings thought out and the participants convinced of the worthwhileness from their point of view. They must be given time to understand the change proposals, and to 'digest' the changes after they have been made. Do not make changes too frequently. They are too hard to digest and will become disfunctional or cosmetic.

Principle Two: Organizations are occupational and political systems as well as rational resource-allocation ones. Every reaction to a change proposal must be interpreted not only in terms of the rational arguments of what is best for the firm (which are the ones actually used). The reactions must also be understood in relation to the occupational system (how will it affect the ways of working, number of jobs, career prospects, motivation, of the particular person or group whose arguments are being heard) and the political system (how will it affect the power, status, prestige of the group?)

Principle Three: All members of an organization operate simultaneously in all three systems—the rational, the occupational and the political ones. Do not make the mistake of becoming cynical and thinking that the occupational and political aspects are all that matter, and that rational arguments are merely rationalizations to defend a particular position. The arguments by which the Personnel Manager, for example, resists a diminution in the department's functions will be real ones, even though they will inevitably be suffused with occupational and political considerations.

Principle Four: Change is most likely to be acceptable and effective in those people or departments who are basically successful in their tasks but who are experiencing tension or failure in some particular part of their work. They will have the two basic ingredients of confidence in their ability and motivation to change. The next most likely to change are the successful. They will have the confidence but must be interested in developing the motivation. The least likely to understand and accept change are the unsuccessful. They will attempt to protect themselves by their rigidity.

These principles are very important in designing a change process, in deciding where to start and what methods to use.

For effective change to take place, therefore, a manager must *anticipate* the need for change so that time is available, and *manage* the process over that time so that the two relevant characteristics of the people involved (i) their confidence in their ability and (ii) their motivation to change, can be maintained and developed.

Here are six rules for managing change effectively:

Rule One: Work hard at establishing the need for change. This may seem hardly necessary to the change proposer, but what may be an obvious need to him/her may not be seen as such by the others involved. What may be seen as an obvious need for improvement in their control procedures by the accountants may be seen by the marketing staff as yet another attempt to reduce their autonomy and responsibilities.

Effective reasons for changes are those that can be accepted by many of the interest groups and people who will be involved. For example, needs which can be demonstrated to flow from changes in the firm's environment (changes in customers' behaviour, competitors' tactics, Government policies) will find greater acceptability as being relevant to all, than purely internally generated changes which are more likely to be viewed in the political system.

Rule Two: Don't only think out the change, THINK THROUGH IT. It is not enough to think out what the change will be and calculate the benefits and costs from the proposer's point of view. The others involved will almost inevitably see the benefits as less and the costs as greater. By 'thinking through' is meant the need to consider consciously and systematically what the change will mean for all the parties involved, or what they will see as their costs and benefits.

For example, consider systematically for all groups involved:

will the change alter job content
will it introduce new and unknown tasks
will it disrupt established methods of working
will it rearrange group relationships
will it reduce autonomy or authority
will it be perceived to lower status
will it be established without full explanation and discussion?

It is in the answers to these questions, which identify the potential points of resistance to the change, that the manager can get a fuller understanding of what is involved for all. And on the other side he needs to ask what are the benefits in pay, status, job satisfaction, career prospects which are generated as well as the increase in performance.

Rule Three: Initiate change through informal discussion to get feedback and participation. No one person or group can hope to foresee correctly all the ramifications of a real change in policy, structure, procedures or products. So it is important to get discussions going to get feedback to enable the manager to evaluate the proposal fully from all points of view. He/she needs to discover whether the change is correct in principle or not, and what modifications, if any, will improve it.

In addition, in modern organizations effective change is a participative process. Early discussion allows the necessary participation of those affected to take place, since this is what generates commitment to the changes and develops the motivation to make them work. The change proposer has participated a lot if it is his/her idea, that is why he/she is committed to it. Others must have the opportunity to go through this process too.

Rule Four: Positively encourage those concerned to give their objections. This rule may be regarded as rather perverse by an enthusiastic manager who is pushing the change proposal and whose natural inclination is to ride over or belittle objections. But it is an important part of an effective change process for two reasons.

First, because people who have a change pushed on them without account being taken of their objections inevitably lose some confidence in their abilities ('If we are good, why is that nobody listens to us?'). This leads to rigidity. Flexibility is encouraged by people seeing that they can contribute and make an impact.

Second, any current situation is the resultant of a balance of forces. If the forces pressing for change are increased, the forces resisting change do not go away even if they are not brought out into the open. It is important to ensure that the resisting forces are identified and dealt with in their own right.

For example, a change proposal may lead a departmental group to be concerned with their ability to work a new system or to doubt its appropriateness.

This may be tackled as a problem in its own right by means of a trial run and a training programme. Or a proposal which leads to a reduction in autonomy on one aspect of a job may be compensated for by increased autonomy in another aspect.

Rule Five: Be prepared to change yourself. This is probably the most important rule of all. Modern managers cannot afford the luxury of believing that 'change is for other people', since a manager who proposes to initiate change joins in the process and must himself/herself be prepared to change.

There are two corollaries to this rule. *Don't fall in love with your own idea.* It may be good, but it could well be improved after the discussions and objections are taken into account. Overcommitment by the manager at too early a stage leads to rigidity again.

It is essential to split a proposal into its general and specific aspects, starting the discussion on the more general aspects of principles and approach. Do not overplan the details at this stage, leave this until the feedback has shown that the direction is accepted as appropriate. The detailed planning may then take account of the information generated by the whole process.

The second corollary is that change *may be* 'bottom up' *as well as* 'top down'. Change does not have to be initiated from above. A manager who is prepared to change may well consider ideas initiated from below. A very good way of obtaining ideas for improvement is to carry out a survey of subordinates' views. Many managers have been surprised at the quality of proposals which can be unlocked by this method.

Rule Six: Monitor the change and reinforce it. When the change has been carried through, check after a suitable time to see if it is working well and giving the benefits that were argued. If it does not, minor modifications will be in order (but beware of changing in a major way again too quickly).

If the change is working well and the benefits can be demonstrated in, for example, improved efficiency, higher turnover, more satisfaction, *tell every one that this is the case.* This is most important as it gives reinforcement to those involved (who are otherwise more likely to remember the dislocation than the benefits) and for others helps to set up an organizational climate in which change can be seen to be beneficial.

(This chapter was developed from an article which originally appeared in *Accountancy Age*.)

14   A NEW PHILOSOPHY OF MANAGEMENT
F.H.M. Blackler and C.A. Brown

In the early 1970s an account was published[1] of how social scientists, in the mid-1960s, had worked with senior management of a major British oil refining company to formulate a new philosophy of management. Here, we seek to re-examine the success of this project in the light of recent data and to explore briefly the consequences of our analysis for social scientists concerned with strategies for organizational change.

At the time it was undertaken this change programme was unique in the history of management. The publishers of Hill's account went so far as to compare it in importance to the Glacier experiments and the Fawley productivity deals. (Hill's book has undoubtedly contributed to the worldwide interest presently being shown in sociotechnical systems theory.) Certainly the episode has continued to attract the acclaim of social scientists who had been involved.[2, 3, 4] Furthermore there seems little doubt that recent developments at the Shell Sarnia plant in Canada, which have involved the publication of an 'organizational philosophy',[5] have been directly influenced by the programme.

Yet important aspects of the story have never been told and the implications it may have for present day theory and practice have not, therefore, been fully explored. Occasional comments on certain disappointments associated with it have appeared[6, 7] yet these add little to Hill's original account. To date what has been published are generally optimistic and somewhat uncritical accounts reported by people themselves involved in promoting the change programme.[8] Hill made his own comment towards the end of his book:

> Whether, therefore, the values and concepts of the philosophy statement are now sufficiently well embodied in the organisation to withstand future setbacks it is still too early to judge. The indications are that they are, but the next five years will show.[9]

Six years after this was published we were given the opportunity to find out what

Blackler, F. H. M. and Brown, C. A. (1981) A new philosophy of management: Shell revisited, *Personnel Review*, Vol. 10, No. 1, pp 15–21. Reprinted by permission of MCB University Press had taken place in this period. In this chapter we outline some of our findings (the full account is in Blackler and Brown[10]).

METHODOLOGY

To reconstruct the main events that had taken place at Shell UK Refining Ltd at the time of the philosophy exercise, we interviewed during 1977 a number of managers, union officials and more junior level staff who could provide information on relevant aspects of the exercise. We also consulted a number of published and unpublished reports of relevant events. It should be stressed that we were not intending to conduct an opinion survey amongst members of the organization. Such a strategy would have been misplaced, since it soon became apparent, due to the high mobility of labour, that many members had never heard of the project which had begun over a decade before. The task we set ourselves was to prepare a detailed case study of the exercise.

The group of people we spoke to was chosen as follows. At our request senior officials in the relevant personnel departments arranged for us to speak with people with special knowledge of the philosophy programme. Given our wish to speak to key actors in the story there was often little question to whom we should speak; for example, any top manager from the mid-1960s still with the company, staff who had run the philosophy conferences, union officials and representatives who had been involved. In addition, to acquaint ourselves with both sides of any arguments, we asked to see some people known to be supportive and some known to be critical of the ideals of the philosophy. Later, to follow up issues of importance or aspects we had insufficient information about, we asked for a number of additions to these lists. Concentrating on the main locations for the change programme in this way we spoke in detail with 24 people at the Stanlow refinery, 9 at the Shell Haven refinery, 2 at Teesport, 4 managers from Head Office who had been involved, and a member of the Tavistock Institute's advisory group to Shell in the mid-1960s.

Our preliminary analysis of these data indicated a surprising degree of agreement amongst our respondents. However, as we describe in more detail later, our conclusions as to the effectiveness of the philosophy programme were strongly negative. Accordingly we attempted to recheck the accuracy of our conclusions by going to considerable lengths to obtain comments on our draft report from informed parties. As a result of this we were able to correct certain minor inaccuracies and to confirm the factual accuracy of our description of events.

BACKGROUND TO THE PHILOSOPHY EXERCISE

In the early 1960s the oil industry was changing rapidly. Suez, the beginning of OPEC, the nationalization of oil companies by oil-producing countries and price wars in the UK provided the background to this story. At Shell UK Refining attempts to improve financial performance had led to an unprecedented programme of voluntary and compulsory redundancies. Furthermore, Shell's main rival Esso was known to have negotiated far-reaching productivity deals with employees.[11] Within Shell, however, no such deal had yet been agreed and job demarcations and wages drift were serious and continuing problems for management. To deal with manpower difficulties an advisory group, Employee Relations Planning (ERP), was established in the company in 1964. This group was formed to initiate long-term thinking on industrial relations issues and initial analysis led to recommendations that unfavourable worker attitudes and ineffective restrictive practices could be overcome if the company adopted a participatory management style and introduced a series of productivity bargains. To restore the effectiveness of management's calls to collective endeavours the ERP recommended that emerging behavioural science ideas should be incorporated into a specially written philosophy of management.

At the Tavistock Institute these proposals found receptive ears. At that time Emery and Trist had been working on a wide-ranging analysis of social and organizational problems and on ways to combat them. Their views[12] were that modern organizations function increasingly under conditions of great instability. Collaboration, they felt, rather than the traditional competition between different organizations was necessary to overcome the resulting managerial problems. New values needed to be instilled in organizations through, for example, sociotechnical job redesign. Further, Emery and Trist believed that urgent research was needed to study the processes associated with the successful introduction of social changes of these kinds. For the Tavistock team, therefore, the Shell project offered them the exciting opportunity to draft a statement outlining a new role and new approaches to management for major companies in the modern world, and to be closely involved in the first attempt to introduce such thinking in a technologically advanced 'post-industrial' organization.

THE LAUNCHING OF THE PHILOSOPHY PROGRAMME

Between 1965 and 1967 the philosophy the Tavistock theorists outlined was debated in the company. Early indications suggested that it was being well received. Later, four 'channels of implementation' emerged through which it was hoped the philosophy would be put into practice. Figure 14.1 indicates the nature of these channels and presents a comparison of comments Hill made about the progress of the philosophy with those made by people we spoke to in our retrospective study.

While Hill's report makes it clear that both the Tavistock consultants and the ERP personnel who ran the conferences were impressed with the philosophy's initial reception, with the benefit of hindsight it would appear that this reception was much less positive than had first appeared. A senior manager from Shell Haven, present at the very first conference (that for the managing director and his immediate subordinates), described how people from the Stanlow refinery had been immediately enthusiastic but that those from Shell Haven were far less so. He said: 'We had to do something. The ideas had been sold well to the boss of manufacturing. We had to do something as the top man wanted to go this way. Given a free choice I'm not sure what we would have done.'

Yet while top management's views had been divided, at later conferences many

Figure 14.1   Channels of implementation

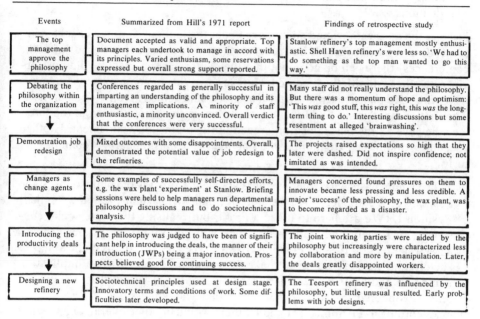

Events	Summarized from Hill's 1971 report	Findings of retrospective study
The top management approve the philosophy	Document accepted as valid and appropriate. Top managers each undertook to manage in accord with its principles. Varied enthusiasm, some reservations expressed but overall strong support reported.	Stanlow refinery's top management mostly enthusiastic. Shell Haven refinery's were less so. 'We had to do something as the top man wanted to go this way.'
Debating the philosophy within the organization	Conferences regarded as generally successful in imparting an understanding of the philosophy and its management implications. A minority of staff enthusiastic, a minority unconvinced. Overall verdict that the conferences were very successful.	Many staff did not really understand the philosophy. But there was a momentum of hope and optimism: 'This *was* good stuff, this *was* right, this *was* the long-term thing to do.' Interesting discussions but some resentment at alleged 'brainwashing'.
Demonstration job redesign	Mixed outcomes with some disappointments. Overall, demonstrated the potential value of job redesign to the refineries.	The projects raised expectations so high that they later were dashed. Did not inspire confidence; not imitated as was intended.
Managers as change agents	Some examples of successfully self-directed efforts, e.g. the wax plant 'experiment' at Stanlow. Briefing sessions were held to help managers run departmental philosophy discussions and to do sociotechnical analysis.	Managers concerned found pressures on them to innovate became less pressing and less credible. A major 'success' of the philosophy, the wax plant, was to become regarded as a disaster.
Introducing the productivity deals	The philosophy was judged to have been of significant help in introducing the deals, the manner of their introduction (JWPs) being a major innovation. Prospects believed good for continuing success.	The joint working parties were aided by the philosophy but increasingly were characterized less by collaboration and more by manipulation. Later, the deals greatly disappointed workers.
Designing a new refinery	Sociotechnical principles used at design stage. Innovatory terms and conditions of work. Some difficulties later developed.	The Teesport refinery was influenced by the philosophy, but little unusual resulted. Early problems with job designs.

junior staff were either to feel ambivalent towards or to resent the exercise and the following two quotations are not atypical. One section head said:

> The ideals, then, were above my head. All I was interested in was how it affected my section, what I could get out of it. I came away with the feeling I got nothing out of it. It was not presented at a low enough level. There was a lot of mistrust at that level of management. What was the need for it? Was there something to be found? Is the mileage that we are putting in not adequate? I suppose it was done to provide the spurt via a rest-cure holiday. Generally it was not accepted by people at that level. There was a feeling it was brain-washing. It did not reduce the barriers between management and the rest. In fact, it did exactly the opposite. It led to a polarisation.

A shift supervisor commented:

> A little bit must stick whatever you feel at the time. I don't remember what I thought was good but I was not very impressed. The general reaction of people was 'it's a bit of a giggle'. The only enthusiastic people there were the lecturers. Possibly other people were enthusiastic but I didn't meet any. We were there for a purpose. We were being indoctrinated on the role of Shell in the community, to shareholders, to employees. Some of the ideas were good but whether they are ever followed up when you get back from these courses is questionable. I was suspicious because the 1964 'Golden Handshake' [a redundancy programme to reduce manning levels] had been preceded by con-

sultants doing something and other company exercises were followed by reductions.

Despite the reservations one might have about the factual accuracy of such comments describing how people had reacted (they were made over a decade after the conferences) there can be no doubt that the conference programme did not convince people as it initially appeared. Here are two sets of comments by managers who, with ERP and advisers from the Tavistock, had helped to run the conferences. The first, a manager at Shell Haven, describes in this quotation from the interview he gave us the basic position argued in the philosophy document. He then speculates about the extent of people's actual (as against apparent) commitment to it:

The whole basis was, what business are we in? What is the philosophy of the company? 'We are here to make a profit', that was basically (what we called) Position I. 'We are here to make a profit, but realising there are social constraints of society and employees which will impose a limit on our profits.' That was Position II. And Position III was: 'We are custodians of the assets of society and we may not even make profits at its expense.' The implication being you had to be successful at making profits but within that framework. And I wondered in retrospect whether that was understood.

According to Positions I, II and III there would be some overall and specific objectives which recognise the characteristics of the oil industry, and certain kinds of recognisable actions to meet these. So, the first thing to debate was, do we believe that Position III (or II, or I) is what we are in and where we should be? Now that's where I believe that however many hands went up the consensus was never more than Position 2½, perhaps only Position 2.1! But we all said we believed in Position III . . . I would put it this way. There were probably 50 per cent who really wanted to make Position III a go and thought they could. There were 25 per cent who would like to but didn't think it had much hope. And there were 25 per cent who didn't think it was right anyway, but weren't going to say so . . . although you had better not take this as literally as I have said it.

The second manager we quote here helped to run many of the conferences for people in the Stanlow refinery. In what follows, he speculates about the extent to which people there fully understood the concept of the 'joint optimization' of the social and technical systems, the second key element in the philosophy statement.

Looking back I would say that really only about 5 per cent of the people who attended the conferences really understood it. My manager kept saying 'It is not a "be nice" policy, but it is a philosophy for getting the best out of people.' But the idea of joint optimisation was not really understood. Engineers could not grasp the idea of optimising what can't be measured! It actually did become a 'be nice to people' philosophy I suppose. Then later on when this manager retired, there was a rumour he was studying for a degree in social work or something similar. This confirmed the image of 'being nice' in people's minds.

... If you mention the notion of joint optimisation now, you get a snort of laughter.

Why, we wondered, had the conferences initially appeared to be more success-ful? The first of the two managers we have just quoted (and who emphasized to us that at the time the conferences were running, he himself had felt they were going rather well) made further observations relevant to this point. Why did people say they went along with Position III if they did not actually agree with it?

> If you go along to one of Billy Graham's meetings and you're the only one who hasn't gone down to be saved do you think you can sit there? They were, I would think, a bit like that. I mean it wasn't revivalist. But that was the pressure. That's what I meant when I said 'hands went up'.

Where then was this pressure coming from? 'I would think the pressure, I would certainly like to think this, the pressure was from people who felt, like me, that this *was* good stuff, this *was* right, this *was* the long-term thing to do.'

It is fair to say that this was the only time any of the people we spoke to about the conferences described the pressures on people in quite such terms, yet other similar observations were made to us. Two other people associated with running the conferences, one at that time with the ERP Unit the other with the Tavistock Institute, agreed that while dissent was discussed, as a general rule its persistence was not fully recognized as legitimate. It does seem that expressions of disagree-ment with the philosophy tended to be given the status of 'problems' that people were having with it, rather than being respected as expressions of legitimate alternatives.

The euphoria which seems to have characterized some of these conferences is perhaps illustrated in this recollection by a (then) shift supervisor:

> Most of us found it very convincing. We felt it was good, it could be a very good thing. The bit about responsibility to the community was sensible you know. And there were some good ideas coming out of it, like no clocking on, and the idea we are all professional people. Remember Shell used to be pater-nalistic, anti-union. In those days the 'boss man' counted. But at the con-ference they said 'You call me Eddie, I'll call you Jack.' We thought, what the bloody hell is going on here? But it made you feel good. Then we all got drunk!

PUTTING THE PHILOSOPHY INTO PRACTICE

It was not intended that the philosophy conferences should be regarded as ends in themselves. It was hoped that significant advances would come after the theory of the philosophy was realized in everyday actions.

Four main channels of implementation of the philosophy emerged. In his 1971 account Hill acknowledges problems with two of these, demonstration job redesign projects and the design of a new refinery at Teesport, although evidence we collected suggests he did not fully appreciate their significance. However, we wish to concentrate on the other two aspects. These were the expectation that

managers should act as change agents (manage their departments by the principles of the philosophy) and the introduction of joint working parties of management and worker representatives (to explore possible new working arrangements
prior to negotiating productivity deals). Both were clearly crucial for the success
of the programme.

Managers as Change Agents

Hill's comments on this include reference to some successes but mainly include
descriptions of how briefing sessions were run to help managers discuss the
philosophy with their staff and to understand the sociotechnical theory of job
design. He later notes how top level support for the whole exercise was to wane
and how rapid staff movements mitigated against the consolidation of new ideas.
Our study indicated this 'channel of implementation' was soon to dry up and
Figure 14.2 summarizes how the hope that departmental managers would
transform the company was not be realized.

Progress towards the Productivity Deals

As Hill suggested, and our enquiries confirmed, the philosophy exercise did help
the introduction of the productivity deals. Joint working parties of management
and worker representatives were a new departure in the company. To an
unprecedented degree management was discussing and explaining its plans to
workers in these committees. Yet our study produced strong evidence that all was
not what it may have appeared in this respect. The JWPs first met in 1966, were
halted because of industrial action in 1967, then met again through 1968. (The
deals were signed in 1969 and 1970.) Reflecting on the slow progress of 1966 a
management representative was later to say in a paper to his colleagues:

> It is as well to remind you that at this stage the company had not fed in the con-
> cepts it had in mind, in other words we went into bat with the working parties
> with the blank piece of paper approach, except that the management represen-
> tatives declared what they felt were impediments to efficiency, for example,
> restriction practices, overtime. In hindsight we feel it would have speeded up
> the discussion had we exposed the concepts we had in mind at the outset and
> used the working parties to ferret out other concepts and to graft flesh on to
> bones. However, you will recall that at this time the wage freeze was imposed
> upon us and perhaps this gave us a false impression that we had all the time in
> the world to allow participation/involvement to take its natural course. For the
> first few months of the meetings which took place once a week (half day), most
> of the ideas being generated came from the management representatives, some
> of whom, you will recall, were present on all working parties. Obviously they
> were gently feeding in the concepts of the embryo plan and ensuring that cross
> fertilisation between the JWPs was taking place.

To describe this as 'participation' sounds somewhat dubious, even allowing for
the fact that the level of openness between management and the worker that did

Figure 14.2. Events associated with managers as change agents

The philosophy had been launched with a 'fanfare of trumpets'. The support of top management had been carefully wooed, though even here was *some* evidence of bulldozer tactics. Later certainly the sell was to become harder.

Reactions to the philosophy varied though supporters seemed to be winning the day. Some people did not understand it. Others saw it in the context of the period of relative austerity the company had just passed through.

Managers were encouraged to become more participative. Problems here led to a feeling that early experiences were patchy in their success.

In the absence of social-skills training all people were given were exhortations and the impression that failures were not respectable.

Many managers involved were technical men. For them the immense work load put on them after the conferences seemed to be producing slow results.

People thought there may have been more for those paid weekly (in, e.g., equal status) from the philosophy than was true for staff, but it was difficult to get those paid weekly to see this.

The demonstration job redesign projects did not inspire confidence.

People looked to their supervisors' behaviour to assess how worthwhile continued effort would be. Important inconsistencies were seen.

Rapid staff movements were taking place at this time. Commitment to the philosophy was not a relevant factor for appointment at senior level in Shell Refining, nor for success in a career in the broader Royal Dutch/Shell group.

By 1970 the refinery managers at both Stanlow and Shell Haven were known as unsympathetic to the philosophy. No support from higher levels was visible.

In 1972 reports (Taylor 1972a and 1972b) were published of an alleged success in participation in the Stanlow wax plant. At this time serious problems at the plant led many to believe that, on the contrary, the wax plant was an example of the 'be nice' philosophy coming unstuck.

exist at this time was greater than ever before. By 1968, however, delays had been such that management had been spurred on, secretly and unilaterally, to decide what it wanted. The manager from whose report we have just quoted said to us in interview:

From about 1968 management took the initiative. We went along to the meetings with blank sheets of paper, just like before. Our minds too had to appear to be blank! But it was really a process of re-education we were in from now on. Management knew what they wanted by now, but we had to lead the men. Change had to emanate from the same union as the men belonged to. A number of items appeared on the agenda, but we presented ideas as if they were off the top of our heads. Really, the second set of working parties was just a gimmick. They were just a way of moving towards the productivity deals.

Comments by a union representative about this period provides a clue as to how this apparent spontaneity was engineered. While he fully understood that the philosophy had been launched in 1966 this interviewee nevertheless maintained that as a real influence it did not emerge until after an industrial dispute in mid 1967. 'After that,' he said, 'it led to the productivity deal.' Reports such as these, taken with the close links most people we interviewed saw between the philosophy and the productivity deals, tend to suggest that references to the 'spirit of the philosophy' were regularly being made at that time as part of a management effort to formulate and implement the revised union agreements it desired; a manipulative rather than a collaborative element was predominant in management's dealings with the unions.

Later that good will which had been built up through the productivity deals was not to last. At the time of our survey in most ways the 'pre-deal orthodoxy' had been re-established in shop-floor working. Commenting on such developments an ex-union negotiator said:

Up till 1969 there had been wage freezes. So the pressures were great to sign for money. But many people believed in the deal then because it was a change in our position and status in the company, and because the company assured us 'this was not the end, but the beginning!' But look at the value of the productivity deals then, and now! And look at the erosion of the differentials! The company was not willing to try to keep it alive. . . . The company doing nothing has left a bitter taste. We (operators at Shell Haven) have had only one strike in all this time, but that is not due to the company being good!

Included in the deals was the provision that employees should be paid an annual salary rather than a weekly wage. As part of this change paid overtime was replaced by a 'time off in lieu' provision. The abolition of paid overtime ended any mechanism by which shop-floor employees could be paid more money short of increasing their annual salaries. Successive years of UK government pay policy prevented this latter course of action, and early reviews of annual salary levels (conducted in 1971 and 1972 between governmental pay pauses) produced settlements described as 'penny pinching'. While Shell's original deal had made them leaders, within 12 months or so other companies caught and passed them without requiring concessions of workers that were built into Shell's deals and, importantly, without abolishing paid overtime. 'In the early days the operators made it work,' said a plant manager, 'then they looked for the rewards and did not get them.'

DISCUSSION

The following summarizes the points made about the philosophy programme:

1. Top management and their social science advisers had somewhat different perspectives on the activities in which they were jointly engaged.
2. In contradiction to early and optimistic reports of the project and its achievements it never really 'took off' and, as a force for widespread change, soon faded away in Shell.
3. Despite the good intentions of the architects of the philosophy, championing the values of mutual respect and partnership, a manipulative element became a feature of the exercise.

The last of these points is perhaps the most interesting and in the remainder of this chapter we comment upon it in more detail.

Of course it was never the intention of the Tavistock group unfairly or insidiously to manoeuvre people. The series of events associated with the development of the productivity deals that we describe was certainly not what they would have wished. But while this episode serves as a reminder of the reality of the industrial relations situation in the company and of problems for genuine participation within it other, more subtle, opportunities for the exercise to be used manipulatively had been present from the start.

Pressure by the conference organizers for support of the point of view they were presenting, as we noted, was remembered with resentment by several of our interviewees. While the ostensible purpose of the conferences was to enable people to discuss and freely to accept or reject the philosophy, it seems likely that the manner in which these conferences were conducted suggested something else to the conference participants. Time provided off work, generous hotel accommodation at the philosophy conferences, expenses paid, backing for the philosophy from top management, authority for it from eminent social scientists, the confidence of the company officials who ran the discussions, were features much in evidence. Such factors implied that acceptance of the philosophy, if not actually to be expected, was certainly much to be encouraged. Moreover, within the philosophy statement itself a reconciliation of potentially troubling problems was achieved as both the profit motive and social responsibility were used to justify company activities. Any potential dissident, therefore, would have found the forum of the conferences an unsympathetic environment in which to express his doubts. Such doubts, if forcibly expressed, might have seemed to imply that Shell's role in society was not without its problems, evidently a difficult position to maintain in such a gathering of well-meaning company men. Here, indeed, are many of the conditions supporting what Janis[13] has called 'groupthink'. In such circumstances, while some people certainly did express disagreements, it hardly seems surprising that many doubters appear to have acquiesced or suspended judgement.

Later, as managers were asked to act as agents for change and to take responsibility for implementing the philosophy, other pressures may have been experienced by them. A quotation from the interviewee at Shell Haven whom we reported earlier as saying 'we had to do something as the top man wanted to go this way' supports this point. Commenting on the way Shell Haven managers were less keen than their counterparts at Stanlow he said:

> We were more sluggish getting off the mark than Stanlow was. We weren't sure how to handle it. We had the Tavistock people over for a few days but I blew my top at them! They wouldn't give us an opinion as to what we ought to do. 'What are we paying you for?' I exploded! They explained they were working only as catalysts and we had to take responsibilities for any programme.

Nondirective counselling in organizational change programmes, especially since Argyris's book,[14] has been well-known and practised by change agents. According to Argyris the process involves helping people make free and informed choices to which they can feel committed; it is not the consultant's job to impose his/her own analysis and solutions on the people he/she is serving. In the incident reported here, while superficially it may seem that the Tavistock consultants were operating in a nondirective style it is clear they were not. Refusing to translate their philosophy into a statement of necessary action was not enough; all strategic choices had already been taken once the philosophy had been formulated by the Tavistock and ERP and then approved as policy. The extent of the choice open to managers asked now to be 'change agents' was to take or leave the package on offer. People were presented with a puzzle they had not devised which, they were told, it was theirs to take or leave but which in practice it was clearly apparent they had better solve anyway. The fact that at least one such manager 'blew his top' seems quite understandable!

Three factors may explain why manipulation became such a significant part of the Shell philosophy story. In the first place there is the confidence of the philosophy's presenters. The Tavistock theorists believed in the pressing need for companies to adopt new social roles and internal organizational arrangements. Members of the ERP unit believed new management practices would help restore organizational harmony and effectiveness. Thus the Tavistock group as authors in search of a character and the members of ERP as characters in search of an author came together with a shared sense of urgency. For the members of both groups, albeit for different reasons, the philosophy amounted to nothing less than a blueprint for a new social order. And for both groups questions about the ease with which others could be convinced of the appropriateness of their ideas were of greater significance than the need to evaluate the quality of the ideas themselves.

The second factor is related to the first. Given an awareness of the joint sense of urgency, the Tavistock theorists failed to appreciate the significance of differences between their objectives and those of Shell's management. These differences are most obviously visible when one reflects on the ideas that 'emerged' through which the philosophy was to be put into action after the conferences. The ideas of more participative management and of a 'jointly optimized' social and technical system which characterized each of the four channels Hill discusses were certainly considered important ways by which the philosophy should be acted out. Yet a pivotal notion in the philosophy was that the company should act as 'the custodian of the assets of society and should not make a profit at its expense'. This idea of 'stewardship' was intended to suggest important new objectives for the company. (Hill himself mentioned concern for the appropriate treatment of materials, money and the environment.[15] Yet no 'main channel' emerged by which progress towards such objectives was to be managed and monitored. Challenging debating points were undoubtedly posed at the conferences yet no project groups were formed as a result of them to review Shell's broad social role. In practice the philosophy exercise developed in ways consistent with the ERP unit's original brief. It was an inward looking exercise concerned with personal values and managerial styles.

In conjunction with the enthusiasm of the philosophy's presenters and the failure of the Tavistock group to heed the difference between their objectives and those of the ERP unit a third factor helps account for the manipulative aspects of the philosophy exercise. This was the naïveté and hence the theoretical inadequacy of the ideas inspiring the philosophy itself. Regarding the notion of 'stewardship', it now seems plain enough that the overwhelmingly important resource to which an oil company has access is oil itself. An oil company which was seriously to consider ways by which it might respect the claims of others to this finite commodity would evidently seek to ensure its exploitation in a more or less rational and planned way. Thus, through action regarding prices, availability and distribution, as well as by advising and negotiating with governments and other interest groups it would attempt to balance various social considerations. The issues would by no means be uncontroversial for, arguably, such considerations would include debating the needs of oil producing as well as of oil using states, of the needs of underdeveloped countries, as well as of developed ones, and of the needs of future as well as of present generations for this vital, scarce, and nonrenewable resource. Indeed, given the limits of manoeuvre Shell UK refining would experience as a consequence of its position in the broader Royal Dutch Shell group, much work would be involved in making the 'stewardship' concept a reality. Yet as we have seen, the Tavistock people seem neither to have appreciated this nor to have understood the essentially political nature of the role they wished the company to assume.

Such naïveté was also associated with the second core concept of the philosophy, that the social and technical systems of the company should be 'jointly optimized'. Important as the observation was that human needs deserve as much consideration in the planning of the company's organization as technical ones, in retrospect it is clear that without further detailed application this concept was inadequate as a basis for an organizational philosophy. Emphasizing (probably correctly) that much more scope for accommodating organizational and individual needs existed than had been previously recognized, the philosophy nonetheless failed to note that factors other than technology mitigated against a wholehearted 'joint optimization' of them. While Emery and Trist could write of the need for differing interest groups between organizations to negotiate over their varying but legitimate interests they did not, in the philosophy they wrote for Shell, recognize the implications of such an analysis for affairs within the company itself. In the philosophy statement, although safety and security needs of employees were mentioned, the psychology from which all significant action followed emphasized the values of achievement, responsibility and personal growth through work. Yet the employees of Shell, *en masse*, did not demand redesigned jobs, managers who tried to adopt more participative styles were not always rewarded by more cooperative staff, and the productivity bargains began to look less and less like bargains to the people whose income was determined by them.

CONCLUSIONS

It has not been our intention to be unnecessarily critical in discussing disappointments associated with the philosophy programme. In its day the exercise was a brave attempt in what it tried to do and there may be much to learn by treating it as a 'gallant failure'. Yet to the extent that the mistakes of the Shell project were easily made the story will be of recurring interest. For people concerned both with genuinely social applications of social scientific ideas and with the vigorous development of the ideas themselves the Shell project must stand as something of a cautionary tale; most especially because:

1. The case illustrates a dilemma for applied social scientists. To become closely involved in an action programme requires scientists to be committed to the work undertaken; yet to the extent that they are more scientist than salesman scientists will need to recognize the possibility of error in their work and will seek to cultivate a reflective approach towards it. The Shell story provides an example of a failure to cope satisfactorily with this problem.
2. The case also shows how easily disappointments may arise if, even for the best intentions, social science consultants address themselves to a different set of problems than those which are preoccupying their clients.
3. While the attempt to 'jointly optimize' employee satisfactions and organizational effectiveness is clearly a commendable thing to do, it may be an occupational hazard for people so engaged to overestimate the significance of their work and to underestimate its limitations. The Shell story illustrates how, despite hopes that employees' quality of working life would be improved by the application of certain social scientific theories, such ideas introduced in a naïve fashion can have the effect of reinforcing the power of one group over another.

REFERENCES

1. Hill, C.P. (1971) *Towards a New Philosophy of Management*, Gower Press, Farnborough

2. Emery, F.E. and Trist, E.L. (1972) *Towards a Social Ecology*, Plenum Press, London

3. Trist, E.L. (1979) Collaboration in work settings: a personal perspective, *Journal of Applied Behavioral Science*, Vol. 13, pp 292–302

4. Emery, F.E. (1978) The search for a better kind of planning, *International Management*, Vol. 33, pp 58–9

5. Davis, L.E. and Sullivan, C.S. (1980) A labour-management contract and the quality of working life, *Journal of Occupational Behaviour*, Vol. 1, pp 29–41

6. Walton, R.E. (1975) The diffusion of new work structures: explaining why success didn't take, *Organisational Dynamics* (Winter) pp 3–22

7. Herbst, P. G. (1976) *Alternatives to Hierarchies*, Nijhoff, The Hague

8. Taylor, L.K. (1972a) *Not for Bread Alone: An Appreciation of Job Enrichment*, Business Books, London; Taylor, L. K. (1972b) Job enrichment at Shell Stanlow, *Hydrocarbon Processing* (June) pp 140–4

9. Hill, C. P., *op. cit.* p 186

10. Blackler, F.H.M. and Brown C.A. (1980) *Whatever Happened to Shell's New Philosophy of Management? Lessons for the 1980s from a Major Socio-Technical Intervention of the 1960s*, Saxon House, Farnborough

11. Flanders, A. (1964) *The Fawley Productivity Agreements*, Faber and Faber, London

12. Emery, F.E. and Trist, E.L. (1965) The causal texture of organisational environments, *Human Relations*, Vol. 18, pp 12–32

13. Janis, I.L. (1972) *Victims of Groupthink: a psychological study of foreign policy decisions and fiascos*, Houghton Mifflin, Boston, MA

14. Argyris, C. (1970) *Intervention Theory and Method: A Behavioral Science View*, Addison Wesley, Reading, MA

15. Hill, C. P., *op. cit.* p 70

15 CHOOSING STRATEGIES FOR CHANGE
John P. Kotter and Leonard A. Schlesinger

'From the frying pan into the fire,' 'let sleeping dogs lie,' and 'you can't teach an old dog new tricks' are all well-known sayings born of the fear of change. When people are threatened with change in organizations, similar maxims about certain people and departments are trotted out to prevent an alteration in the status quo. Fear of change is understandable, but because the environment changes rapidly, and it has been doing so increasingly, organizations cannot afford not to change. One major task of a manager, then, is to implement change, and that entails overcoming resistance to it. In this chapter, we describe four basic reasons why people resist change. We also describe various methods for dealing with the resistance and provide a guide to what kinds of approaches will work when the different types of resistance occur.

'It must be considered that there is nothing more difficult to carry out, nor more doubtful of success, nor more dangerous to handle, than to initiate a new order of things.'[1]

In 1973, The Conference Board asked 13 eminent authorities to speculate what significant management issues and problems would develop over the next 20 years. One of the strongest themes that runs through their subsequent reports is a concern for the ability of organizations to respond to environmental change. As one person wrote:

> It follows that an acceleration in the rate of change will result in an increasing need for reorganization. Reorganization is usually feared, because it means disturbance of the status quo, a threat to people's vested interests in their jobs, and an upset to established ways of doing things. For these reasons, needed reorganization is often deferred, with a resulting loss in effectiveness and an increase in costs.[2]

Subsequent events have confirmed the importance of this concern about organizational change. Today, more and more managers must deal with new government regulations, new products, growth, increased competition, technological developments and a changing work force. In response, most companies or divisions of major corporations find that they must undertake moderate organizational changes at least once a year and major changes every four or five.[3]

Few organizational change efforts tend to be complete failures, but few tend to be entirely successful either. Most efforts encounter problems; they often take longer than expected and desired, they sometimes kill morale, and they often cost a great deal in terms of managerial time or emotional upheaval. More than a few organizations have not even tried to initiate needed changes because the managers involved were afraid that they were simply incapable of successfully implementing them.

In this chapter, we first describe various causes for resistance to change and then outline a systematic way to select a strategy and set of specific approaches for implementing an organizational change effort. The methods described are based on our analyses of dozens of successful and unsuccessful organizational changes.

DIAGNOSING RESISTANCE

Organizational change efforts often run into some form of human resistance. Although experienced managers are generally all too aware of this fact, surprisingly few take time before an organizational change to assess systematically who might resist the change initiative and for what reasons. Instead, using past experiences as guidelines, managers all too often apply a simple set of beliefs—such as 'engineers will probably resist the change because they are independent and suspicious of top management.' This limited approach can create serious problems. Because of the many different ways in which individuals and groups can react to change, correct assessments are often not intuitively obvious and require careful thought.

Of course, all people who are affected by change experience some emotional turmoil. Even changes that appear to be 'positive' or 'rational' involve loss and uncertainty.[4] Nevertheless, for a number of different reasons, individuals or groups can react very differently to change—from passively resisting it, to aggressively trying to undermine it, to sincerely embracing it.

To predict what form their resistance might take, managers need to be aware of the four most common reasons people resist change. These include: a desire not to lose something of value, a misunderstanding of the change and its implications, a belief that the change does not make sense for the organization, and a low tolerance for change.

Parochial Self-interest

One major reason why people resist organizational change is that they think they will lose something of value as a result. In these cases, because people focus on their own best interests and not on those of the total organization, resistance often results in 'politics' or 'political behaviour.'[5] Consider these two examples:

First, after a number of years of rapid growth, the president of an organization decided that its size demanded the creation of a new staff function—new product-planning and development—to be headed by a vice president. Operationally, this change eliminated most of the decision-making power that the vice presidents of marketing, engineering and production had over new products. Inasmuch as new products were very important in this organization, the change also reduced the vice presidents' status which, together with power, was very important to them.

During the two months after the president announced his idea for a new, product vice president, the existing vice presidents each came up with six or seven reasons the new arrangement might not work. Their objections grew louder and louder until the president shelved the idea.

Second, a manufacturing company had traditionally employed a large group of personnel people as counsellors and 'father confessors' to its production employees. This group of counsellors tended to exhibit high morale because of the professional satisfaction they received from the 'helping relationships' they had with employees. When a new performance appraisal system was installed, every six months the counsellors were required to provide each employee's supervisor with a written evaluation of the employee's 'emotional maturity', 'promotional potential', and so forth.

As some of the personnel people immediately recognized, the change would alter their relationships from a peer and helper to more of a boss and evaluator with most of the employees. Predictably, the personnel counsellors resisted the change. While publicly arguing that the new system was not as good for the company as the old one, they privately put as much pressure as possible on the personnel vice president until he significantly altered the new system.

Political behaviour sometimes emerges before and during organizational change efforts when what is in the best interests of one individual or group is not in the best interests of the total organization or of other individuals and groups.

While political behaviour sometimes takes the form of two or more armed camps publicly fighting things out, it usually is much more subtle. In many cases, it occurs completely under the surface of public dialogue. Although scheming and ruthless individuals sometimes initiate power struggles, more often than not those who do are people who view their potential loss from change as an unfair violation of their implicit, or psychological, contract with the organization.[6]

Misunderstanding and Lack of Trust

People also resist change when they do not understand its implications and perceive that it might cost them much more than they will gain. Such situations often occur when trust is lacking between the person initiating the change and the employees.[7] Here is an example:

When the president of a small midwestern US company announced to his managers that the company would implement a flexible working schedule for all employees, it never occurred to him that he might run into resistance. He had been introduced to the concept at a management seminar and decided to use it to make working conditions at his company more attractive, particularly to clerical and plant personnel.

Shortly after the announcement, numerous rumours begin to circulate among plant employees—none of whom really knew what flexible working hours meant and many of whom were distrustful of the manufacturing vice president. One rumour, for instance, suggested that flexible hours meant that most people would have to work whenever their supervisors asked them to—including evenings and weekends. The employee association, a local union, held a quick meeting and then presented the management with a nonnegotiable demand that the flexible hours concept be dropped. The president, caught completely by surprise, complied.

Few organizations can be characterized as having a high level of trust between employees and managers; consequently, it is easy for misunderstandings to develop when change is introduced. Unless managers surface misunderstandings and clarify them rapidly, they can lead to resistance. And that resistance can easily catch change initiators by surprise, especially if they assume that people only resist change when it is not in their best interest.

Different Assessments

Another common reason people resist organizational change is that they assess the situation differently from their managers or those initiating the change and see more costs than benefits resulting from the change, not only for themselves but for their company as well. For example:

The president of one moderate-size bank was shocked by his staff's analysis of the bank's real estate investment trust (REIT) loans. This complicated analysis suggested that the bank could easily lose up to $10 million, and that the possible losses were increasing each month by 20 per cent. Within a week, the president drew up a plan to reorganize the part of the bank that managed REITs. Because of his concern for the bank's stock price, however, he chose not to release the staff report to anyone except the new REIT section manager.

The reorganization immediately ran into massive resistance from the people involved. The group sentiment, as articulated by one person, was: 'Has he gone mad? Why in God's name is he tearing apart this section of the bank? His actions have already cost us three very good people [who quit], and have crippled a new program we were implementing [which the president was unaware of] to reduce our loan losses.'

Managers who initiate change often assume both that they have all the relevant information required to conduct an adequate organization analysis and that those who will be affected by the change have the same facts, when neither assumption is correct. In either case, the difference in information that groups work with often leads to differences in analyses, which in turn can lead to resistance. Moreover, if the analysis made by those not initiating the change is more accurate than that derived by the initiators, resistance is obviously 'good' for the organization. But this likelihood is not obvious to some managers who assume that resistance is always bad and therefore always fight it.[8]

Low Tolerance for Change

People also resist change because they fear they will not be able to develop the new skills and behaviour that will be required of them. All human beings are limited in their ability to change, with some people much more limited than others.[9] Organizational change can inadvertently require people to change too much, too quickly.

Peter F. Drucker argues that the major obstacle to organizational growth is managers' inability to change their attitudes and behaviour as rapidly as their organizations require.[10] Even when managers intellectually understand the need for changes in the way they operate, they sometimes are emotionally unable to make the transition.

It is because of people's limited tolerance for change that individuals will sometimes resist a change even when they realize it is a good one. For example, a person who receives a significantly more important job as a result of an organizational change will probably be very happy. But it is just as possible for such a person also to feel uneasy and to resist giving up certain aspects of the current situation. A new and very different job will require new and different behaviour, new and different relationships, as well as the loss of some satisfactory current activities and relationships. If the changes are significant and the individual's tolerance for change is low, he/she might begin actively to resist the change for reasons even he/she does not consciously understand.

People also sometimes resist organizational change to save face; to go along with the change would be, they think, an admission that some of their previous decisions or beliefs were wrong. Or they might resist because of peer group pressure or because of a supervisor's attitude. Indeed, there are probably an endless number of reasons why people resist change.[11]

Assessing which of the many possibilities might apply to those who will be affected by a change is important because it can help a manager select an appropriate way to overcome resistance. Without an accurate diagnosis of possibilities of resistance, a manager can easily get bogged down during the change process with very costly problems.

DEALING WITH RESISTANCE

Many managers underestimate not only the variety of ways people can react to organizational change but also the ways they can positively influence specific individuals and groups during a change. And, again because of past experiences, managers sometimes do not have an accurate understanding of the advantages and disadvantages of the methods with which they *are* familiar.

Education and Communication

One of the most common ways to overcome resistance to change is to educate people about it beforehand. Communication of ideas helps people see the need for and the logic of a change. The education process can involve one-on-one discussions, presentations to groups or memos and reports. For example:

As a part of an effort to make changes in a division's structure and in measurement and reward systems, a division manager put together a one-hour audiovisual presentation that explained the changes and the reasons for them. Over a four-month period, he made this presentation no less than a dozen times to groups of 20 or 30 corporate and division managers.

An education and communication programme can be ideal when resistance is based on inadequate or inaccurate information and analysis, especially if the initiators need the resistors' help in implementing the change. But some managers overlook the fact that a programme of this sort requires a good relationship between initiators and resistors or that the latter may not believe what they hear. It also requires time and effort, particularly if a lot of people are involved.

Participation and Involvement

If the initiators involve the potential resistors in some aspect of the design and implementation of the change, they can often forestall resistance. With a participative change effort, the initiators listen to the people the change involves and use their advice. To illustrate:

The head of a small financial services company once created a task force to help design and implement changes in his company's reward system. The task force was composed of eight second- and third-level managers from different parts of the company. The president's specific charter to them was that they recommend changes in the company's benefit package. They were given six months and asked to file a brief progress report with the president once a month. After they had made their recommendations, which the president largely accepted, they were asked to help the company's personnel director implement them.

We have found that many managers have quite strong feelings about participation—sometimes positive and sometimes negative. That is, some managers feel that there should always be participation during change efforts, while others feel this is virtually always a mistake. Both attitudes can create problems for a manager, because neither is very realistic.

When change initiators believe they do not have all the information they need to design and implement a change, or when they need the wholehearted commitment of others to do so, involving others makes very good sense. Considerable research has demonstrated that, in general, participation leads to commitment, not merely compliance.[12] In some instances, commitment is needed for the change to be a success. Nevertheless, the participation process does have its drawbacks. Not only can it lead to a poor solution if the process is not carefully managed but it can be enormously time-consuming. When the change must be made immediately, it can take simply too long to involve others.

Facilitation and Support

Another way that managers can deal with potential resistance to change is by being supportive. This process might include providing training in new skills or giving employees time off after a demanding period or simply listening and providing emotional support. For example:

Management in one rapidly growing electronics company devised a way to help people adjust to frequent organizational changes. First, management staffed its human resource department with four counsellors who spent most of their time talking to people who were feeling 'burnt out' or who were having difficulty adjusting to new jobs. Second, on a selective basis, management offered people four-week mini-sabbaticals that involved some reflective or educational activity away from work. And, finally, it spent a great deal of money on in-house education and training programmes.

Facilitation and support are most helpful when fear and anxiety lie at the heart of resistance. Seasoned, tough managers often overlook or ignore this kind of resistance, as well as the efficacy of facilitative ways of dealing with it. The basic drawback of this approach is that it can be time-consuming and expensive and still fail.[13] If time, money, and patience just are not available, then using supportive methods is not very practical.

Negotiation and Agreement

Another way to deal with resistance is to offer incentives to active or potential resistors. For instance, management could give a union a higher wage rate in return for a work rule change; it could increase an individual's pension benefits in return for an early retirement. Here is an example of negotiated agreements:

In a large manufacturing company, the divisions were very interdependent. One division manager wanted to make some major changes in his organization. Yet, because of the interdependence, he recognized that he would be forcing some inconvenience and change on other divisions as well. To prevent top managers in other divisions from undermining his efforts, the division manager negotiated a written agreement with each. The agreement specified the outcomes the other division managers would receive and when, as well as the kinds of cooperation that he would receive from them in return during the change process. Later, whenever the division managers complained about his changes or the change process itself, he could point to the negotiated agreements.

Negotiation is particularly appropriate when it is clear that someone is going to lose out as a result of a change and yet his or her power to resist is significant. Negotiated agreements can be a relatively easy way to avoid major resistance, though, like some other processes, they may become expensive. And once a manager makes it clear that he/she will negotiate to avoid major resistance, he/she opens himself/herself up to the possibility of blackmail.[14]

Manipulation and Cooptation

In some situations, managers also resort to covert attempts to influence others. Manipulation, in this context, normally involves the very selective use of information and the conscious structuring of events.

One common form of manipulation is cooptation. Coopting an individual usually involves giving him or her a desirable role in the design or implementation of the change. Coopting a group involves giving one of its leaders, or someone it respects, a key role in the design or implementation of a change. This is not a form of participation, however, because the initiators do not want the advice of the coopted, merely his or her endorsement. For example:

One division manager in a large multibusiness corporation invited the corporate human relations vice president, a close friend of the president, to help him and his key staff diagnose some problems the division was having. Because of his busy schedule, the corporate vice president was not able to do much of the actual information gathering or analysis himself, thus limiting his own influence on the diagnoses. But his presence at key meetings helped commit him to the diagnoses as well as the solutions the group designed. The commitment was subsequently very important because the president, at least initially, did not like some of the proposed changes. Nevertheless, after discussion with his human relations vice president, he did not try to block them.

Under certain circumstances cooptation can be a relatively inexpensive and easy way to gain an individual's or a group's support (cheaper, for example, than negotiation and quicker than participation). Nevertheless, it has its drawbacks. If people feel they are being tricked into not resisting, are not being treated equally or are being lied to, they may respond very negatively. More than one manager has found that, by his/her effort to give some subordinate a sense of participation through cooptation, he/she created more resistance than if he/she had done nothing. In addition, cooptation can create a different kind of problem if those coopted use their ability to influence the design and implementation of changes in ways that are not in the best interests of the organization.

Other forms of manipulation have drawbacks also, sometimes to an even greater degree. Most people are likely to greet what they perceive as covert treatment and/or lies with a negative response. Furthermore, if a manager develops a reputation as a manipulator, it can undermine his/her ability to use needed approaches such as education/communication and participation/involvement. At the extreme, it can even ruin a career.

Nevertheless, people do manipulate others successfully—particularly when all other tactics are not feasible or have failed.[15] Having no other alternative, and not enough time to educate, involve or support people, and without the power or other resources to negotiate, coerce or coopt them, managers have resorted to manipulating information channels in order to scare people into thinking there is a crisis coming which they can avoid only by changing.

Figure 15.1 Methods for dealing with resistance to change

Approach	Commonly used in situations	Advantages	Drawbacks
Education + communication	Where there is a lack of information or inaccurate information and analysis	Once persuaded, people will often help with the implementation of the change	Can be very time-consuming if lots of people are involved
Participation + involvement	Where the initiators do not have all the information they need to design the change, and where others have considerable power to resist	People who participate will be committed to implementing change, and any relevant information they have will be integrated into the change plan	Can be very time-consuming if participators design an inappropriate change
Facilitation + support	Where people are resisting because of adjustment problems	No other approach works as well with adjustment problems	Can be time-consuming, expensive and still fail
Negotiation + agreement	Where someone or some group will clearly lose out in a change, and where that group has considerable power to resist	Sometimes it is a relatively easy way to avoid major resistance	Can be too expensive in many cases if it alerts others to negotiate for compliance
Manipulation + cooptation	Where other tactics will not work, or are too expensive	It can be a relatively quick and inexpensive solution to resistance problems	Can lead to future problems if people feel manipulated
Explicit + implicit coercion	Where speed is essential and the change initiators possess considerable power	It is speedy, and can overcome any kind of resistance	Can be risky if it leaves people angry with the initiators

Explicit and Implicit Coercion

Finally, managers often deal with resistance coercively. Here they essentially force people to accept a change by explicitly or implicitly threatening them (with the loss of jobs, promotion possibilities and so forth) or by actually firing or transferring them. As with manipulation, using coercion is a risky process because inevitably people strongly resent forced change. But in situations where speed is essential and where the changes will not be popular, regardless of how they are introduced, coercion may be the manager's only option.

Successful organizational change efforts are always characterized by the skilful application of a number of these approaches, often in very different combinations. However, successful efforts share two characteristics: managers employ the approaches with a sensitivity to their strengths and limitations (see Figure 15.1) and appraise the situation realistically.

The most common mistake managers make is to use only one approach or a limited set of them *regardless of the situation*. A surprisingly large number of managers have this problem. This would include the hard-boiled boss who often coerces people, the people-oriented manager who constantly tries to involve and support his people, the cynical boss who always manipulates and coopts others, the intellectual manager who relies heavily on education and communication, and the lawyerlike manager who usually tries to negotiate.[16]

A second common mistake that managers make is to approach change in a disjointed and incremental way that is not a part of a clearly considered strategy.

CHOICE OF STRATEGY

In approaching an organizational change situation, managers explicitly or implicitly make strategic choices regarding the speed of the effort, the amount of preplanning, the involvement of others and the relative emphasis they will give to different approaches. Successful change efforts seem to be those where these choices both are internally consistent and fit some key situational variables.

The strategic options available to managers can be usefully thought of as existing on a continuum (see Figure 15.2).[17] At one end of the continuum, the change strategy calls for a very rapid implementation, a clear plan of action and little involvement of others. This type of strategy mows over any resistance and, at the extreme, would result in a fait accompli. At the other end of the continuum, the strategy would call for a much slower change process, a less clear plan and involvement on the part of many people other than the change initiators. This type of strategy is designed to reduce resistance to a minimum.[18]

The further to the left one operates on the continuum in Figure 15.2, the more one tends to be coercive and the less one tends to use the other approaches—especially participation; the converse also holds.

Organizational change efforts that are based on inconsistent strategies tend to run into predictable problems. For example, efforts that are not clearly planned in advance and yet are implemented quickly tend to become bogged down owing

Figure 15.2 Strategic continuum

Fast	Slower
Clearly planned	Not clearly planned at the beginning
Little involvement of others	Lots of involvement of others
Attempt to overcome any resistance	Attempt to minimize any resistance

Key situational variables

The amount and type of resistance that is anticipated

The position of the initiators vis-à-vis the resistors (in terms of power, trust and so forth)

The locus of relevant data for designing the change, and of needed energy for implementing it

The stakes involved (e.g., the presence or lack of presence of a crisis, the consequences of resistance and lack of change)

to unanticipated problems. Efforts that involve a large number of people, but are implemented quickly, usually become either stalled or less participative.

Situational Factors

Exactly where a change effort should be strategically positioned on the continuum in Figure 15.2 depends on four factors:

1. The amount and kind of resistance that is anticipated. All other factors being equal, the greater the anticipated resistance, the more difficult it will be simply to overwhelm it, and the more a manager will need to move toward the right on the continuum to find ways to reduce some of it.[19]
2. The position of the initiator vis-à-vis the resistors, especially with regard to power. The less power the initiator has with respect to others, the more the initiating manager *must* move to the left on the continuum.[20] Conversely, the stronger the initiator's position, the more he or she can move to the right.
3. The person who has the relevant data for designing the change and the energy for implementing it. The more the initiators anticipate that they will need information and commitment from others to help design and implement the change, the more they must move to the right.[21] Gaining useful information and commitment requires time and the involvement of others.
4. The stakes involved. The greater the short-run potential for risks to organizational performance and survival if the present situation is not changed, the more one must move to the left.

Organizational change efforts that ignore these factors inevitably run into problems. A common mistake some managers make, for example, is to move too quickly and involve too few people despite the fact that they do not have all the information they really need to design the change correctly.

Insofar as these factors still leave a manager with some choice of where to operate on the continuum, it is probably best to select a point as far to the right as possible for both economic and social reasons. Forcing change on people can have just too many negative side effects over both the short and the long term. Change efforts using the strategies on the right of the continuum can often help develop an organization and its people in useful ways.[22]

In some cases, however, knowing the four factors may not give a manager a comfortable and obvious choice. Consider a situation where a manager has a weak position vis-à-vis the people whom he thinks need a change and yet is faced with serious consequences if the change is not implemented immediately. Such a manager is clearly in a bind. If he somehow is not able to increase his power in the situation, he will be forced to choose some compromise strategy and to live through difficult times.

Implications for Manager

A manager can improve his/her chance of success in an organizational change effort by:

1. Conducting an organizational analysis that identifies the current situation, problems, and the forces that are possible causes of those problems. The analysis should specify the actual importance of the problems, the speed with which the problems must be addressed if additional problems are to be avoided, and the kinds of changes that are generally needed.
2. Conducting an analysis of factors relevant to producing the needed changes. This analysis should focus on questions of who might resist the change, why, and how much; who has information that is needed to design the change, and whose cooperation is essential in implementing it; and what is the position of the initiator vis-à-vis other relevant parties in terms of power, trust, normal modes of interaction and so forth.
3. Selecting a change strategy, based on the previous analysis, that specifies the speed of change, the amount of preplanning and the degree of involvement of others; that selects specific tactics for use with various individuals and groups; and that is internally consistent.
4. Monitoring the implementation process. No matter how good a job one does of initially selecting a change strategy and tactics, something unexpected will eventually occur during implementation. Only by carefully monitoring the process can one identify the unexpected in a timely fashion and react to it intelligently.

Interpersonal skills, of course, are the key to using this analysis. But even the most outstanding interpersonal skills will not make up for a poor choice of strategy and tactics. And in a business world that continues to become more and more dynamic, the consequences of poor implementation choices will become increasingly severe.

REFERENCES

1. Niccolò Machiavelli, *The Prince*
2. Marvin Bower and C. Lee Walton, Jr. (1973) *Gearing a business to the future*, in Challenge to Leadership, The Conference Board, New York, p 126

3. For recent evidence on the frequency of changes, see Stephen A. Allen (1978) Organizational choice and general influence networks for diversified companies, *Academy of Management Journal* (September) p 341

4. For example, see Robert A. Luke, Jr (1973) A structural approach to organizational change, *Journal of Applied Behavioral Science* (September/October) p 611

5. For a discussion of power and politics in corporations, see Abraham Zaleznik and Manfred F.R. Kets de Vries (1975) *Power and the Corporate Mind* Houghton Mifflin, Boston, chapter 6; and Robert H. Miles (1978) *Macro Organizational Behavior*, Goodyear, Pacific Palisades, CA, chapter 4

6. See Edgar H. Schein (1965) *Organizational Psychology*, Prentice-Hall, Englewood Cliffs, NJ, p 44

7. See Chris Argyris (1970) *Intervention Theory and Method*, Addison-Wesley, Reading, MA, p 70

8. See Paul R. Lawrence (1954) How to deal with resistance to change, *HBR* (May–June) p 49; reprinted as HBR Classic, January–February 1969, p 4

9. For a discussion of resistance that is personality based, see Goodwin Watson (1969) Resistance to change, in *The Planning of Change*, eds. Warren G. Bennis, Kenneth F. Benne, and Robert Chin, Holt, Reinehart, and Winston, New York, p 489

10. Peter F. Drucker (1954) *The Practice of Management*, Harper and Row, New York

11. For a general discussion of resistance and reasons for it, see chapter 3 in Gerald Zaltman and Robert Duncan (1977) *Strategies for Planned Change*, John Wiley, New York

12. See, for example, Alfred J. Marrow, David F. Bowers, and Stanley E. Seashore (1967) *Management by Participation*, Harper and Row, New York

13. Zaltman and Duncan, *Strategies for Planned Change*, chapter 4

14. For an excellent discussion of negotiation, see Gerald I. Nierenberg (1968) *The Art of Negotiating*, Cornerstone, Birmingham, AL

15. See John P. Kotter (1977) Power, dependence, and effective management, *HBR* (July–August) p 125

16. *Ibid.*, p 135

17. See Larry E. Greiner (1967) Patterns of organization change *HBR* (May–June) p 119; and Larry E. Greiner and Louis B. Barnes (1970) *Organization change and development* in Gene W. Dalton and Paul R. Lawrence (Eds) Organizational Change and Development, Irwin, Homewood, IL, p 3

18. For a good discussion of an approach that attempts to minimize resistance, see Renato Tagiuri (1979) *Notes on the management of change: implication of postulating a need for competence*, in John P. Kotter, Vijay Sathe, and Leonard A. Schlesinger, Organization Irwin, Homewood, IL

19. Jay W. Lorsch (1976) *Managing change*, in Paul R. Lawrence, Louis B. Barnes, and Jay W. Lorsch (Eds) Organizational Behavior and Administration, Irwin, Homewood, IL, p 676

20. *Ibid.*

21. *Ibid.*

22. Michael Beer (1979) *Organization Change and Development: A Systems View*, Goodyear, Pacific Palisades, CA

16 MAKING NEW THINGS HAPPEN
Tudor Rickards

There is a widespread and deep-rooted assumption about 'the way things get done' in organizations. The process whereby an idea becomes an accepted innovation is assumed to be a *sequential* one. First there is a discovery, then there are various stages of testing, checking, refining and the like. Many problem-solving models reflect this sequential thinking and include an 'acceptance seeking' stage for a favoured idea or solution. At its crudest, such linear thinking can lead to coercion and 'selling' of ideas to a resistant community involved in the process. This is not the only possible approach to innovation, and we will be looking at three overlapping ones:

1. The contractual or mission-oriented approach
2. The negotiative approach
3. The participative approach

An innovation project may be influenced by all three approaches, but it is often possible and revealing to identify a dominant influence.

The contractual approach reflects the sequential viewpoint already mentioned. The basic assumption is that the problem can be analyzed into reasonably well-defined bits which can then be worked on by assigned individuals or teams skilled in the key disciplines identified. Furthermore, once the subproblems have been solved, the process has brought about the desired solution (or implemented the innovation task). The analytic weapons of the contractual approach include control charts, coordination devices, professional expertise and 'know how'. Sometimes the technological problems of an innovation project can be dealt with excellently though the research and development facilities of an organization, and the results are then made available to a further contractual group involving marketing and advertising specialists. The contractual approach is characterized by highly professional people working to a provided brief. If, as often happens, 'outsiders' fail to understand the importance or relevance of the work, and do not

Rickards, T. (1985) Making new things happen, *Technovation*, Vol. 3, pp 119–31 assist in its goals, there is an *implementation* problem often seen from within as a matter of selling, influencing or coercing the outsider, in order to achieve the contractual goals. (It is not uncommon to hear a professional say 'It's not my job to worry about what *they* want. That's their problem. We've got a brief of our own to worry about'.)

The negotiative approach can arise when professionals have assumed that their brief is a clear-cut one (a contractual situation), but have discovered subsequently that some modification to the original proposal might give results that are more acceptable to the client and to themselves as the appointed experts and project executors. This situation often arises in design and engineering projects, and has been modelled elegantly by the leading systems thinker West Churchman.

His model is one of *implementation*, and has influenced many professional consultants, particularly with operations-research backgrounds. We can understand the main point by considering a professional (or researcher) supplied with a problem from a manager (or client). Each of the two parties may understand, or fail to understand the other. To break out of the problems of *persuading* or *telling*, each party has to seek to understand the other. The consequence is mutual learning and problem-solving which is negotiative, but also creative. The expert does provide expert advice, but in the spirit of offering the means which require imaginative coupling with client needs to achieve the recurring innovation equation: means + needs = innovation. Other innovation workers share Churchman's awareness of the importance of resolving the possible conflicts between major subsystems within the general innovating system. The sociotechnical approach does so by reconciling technological and human needs. My own work with John Carson (Scimitar) seeks to integrate the resources of an organization with the needs of its environment.[23]

Participative thinking can be distinguished from negotiative thinking as being more firmly located in the action-research tradition. The professional expertise is that of *process facilitator* concerned with bringing about mutual understanding *within* the innovating system, rather than identifying a preferred technology or design for proceeding. (There will in practice be overlap between the two approaches, as we will see later.) The most important feature of such an approach is that implementation of an idea becomes a quite different concept. Instead of implementation being something tacked on, to bring about an identified and desirable change in a system, innovation *emerges* from the process which is taking place, as starting ideas are modified and reshaped. In a paradoxical way, implementation is diminished as a concluding stage of innovative problem-solving, but the requirement to change influences the behaviours and thinking of subgroups *pervasively* and from the start of the innovation activity.

It is not my intention to put forward one of these types of thinking as the 'best' for innovation. Mission-oriented teams have been responsible for many technological triumphs over the last two decades. I am more comfortable working within a participative mode, but have also been heavily involved in various projects requiring negotiative approaches. Furthermore, these projects tend to identify aspects of the whole which could be closely defined as bounded problems and well-suited for mission-oriented attack. By an awareness of the possibilities, a manager can avoid the trap of assuming his or her preferred way of seeking innovation is the only way—particularly when 'stuck'—there are always other ways, and there are often better untested ways. Let us now look at examples of innovation which capture some aspects of each of the approaches. The examples have been chosen as representative, and could easily be replaced with a different set, without hiding their instructive messages for other innovators.

MISSION-ORIENTED APPROACHES TO INNOVATION

Let us look very briefly at two well-known, large mission-oriented projects, one successful, one less so; and then two much smaller projects.

Paul Lawrence from Harvard, with co-researchers from England and Canada studied NASA's moon programme and other very large-scale projects such as the artificial heart programme.[4] In the 1960s it had been proposed that the artificial heart programme and the moon-shot project had essentially similar technical logics. Each had a clearly defined mission, and a number of identifiable non-interacting subsystems. Each seemed likely candidates for mission-oriented projects. One advocate, who was also a Nobel Laureate, suggested to the director of the US Heart Institute that it would be a great pity 'to neglect the opportunity of a systems response to what is now a well-defined technical problem, which is so much a matter of engineering design, material development and empirical testing, and should not be confused with the basic research that was needed at its foundations.' The master plan, finally accepted, was for a ('hard') systems approach in which phase one would assess the state of invited competitive proposals for the entire system. Phase three would design and develop several prototypes. Phase four would implement the mass production of medically acceptable artificial hearts. The project, in lunar terms, never got off the ground. it never even built a space craft. Lawrence and his team summed up the failure as follows.

> The system required to put a man on the moon can be visualised as a black box in its environment, the solar system. . . . The ability to isolate the black box for design purposes made possible a view of the development process as optimisation within known stable constraints. The artificial heart could not, and still cannot, be isolated as a black-box problem. . . . The Artificial Heart Program's defined task simply did not fit the state of knowledge of the physical phenomena.

In other words, the 'man on the moon' project, while historic in impact, was essentially a *well-defined and bounded project*. The innovative component was where the system went, not how the system was created. The mission-oriented approach worked within the black boxes, which were capable of being coordinated to achieve higher-order system objectives.

But why did the moon programme work when the artificial heart one did not? Lawrence concluded that the overall organizational system engaged in some purposive attempt to innovate incorporates a *technical* logic which has often been overstudied at the expense of other dimensions, and it also includes a *political* logic, and an *organizational* logic. The organizational and political logics of the moon programme were nonproblematic because of the charismatic sponsorship and decision-making imposed by presidential decree. Under these circumstances the technical logic can become what is sometimes called a *technological impera-tive*. Problem definitions tend to be technical, and highly suited for turning into mission-oriented projects, by virtue both of a relatively well-bounded character, and the absence of intrusive political or organizational 'logics' (or subsystems).

It is also possible to find much smaller schemes which have successfully stimulated innovation through providing technological expertise, although the procedures will be strongly dependent on local conditions. We will compare an American and a UK scheme, each of which has been identified with a technologi-cal university. The Rennselaer Polytechnic Incubator programme (the RPI scheme) is the brainchild of Pier Abetti, who is professor in the management of technology at Rennselaer Technical University.[5] He had argued that innovation requires 'an existing or potential market need, determined by the conditions of the economy; new (relative to that market or industry) technical means, determined by the status of the technology; and an entrepreneur who initiates and carries through the innovation process.' The objective of the RPI programme was to fulfil the university's commitment as a technological resource base for its local com-munity. The major deficiency in existing schemes was identified as absence of the equivalent to the large-firm's R&D environment which can nurture a new idea until it reaches precommercialization, as a tested new product. The *incubation* stage set out to meet that need.

RPI evolved five criteria to assist in selecting the schemes for its 'hot house'. It was only concerned with ideas of some *technological novelty*. However, existing applications of the technology were considered important as evidence of techni-cal *feasibility*. Clear perception and understanding of the *market place* by the entrepreneur were also considered to be important. The *people* involved were evaluated for 'match' with the project by experience and background. Finally a match with the RPI *resources* was considered. Applicants provided information in a business plan which explored these criteria, as a course screen of initial appli-cants, and then in more detail. Even applying these filters, a growing number of entrepreneurs contacted the programme, and were accepted. The pilot scheme began in a small storage building and ran with a support grant shared between the university and a government agency. It rapidly expanded into larger premises, still within the university campus, while maintaining the concept of low-cost 'shell' accommodation. Technical and administrative support came through a small committee comprising a coordinator, and three others supplying technical, business and finance aid. In a series of meetings the business plan is developed, and those projects failing to satisfy the criteria are discontinued. About 1 in 10 proposals pass through this stage and are accepted as ventures. A milestone occurs as first business orders arrive, and transition to an established organiza-tion draws near. This may take 6–24 months, during which time the business plan is also being upgraded for raising finance for full commercial operations. The support of the incubator committee extends to this stage, but the final responsibility for selling the plan to potential partners and backers rests with the emerging company.

By the second year of operation (1983), several of the high technology 'start ups' showed all the signs of growth possibilities, and 50 jobs had been created. The business planning cycle is highly goal-orientated, with a 'mission' to arrive at a viable business. Although high technology was taken as a starting criterion, the overall procedure resembles a problem-solving approach in which a 'bright idea' is implemented and protected from premature market and political complications.

In the United Kingdom, an interesting and notable example of stimulating regional innovation has come from Salford, a small city merging with its much larger neighbour Manchester, but fiercely independent of it. Its industrial history is an heroic one from the early days of the industrial revolution, perhaps best known for Engel's famous works on the condition of its working classes. In more recent and folk culture it is famed as the home of the English painter L. S. Lowrey, and of the television soap opera *Coronation Street*. Urban problems are as severe and persistent as any in the UK, and its long-established polytechnic acquired the status of a university in the 1960s. From that time it has acquired an enviable reputation for its university/industry links. Interestingly, this policy has not been matched by generosity from the university grants committee, which has reduced Salford's grants, favouring the more traditional universities, in which the pursuit of scholarship is uncontaminated by responses to industry's practical needs.

Salford University Industrial Centre (SUIC) was set up in 1967 as a business subsidiary to seek out industrial consultancy, drawing on the university's technological skills.[6] It rapidly found markets for design and development work and later for exploiting the university's ideas in fields such as mechanized assembly, vibration and corrosion control, ion plating and integrated computer-aided manufacture. Its local clients were augmented by large organizations such as the US Air Force, the National Coal Board, Siemens, Kodak and the UKAEA. By 1979 there were 20 full-time commercial and technical staff, and by 1984 the numbers had risen to 43, despite the fierce impact of the recession on industrial firms in the region over the intervening years. The centre's director, Barry Richardson, believes that the key to making innovation happen lies in finding a match between what industry wants and the high technology environment available within the university. He sees his primary responsibility as 'getting the people and the environment right' and providing some rules and measures to make this happen.

SUIC has a more eclectic approach to projects than RPI, and has no preconceived project or business plan. Some of the most commercially successful projects were initiated by a postgraduate student with a research idea; others have come from 'responsive consultancy' (which is more akin to the negotiative style to be considered next). 'Getting the environment right' has been assisted by a supportive, but noninterfering relationship with the University of Salford (in direct contrast to many other university innovation schemes, which seem to accrue stultifying management committees of worthy academics and academic administrators). 'Getting the right people' involves cultivating 'product champions'—either from the university or industry and establishing acceptable reward systems. Two university-linked schemes exist, each successful in the management of innovation. They share a concern for active matching of market needs and technical means, and for establishing a supportive climate for product champions/business entrepreneurs. Both might be said to reduce the innovation process to manageable and well-bounded projects, yet in approach they have strong individual styles, once again illustrating the folly of seeking any one *correct* set of operational procedures for stimulating innovation.

NEGOTIATIVE THINKING

The various innovation activities just described appear superficially to be driven by a technological 'logic'. High technological (and in some cases scientific) skills have been necessary for their successes. Yet as we have seen, this is only a partial picture. Closer inspection reveals that the projects have been constructed to exploit these skills by isolating and defining the technological component of innovation into well-defined projects. When this proves difficult (as in the case of the artificial heart programme) other logics intrude. Some approaches to innovation have concentrated on identifying the potentially conflicting logics, as a prelude to resolving them creatively. An early example of this is Trist and Bamforth's work with coalminers facing social changes imposed by new technology.[7] They resolved the conflict by recognizing and merging social and technical needs, thus pioneering sociotechnical studies of organizations. Let us now look at two rather different and more modern approaches which have in common a systematic attempt to understand and reconcile differing system logics.

The ETHICS approach has been developed by Professor Enid Mumford at Manchester Business School as a means of enhancing the design of computer systems through greater user-involvement.[8] ETHICS stands for Effective Technical and Human Implementation of Computer-based Systems, and has found wide acceptance in European and American projects. Because of its great value as a method of *implementing* new technology it is being presented here as an example of *negotiative* rather than *participative* methodology for innovation, although the distinction is again fuzzy, and the originator has pointed out how the reality of most participative change situations is a negotiated outcome. According to her, ETHICS

> is a way of enabling everyone concerned with the introduction of new technology to consider human as well as technological factors when embarking on the design of a new (computer-based work) system ... such an approach takes account of the fact that different individuals and groups have their own needs, interests and values and that these must be met if employees are to accept major change enthusiastically and willingly.

The matching process of technical and social factors involves the systematic diagnosis of business and social needs and problems; setting efficiency and social objectives; closing a strategy which best achieves both sets of objectives; designing this in detail; implementing the new system; and evaluating it. Mumford developed a range of techniques to assist the process, including facilitation (once again the creative process is enhanced by a process expert); inventories; group discussions; and two-tier systems for effective consultation/participation.

The matching of social and technical requirements of a system reconciles their 'logics', and bears a passing resemblance to the recurring theme of *means* + *needs* = *innovation*. The process is indeed an innovative one. Many managers, even today, are not accustomed to taking social requirements into account as they address the challenges of introducing new technology, and ETHICS offered a substantial advance over previous practices. (This point may not be immediately obvious to Business School students who are accustomed to lectures emphasizing the importance of human factors for job satisfaction and performance effectiveness. Some management science precepts take a long time to percolate through into practical applications.)

A system with some similarities to the ETHICS approach is SCIMITAR (Systematic Creativity and Integrated Modelling of Industrial Technology and Research). The approach was originated by John Carson[2] while working for a UK chemicals company as new products manager, in the 1970s. Since then the system has been applied across a range of industries, and tested in European, American and Japanese organizations as a low-cost approach to finding and commercializing new products. Carson's original concept was to apply the practices and attitudes of the private entrepreneur to the search for innovation within a traditional, medium-sized corporation. He believed that many companies were making innovation even riskier than it need be by poor search and selection strategies. His remedies were to systematize the idea search; to concentrate on matching corporate resources and market needs; to generate promising ideas in sufficient numbers to ensure a flow of products to the market place, eliminating those which fail to meet target deadlines; and to devote the creative and entrepreneurial efforts of a small team, full-time, to achieving these ends, until the projects are ready to be transferred into the routine production and marketing facilities of the organization. The emphasis is on *incremental* innovation (although the system is often used to help a company identify and move into new markets, or new technologies).

A recent survey of 24 companies using SCIMITAR enables some generalizations to be made about the practical procedures followed.[3] Perhaps the most important start-up tasks are those concerning the setting-up of an organizational structure to assist innovation. Regardless of the strongest of advocacy for full-time groups, most (UK) boards of directors are seduced by the attractions of 'doing things on the cheap' and attempt to start with part-time innovation teams. In the sample of 24 organizations, 14 operated part-time committee structures. Many of the subsequent difficulties—for example, of acquiring corporate backing and resources—stem from failures to agree on terms of reference and adequate resources (which in part reflects the difficulty in obtaining a team leader with that entrepreneurial ability of striking a good bargain for his or her group and company).

SCIMITAR's central management aid is the development of a three-dimensional business model which represents the company as it is, and as it might become. Twenty-three of the 24 companies found they were able to build and interpret such a model to produce new business ideas to satisfy the twin criteria of an identified market need and a proposed corporate means of resolving that need. The early work had established a vital principle in the management of innovation: *provided the innovation process is managed as a regular throughput of new product ideas, the overall uncertainties can be minimized, and substituted by assessable, probabilistic risk.* That is to say, for a given set of starting ideas, it becomes possible to *control* the development effort per idea, and *estimate* the yearly output of prototype products for commercialization trials. What remains uncertain is the fate of any particular idea—which is not problematic, provided the numerical weight of ideas progressing through the system ensures sufficient commercially successful ideas over time.

Over many trials over the period 1973–78 it was found that just under a hundred ideas *all of initial promise* were required to ensure that after refinement and critical appraisal one product reached the market place and made profits for the company. This ratio has been quoted in earlier works on innovation without satisfactory explanation, and we have found similar results in other companies ranging from consumer goods to engineering. There is nothing mystical about the ratio, however, which can be modified according to circumstances—by changing the severity of acceptance criteria, for example. I suspect we have to look at the well-known estimating biases, especially of project times, for a partial explanation. The empirically important point is that a new venture team can eventually model and control the flow of new product ideas. Innovation while risky need not be totally uncertain.

The ideas are generated from the three-dimensional model by a systematic exploration of its cells, often by a small team and facilitator following the general principles of creative problem-solving. In the reduction of numbers of ideas the key points are *standardization* (without which assessment is virtually impossible) and setting an agreed target time to produce a prototype from each idea, and to eliminate *all* ideas which fail to be completed on time. This valuable discipline removes at a stroke potentially 'rogue' projects that seem to have intrinsic aspects that result in problems at each stage of progress. The 50 per cent overrun on a three-week development test is trivial, but the 50 per cent overrun to a planned commercial launch can be disastrous. During development, low cost trials are essential to maintain the low cost per project evaluated. Pilot rigs, and trials on plant belonging to potential customers are favoured strategies.

Over 9000 ideas were developed within the 24 trials, and the ratio of commercialized products remained close to one from 88 ideas giving just over 100 new products, of above average contribution to the companies involved. The returns on investment and turnovers are not available, but an assessment of £25 million of combined turnover at maturity has been made. The most successful product, an agricultural chemical with novel delivery system assisting its effectivenss, is selling at a rate of £6 million per annum.

SCIMITAR is an ambitious attempt to provide operating procedures for a generalized approach to industrial innovation. Its emphasis is not mission-oriented, as the iterative process helps redefine and clarify objectives. In practice, the approach involves considerable negotiation ('selling in and selling out'), as the commercialization process proceeds.

THE PARTICIPATIVE INNOVATION APPROACH

Participative approaches to innovation operate on the assumption that innovations *emerge* and that the process is influenced from outsiders only as process consultants or facilitators. Let us look at one project in detail and consider other versions very briefly.

In 1976 a scheme was set up in Holland with government funding to help small firms become more innovative (The PII or Project Industriele Innovation scheme). The results have been described by the project leader Jan Buijs, of the TNO organization, Delft (1984).[9] New technology based firms (NTBFs) tended to need 'expert' consultancy advice on specific commercial issues. In contrast, small- and medium-sized enterprises (SMEs) in mature industries required a *process consultancy* approach that was not available at the time in Holland. Buijs suggests that NTBFs tend to have a core idea and are looking for means of commercializing it (mission orientation), whereas the SMEs have an existing structure, often in declining markets, and need to obtain ideas for new products. To help these latter organizations, PII designed a training programme for process consultants. The scheme was based on a subsidized consultancy approach to selected organizations. Of nearly 300 applicants, about 100 were taken on (from a population of 6000 SMEs with 25–500 employees). For SMEs the subsidies were available for the strategic stages of innovation planning only—on the principle that there were available services (of the expert kind) for subsequent exploitation of the innovation. The consultants were widely recruited from private organizations, and had expert consultancy skills, but had little appreciation of principles of stimulating innovation through process facilitation. About 1600 consultants were identified who had management service skills. These were approached through their professional organizations, about 200 expressed interest, and after interviews 72 were selected to participate. It was felt that economically very vulnerable firms would not be able to benefit from the programme design, and these were excluded. (When this constraint was dropped for a subsequent trial the weaker companies did find difficulty in benefitting from the approach.)

The five elements of the original approach were summarized as:

A step-by-step model of the innovation process based on strategic planning approaches, management of innovation theories and organizational learning

A team approach which involves all functional departments of the company, including the participation of management

A strong external orientation, conditioned by the fact that the reason for most innovation is to be found outside the company and depends on the acquisition of relevant information

The intensive use of appropriate creativity techniques to provide intervention
   methods for the consultant
The process-oriented consulting role

   The eventual allocation of a consultant to an organization was made at the
request of the organization—a point considered important to reinforce commitment on both sides. (A consultant nominated by PII was approved, or a second
one offered. Rejection of four nominees was taken as evidence of something
wrong with the firm, not the consultants.) By 1984 a pattern of progress had been
observed. The inevitable attrition rate of consultants and companies had
occurred, although well over half of firms and consultants persisted. At the end of
round one in 1982, about two thirds of the original 79 firms considered they had
gained a positive innovative contribution from the work. Many of these also considered that a learning process had ensued which would equip them better for
future innovation initiatives. About 20 per cent considered they had gained nothing from the project. These positive results are supported by the fact that the vast
majority of the firms chose to continue the project even after the subsidies for the
consultants ended.
   Four of the five objectives of the programme stated have been confirmed as
contributing to its success of the project, with the application of creativity techniques the 'odd one out'. (I am not at all surprised at this. The evidence from substantial practical experience in the UK is that training facilitators to run
creativity techniques for innovation projects requires considerably more time
than was available to the PII trainers.) In addition, the exit interviews suggested
that many firms (76 per cent) thought the programme had achieved a management development effect. Monitoring the way the consultants operated showed
that the intended facilitative style was by no means followed by all consultants.
However, those consultants who followed classical 'expert' consultancy modes
turned out to be less effective than the process consultants. (A 'mixed' mode,
termed programmatic consultants, also proved more effective than the purely
expert mode of consultancy.)
   Organization of this complex project was through a steering committee representing Dutch industrial organizations, and a smaller executive board.
Deliberate steps have been taken to minimize bureaucracy, by subcontracting out
much of the consulting, keeping permanent staff to a minimum, relocating the
project office away from The Hague, and by setting up a special Foundation for
administrative purposes. Small firms (less than 25 people) were particularly difficult to attract to the programme and, once recruited, required special treatment.
Heavy promotion is necessary to overcome their suspicion of such outside agencies. Modified methods are being tried out to overcome these problems with small
firms, including working with 'sets' from several noncompeting companies assisted by business students (who are cheaper than consultants).
   One of the unique features of the PII project was its large-scale training and
utilization of process consultants to stimulate innovation. When operating in this
mode, each project was self-directing. The consultants were not providing
frameworks such as ETHICS or SCIMITAR, unless some aspect of the project
suggested such aids were *needed* or *appropriate* in which case the format shifted

to what Buijs termed *programmatic* consultancy, involving more active interventions and supply of 'know how' and techniques by the consultant.

Similarities with Revans's well-known action learning approach[10] and JDAs[11] can be noted. Quality circles represents another related participative approach, particularly when they are incorporated into back-up systems which convert the incremental ideas produced by the circles into practice. The practical manager and the political sponsor would like to have evidence that participative systems 'work', and are worthy of support. Although this has prompted some workers to produce evidence in statistical terms (compare Buijs), this seems to me to be only partially satisfactory. The participative approach and to some degree the negotiated approach are attempts to deal with problems that are ill-.defined, and which defy a reductionist treatment. They are closer to the action-research philosophy[12] which deals not in 'proof' but in learned knowledge through experience. It is more in keeping with that paradigm to respond to managers seeking proof by offering instead *action* and *trials*. Adapting any innovation requires a similar act of faith—and among adaptors those with the least faith wait until everyone else has made the leap. Information of what other people have done, as provided in this article, can be taken as supportive evidence in favour of further action-research initiatives, but in the final analysis, the proof of the action will be in the testing. Failure to achieve understanding on this point is failure to achieve Schein's 'psychological contract', a prerequisite to mutual involvement and creative problem-solving.[13]

The descriptions of various ways in which innovation projects have been carried out can be related to many other examples recorded in the literature. The mission-oriented approaches show how innovation can be targeted, under conditions which permit the isolation of well-identified technological objectives from potentially intrusive political and environmental factors. The negotiative approaches show how differing dimensions can be creatively reconciled and how a framework can give freedom as well as structure. The participative approaches require willingness to engage in them, in which case they work—at one level because they are *experienced* as working. Practically, the purposive steps taken by an innovator engaging in his/her trade, will reflect his/her belief system and specific situational factors, especially resources and environment. The technologically oriented manager will be able to identify 'technological imperatives', the trained facilitator will be able to resolve social needs and technical opportunities and so on. But despite widespread assumptions to the contrary:

> There is no such thing as technological innovation, or social innovation or even sociotechnical innovation. There is just technological and social perspectives within a complex system involving interest groups, pluralities of goals, and expectations.

It is hoped that awareness of such multiple possibilities will help practitioners in innovation projects avoid the dangerous error of assuming 'my way is not just my way but the way'.

REFERENCES

1.   Churchman, C. W. (1975) *Theories of implementation*. In R. L. Schultz and D. P. Slevin (Eds.), Implementing Operations Research/Management Science, Elsevier, New York
2.   Carson, J., and Rickards, T. (1979) *Industrial New Product Development*, Gower, Farnborough, UK
3.   Carson, J.W., and Rickards, T. (1983) Scimitar, a state of the art review, *Creativity and Innovation Network*, Vol. 9, No. 3
4.   Lane, H.W., Beddows, R.G., and Lawrence, P.R. (1981) *Managing Large Scale R and D Projects*, SUNY, Buffalo, USA
5.   Abetti, P., and Wacholder, M.H. (1983) The process of technological innovation and its application to the RPI incubator program. Mimeographed summary of a presentation, Dublin, Ireland
6.   Rickards, T. (1985) *Stimulating Innovation*, Frances Pinter, London
7.   Trist, E.A., and Bamforth, K.W. (1951) Some social and psychological consequences of the longwall method of coal-getting, *Human Relations*, Vol. 4, No. 1
8.   Mumford, E. (1983) *Designing Human Systems*, Manchester Business School, Manchester, UK
9.   Buijs, J. (1984) *Innovatie en Interventie*, Kluwer, Deventer, Netherlands
10. Revans, R. (1982) *Origins and Growth of Action Learning*. Chartwell UK
11. Morris, J. (1980) *Joint development activities from practice to theory*. In J. Beck and C. Cox (Eds.), Advances in Management Education. John Wiley, Chichester, UK
12. Susman, G.I. and Evered, R.D. (1978) An assessment of the scientific merits of action-research, *ASQ* (December)
13. Schein, E.H. (1969) *Process Consultation*, Addison Wesley, Reading, MA

17 PEOPLE AND SYSTEMS
R.A. Johnston, F.E. Kast and J.E. Rosenweig

The primary consideration here is the business organization as a social system; we are dealing with man-made systems. Therefore this chapter is devoted to a discussion of the human aspects of the systems concept. Certainly a society which places high value on individual rights and freedoms and is geared primarily to the satisfaction of individual needs must give adequate recognition to the impact of the systems concept upon people. The material on people and systems will be concerned with the following topics:

The human need for systematic relationships
The need for systems change
Human resistance to change
How people resist change
Impact of the systems concept
Human factors in systems design
Open-systems concept as a basis of human integration
Meeting the human and social problems

Application of the systems-management concept has a major impact upon participants at all levels of the organization—the blue-collar worker, foreman, white-collar worker and even middle and upper managememnt. If a concept of systems management is to be applied for greater efficiency and social benefit, recognition must be given to the needs, motivations and aspirations of all these groups.

THE HUMAN NEED FOR SYSTEMATIC RELATIONSHIPS

In discussing the impact of the systems concept on people it should not be assumed that people generally resist systemization. Much of people's conscious activities are geared to creating system out of chaos. They do not resist systemization of their behavioural patterns per se. Rather, the normal human being

Johnston, R. A. et al. (1967) *People and systems*, The Theory and Management of Systems, McGraw-Hill, pp 365–400 seeks satisfactory systems of personal and interpersonal relationships which guide his/her activities. Everyone has been taught or has developed habit patterns which provide a basis for systemizing many of his/her activities. Each human being has, in effect, developed a unique system for relating a number of diverse activities within a broad operational whole—life's activities. Without systemization, behaviour would be random, nongoal-oriented and unpredictable. Certainly the complex modern industrial society demands more structured human behaviour than did older, less structured societies.

Nor should the discussion be confined to talking about the systems by which each individual relates personally to the physical environment. Many actions and much behaviour are dependent upon interpersonal relationships. As Sherif and Sherif have written, 'Many motives of man are products of social interaction and exposure to sociocultural products. These motives of social origin (sociogenic motives) are revealed in our preferences, in the favorable or unfavorable stand we take toward groups and social issues—in brief in what constitutes our social attitudes.'[1]

Thus we are products of our own motives and aspirations, which are modified extensively by sociocultural factors. Every individual develops systems of satisfactory relationships with other members of his/her society. The concept that 'no man is an island' merely means that people are social creatures and take most of their norms and standards of conduct from other members of their society. Everyone has a system of relationships which sets a pattern for his/her life.

Much has been written of the human consequences of the sociocultural changes brought on by advancing technology. One of the earliest and most pessimistic of these research findings was made at the turn of the century by the sociologist Émile Durkheim.[2] In his investigations he found that rapid industrialization brought on by the industrial revolution had broken down the *solidaire* within social groups. Old family and community relationships were destroyed, and the individual was unable to replace these with new satisfactory social interactions. In the US, Mayo said: 'This is a clear statement of the issue the civilized world is facing now, a rapid industrial, mechanical, physiochemical advance, so rapid that it has been destructive of all the historic and social and personal relationships.[3]

The problem, then, is not one of requiring us to change our total pattern of living and to adapt for the first time to the systematic organization of our behaviour. Rather, it is primarily one of people changing from old systems of work and interpersonal relationships to a *new and different systems environment*. Because of the rapidity of change, we cannot make the adjustments over long-time periods. Walker says:

> Rapid change has now left most Americans a little breathless. So complex are effects of changing technology that they have overtaken mankind as problems rather than as opportunities. If men are to utilize technology for the good life, they will have to find a substitute for time, which in the past permitted the human organism, and the community, to adjust to the pace of history.[4]

But it should not be inferred that there is just one major sociocultural system to which each individual member belongs. Every one of us has a number of 'inter-personal systems' which have differing objectives, perform different functions and occupy a different place in our lives. Behavioural scientists call this the iden-tification of the individual with the various groups with which he/she comes into contact. Each of these groups may require the individual to take a different 'role'. Every position in society carries with it certain norms and expectations of behaviour. Thus, a doctor, professor, foreman or clerk are social roles that have well-defined behaviour patterns, Organizations, both formal and informal, have defined roles for participants. 'In organizational settings, highly elaborate defini-tions of positions and roles are transmitted through formal and informal mechanisms. These definitions are intrinsic to the hierarchy and are symbolized in a variety of ways—through dress, physical location, and other status attributes, including age and sex.'[5] Role performance is a means for integration within a group.

It is useful to classify individual identification with various types of system or human group. It would be impossible to do this for all activities. In this respect everyone is unique; no two people have the same set of group associations or sys-tems of interpersonal relationships. We are concerned primarily with the work organization and can classify this identification with various social systems as follows:

Identification with Systems External to the Organization

These systems (for example, family groups, professional associations, com-munity groups, educational groups) of interpersonal relationships are unique to the individual and are largely determined by him/her rather than by the formal organization. However, the systems of interpersonal relationships cannot be separated into neat categories. Most certainly our participation and association with such groups as the church or educational institutions can have a profound effect upon our other organizational relationships.

Identification with the Organization

Identification with the formal organization is one of the strongest systems of interpersonal relationships for most individuals. Ask anyone what he/she is, and he/she will often respond, I work for General Electric, or IBM, or for the Univer-sity of Washington. This apparent dominant need to identify and to maintain satisfactory relationships with the formal organization system is an important characteristic of our industrial society.

Identification with Functional and Task Groups

Even within the complex organization, identification is most frequently made within subgroups. For example, I work for the sales department, or I work in accounting, or I am in the Graduate School of Business Administration. Associa-tion with these functional groups provides a more refined system of relationships for the individual in his/her work environment.

Identification with Informal Groups

All of us recognize the importance of informal interpersonal relationships and how these affect the formal organizational requirements. With whom do we go to lunch? Who shares our coffee break? These are ramifications of the informal social system which is apparent within every formal organization. To be sure, the formal structure sets the broad framework and pattern within which these informal relationships occur, but the individual has a great deal of latitude in his/her participation in informal groups.

Although all of these systems of relationships are basic to the satisfactions of the individual, the work organization continues to be important. Even though rising productivity and output have reduced time on the job and provided for increased leisure-time activities, our work life remains basic to need gratification. Other social relations cannot be substituted completely. Increasing mobility, both social and geographic, makes it difficult for people to establish enduring friendships. Family units often are widely scattered and have become less important as a basis for social activities, identification, and psychological support. Many of our other institutions such as social services, universities and hospitals have become progressively more institutionalized and, although more efficient, are limited in the means of satisfying human social and status needs. Thus the work organization continues to be a basic means of social interactions in the satisfaction of certain needs. Levinson says:

> Affiliation with an organization in which a person works seems to have become a major device for coping with the problems resulting from these economic, social, and psychological changes. Organizations have recognized and fostered the desire of employees to seek financial security in the organization by means of long service. . . .
>
> Many now have an organizational orienting point. They identify themselves with an organization—whether a company, church, university, or government department. In a man's movement from one neighborhood or community to another, the work organization is his thread of continuity and may well become a psychological anchor point for him.[6]

Many forces are geared to maintaining the system of relationships in the formal organization. For example, the organization structure which places each individual in a hierarchical relationship and specifies his/her functions and relationships to other people is one of the vital elements in the system. This structure establishes a common set of expectations as to individual performance. The organization establishes the goals to which the interpersonal systems are directed. Broad policies help establish the system of relationships, as well as the more detailed standard operating procedures and methods. Over all, the organization is a *system* which directly and specifically defines interpersonal relationships for every member.

We have traced some of the interpersonal relationships which tend to systemize individual behaviour. It is not inherent within people to resist the systemization of their activities. Just the opposite, in fact; we seek to establish, in our social and interpersonal relationships, satisfactory and rewarding systems of behaviour. 'Man apparently neither wants nor has experienced this postulated state of complete autonomy. People have always demanded structure in their lives. With few exceptions, men depend on human relationships, some fixity of structure, routine, and habit to survive psychologically.'[7] What then is the major problem in terms of systems and people? It is not one of total resistance to systemization, but of adherence to systems which are already in existence. The crucial problem is ability of the individual and group to change from one type of systematic relationship to another.

A common characteristic in a rapidly advancing society is to make these systems of interpersonal relationships more formal. While many of these systems have been implicit in the past, they are now becoming more explicit. This is one of the major precepts of our systems-management concept: systematic interpersonal relationships are necessary for accomplishing group objectives. Before looking at some of the basic factors which cause us to resist change in our system of relationships, it will be helpful to review briefly some of the reasons why our society has demanded greater change in these systems.

THE NEED FOR SYSTEMS CHANGE

Management in a modern industrial society requires the systematic and coordinated integration of many common elements, both human and physical. Scientific and technological advancements have progressed at an accelerating rate and have fostered wholesale changes. It has been necessary to adopt new managerial, organizational and human relationships in order to meet the requirements of the new technology. The twentieth century has seen enormous advancement affecting everyone. In earlier times, increasing scientific knowledge was rarely, or at best slowly, translated into useful forces for the material betterment of all. Since 1850, however, the time between discovery and utilization of knowledge has been decreasing. Science has become a pervasive force in modern society, with widespread influence over all our activities. The United States provided fertile ground for the exploitation of advancing technology and the changing social structure stemming from the industrial revolution. Our society was favourably inclined toward adaptation and change, a situation infrequently found in other, more restricted cultures.

Scientific and technological achievements have had an obvious impact upon business organizations; indeed, they have been the primary institutions for translating these achievements into goods and services, fundamental indicators of the standard of living. Every industry has seen advancements, not only in its products but also in the means of production. One of the major requirements has been to increase the size and complexity of organizations which in turn creates internal problems of adjustment. Kennedy states:

As systems have become larger and more complex, they have created serious economic, political, social, psychological, and even moral problems in addition to technological problems of engineering design and feasibility. But the most important psychological problem relating to systems arises from the necessity to organize people, to acquire them as system components, to select and classify them, to train them, to keep them working for system goals and to bring their performance to a peak to achieve the system goals.[8]

Hardly a facet of our existence or our social organization has escaped influence by the pervasive effects of advancing science and technology. But these cannot stand alone; they are part of the complex environment of the twentieth century and must be integrated into our overall effort toward a better society. Even though increasing emphasis has been given to science and technology, we must recognize that society without a broad background of human talents would be ill-prepared for the future. Even though society were to allocate all its resources to scientific pursuits and to train the best brains in this direction, the problems of integrating the advancing knowledge into the framework of a complex society would be tremendous.

One of the key elements stemming from the modern industrial society is *change*. It is no longer possible to maintain the *status quo*. We are in a dynamic society; the challenge of change is both a threat and an opportunity. We have evolved a new attitude toward change, one of welcome, of expectation and acceptance, as part of our cultural growth. This has not always been the case. As Drucker suggests, 'Throughout most of history change was considered catastrophe, and immutability the goal of organized human efforts. All social institutions of man for thousands of years had as their first purpose to prevent, or at least to slow down, the onrush of change.'[9] By contrast, in our modern society, change has become 'the accepted pattern of life'.

There is a growing interest in social as well as technical change. During the twentieth century we have moved away from the concept of nonintervention in social affairs which stemmed from the 'natural law' and 'invisible-hand' ideology of the laissez-faire doctrine of automatic adjustment. Today the issue concerns the methods used in planning, controlling, and directing the forces of change. 'Human interventions designed to shape and modify the institutionalized behavior of men are now familiar features of our social landscape.'[10] Increasingly, social scientists are not only studying the social system but are actively engaged in changing and directing its course.

> Behavioral scientists have been drawn, with varying degrees of eagerness and resistance, into activities of 'changing', such as consultation and applied research. 'Helping professionals', 'managers', and 'policy-makers' in various fields of practice increasingly seek and employ the services of behavioral scientists to anticipate more accurately the consequences of prospective social changes and to inform more validly the processes of planning designed to control these consequences.[11]

Indeed, the trend away from depending upon automatic adjustments may be going even further. There is a suggestion that innovative institutions, such as business organizations, must share in the responsibility for the social consequences of the changes they create. Austin makes this point as follows:

> Business is responsible today for incredible technological change. Technological change will continue to cause social change. Social change

brings demands for action to meet or mitigate the effects of social change.

The job of top management today must be broadened to include an awareness of the social change it causes. And that awareness will place new responsibility on business management for intelligent, carefully thought-out decisions as to the basic responsibility for meeting such change.[12]

With advancing technology and the growing emphasis given to increased understanding of the environment, our society and established social organizations will undergo dramatic changes in the future. There is no alternative but to adapt to change. We can no longer rely upon structured systems of interference to ward off the problems of social change which will influence us. The primary question from the viewpoint of systems management in the business organization is to provide a means whereby change can be accomplished with a maximum of benefit to the organization and to the participants and a minimum of penalty to any individual or group. This is the challenge of the systems concept. Before looking at some of the ways in which the change from one system to a new and different type of system can be accomplished with the most advantages and least disadvantages in terms of human relationships, we shall investigate some of the forces which tend to create rigidity or resistance to change.

HUMAN RESISTANCE TO CHANGE

To say that we resist change per se would be an oversimplification of the problem. Certainly, in most activities people welcome and even demand change. Consumers are continually looking for new means and products for expressing their desires for change. Witness the ever-increasing tendency to give formerly standardized products higher style and fashion differentiation. Thus, in many areas, we seem to welcome change. Why, then, is there resistance to technological change within the business organization? Generally, we can make a distinction between these two types of change. The consumers of products have some degree of control over acceptance or rejection of change, whereas, within the organization, technological changes occur which are beyond influence or control of the individual. We tend to resist changes in our interpersonal and job relations because our sense of security and the way in which we have been accustomed to doing things are threatened. People frequently resist changes by indifference or outright opposition and rebellion, because most changes result in a disturbance of the interpersonal equilibrium within the environment in which the individual and social group operates. It is generally not the technological change that is resisted; resistance is generated primarily because of changing sociological relations and because economic well-being may be threatened. In a case study of administering change, Ronken and Lawrence conclude:

So the problems of 'technological change' proved to be the everyday problems of people in an organization, who, like the rest of us, were trying to get along as best they could in the world as they saw it. The increased tempo of change accentuated these problems, and their result was the kind of behavior—uncooperative attitudes', project delays, and even restriction of output—which has led to the cliché that 'people resist change'. Looked at in this broader perspective, the story shows unequivocally that the effects of technological change were not confined to technical materials but were critical largely through their effect on interpersonal relationships.

At each stage the introduction of technological change forced readjustments in the social system. Again and again individuals on the projects found that they had to deal with other individuals who were either new to them or stood in a new relationship to them. That these changes in relationships were the major variable in the introduction of the new product emerged as the most insistent uniformity. [13]

Frequently, management is unaware of the full impact of technological change. It looks primarily at the changes in the physical setup and in the physiological requirement for the individuals on the job. For example, it will require new time-and-motion studies, new job specifications, and other manifestations of the physical change in the work. However, even more important are changes in social equilibrium. Generally, any change will alter the informal or formal social hierarchical relationships which exist between people operating in groups. For some people status may be increased, while for others their positions will be apparently diminished. As Roethlisberger points out, 'Any move on the part of the company may alter the existing social equilibrium to which the employee has grown accustomed and by means of which his status is defined. Immediately this disruption will be expressed in sentiments of resistance to the real or imagined alterations in the social equilibrium.' [14]

This section has suggested that social as well as technological changes are important in understanding resistances. What are some of the more specific reasons for resistance to change?

Economic Security

Undoubtedly, the most obvious causes—also the most readily acknowledged—of resistance to change are those which threaten the economic security of the worker. Any major threat to job security, any possibility that a change might adversely alter the income of the worker, will be met by immediate, intense and determined resistance. Most people are unimpressed by arguments about what is good for them or the country in the long run. They want assurance of economic security and a job for tomorrow, next month, and next year. One of the primary aims of economic activity is to provide the means of obtaining food, clothing, and shelter, that is, to satisfy basic physiological needs. Anything which threatens our ability to meet these needs for ourselves and our families will obviously evoke a major reaction. While it is true that most instances of technological change have a salutary impact upon the welfare of the company and the nation as a whole, it is unrealistic to expect that any individual would be willing to sacrifice his/her own needs and requirements to this greater benefit. He/she simply will not do so, and it is not natural to expect it. He/she will resist the kind of change which threatens to lower one's economic well-being with all the means at his/her disposal, even though to the outside these rections may appear entirely irrational.

However, there generally is a tendency to overrate the importance or impact of economic factors as cause for resistance to change. In reality, much of the resistance, rather than being based upon economic issues or causes, is generated by sociological factors.

Job Status

In a handicraft society, where a craftsman began and completed all phases of his operation, he gained social and egotistic-need satisfaction directly from the products he created.[15] The products were his own work and could be identified as his contribution. However, mass-production techniques changed the social order of work, and workers no longer could feel any particular pride of accomplishment. Workers still gained personal satisfaction from doing a good job, but their accomplishments could not be identified and recognized by others.

Today, workers and managers tend to use other means to symbolize their status. Pride of accomplishment is secondary to pride in the job or position they hold. The job symbols include such things as desk size, parking area, colour of badge, number of subordinates supervised and many other factors. These symbols of status cannot be eliminated or changed without threatening the things for which they stand.

The application of the systems concept through automation, automatic data processing and management science often will upset these symbols and features of job status. It becomes harder and harder for the individual to identify with the job once the job becomes less understandable and influenced by his/her activities.

Uncertainty

'The new way is always strange, threatening, and laden with uncertainties—even if it is an improvement over the old.'[16] A change will create a new situation, and there is conjecturing about the standards of performance and social contact which will be acceptable in the new environment. Anyone with work experience knows the uncertainty that is felt almost instantaneously when change is rumoured. Even if a change is explained and complete information is given, we are not always certain how we will be affected by the change (nor do we always completely accept what we are told). The employee may like his/her present job and work group; a change might involve many unknown consequences. It is common for an employee to worry about seemingly insignificant details, for example, will the new job change my lunch hour? Will I have to park my car on the other side of the plant? Will my payday be the same?

Some people like to go to new places, make new friends and do new things. However, the typical person feels uncertain and insecure when there are drastic changes in his/her familiar environment, unless there are incentives sufficient to overcome this uncertainty.

Increased Complexities

People generally resist and fight any change which makes things more difficult or disagreeable. A period of adjustment is required. It is prudent for management to remember that the old job has become familiar; workers develop certain tricks of the trade and can probably perform quite satisfactorily without concerted and full-time attention. We feel a sense of security and confidence in knowing that we are proficient and capable in our job. Any change requires relearning and therefore greater concentration and uncertainty.

Changed Group Relations

To a major extent, satisfactory group and social relationships have replaced the void left when satisfaction of craftsmanship was destroyed by methods of specialization and mass production. Within most business organizations groups form in order to meet the needs for satisfactory social relationships. Often management is cognizant of the necessity for this in the satisfaction of the workers and provides such things as the coffee break, cafeteria or other eating facilities, recreational areas, bowling teams and a whole host of activities related to the need for and motivation of satisfactory social relationships. Quite often, as a result of the introduction of change, these group and social relationships suffer most severely. People who have worked together and associated closely on the job and have come to understand and value their social interaction often are separated. Perhaps it is no longer possible to go for coffee or to have lunch at the same time or to participate in numerous other activities. Yet the impact of the change in the social relationships is often one that is kept below the surface. It is quite difficult, and even embarrassing, for a worker to explain, for example, his resistance in terms of the fact that he no longer is able to work closely with Joe and the other fellows and is now placed in a group of strangers. He is more likely to explain his resistance in terms of some technical factor, such as his inability to keep up with the pace of the job or complaints about tools or materials.

Disruption of Superior-subordinate Relationships

Change from one system of operation or production to another often requires adjustments and changes in supervisory-subordinate relationships. Even though there is no direct change in a worker's superior, there are often indirect changes in the relationship. For example, during the process of change-over the superior may have to exercise more detailed control over the operations or output of the worker. He/she may be forced to centralize certain decisions in his/her hands and take them away from the employee. The change-over may also require the pre-occupation of the supervisor with technical matters to the extent that he/she has little time for displaying his/her previous personal interest in the worker. Change in these relationships can be a major factor contributing to resistance, yet it is also frequently below the surface.

Union Attitudes

The union has certain institutional needs which must be met if it is to retain its function of leadership for the worker: first, it must represent the workers and be their official spokesperson; second, it must work to improve the status of its members; and finally, it must maintain its membership and bargaining position. When management does not consider a change in terms of the needs of the union, the union will often resist the change, and this resistance will reflect throughout the entire union membership.

The impression should not be left that it is only the work group, particularly blue-collar workers, who are resistant to change. Indeed, all participants in the organization, clerical workers, staff personnel, professionals and the executive group itself, show reluctance to accept change. Scientists and professionals who are frequently the major innovators in our society often are resistant to change in their own interpersonal and social relationships. And these groups typically have more effective means at their disposal to resist change than do production workers.

Thus we see that the primary forces leading to resistance to change are not necessarily technological forces, but rather the pressures on the individual to adjust to new and different social and group relationships. Social psychologists have taken this view of change. Sherif and Sherif, in discussing the impact of change, suggest, 'The effects of technology are always upon individuals interacting with other individuals in group settings with particular organizations, concepts, values, and social norms.'[17]

HOW PEOPLE RESIST CHANGE

Resistance to change can be indicated in many ways. The most obvious manifestation of a resistance to change is by complete disassociation of the worker from the job—he/she quits. This obviously is a major display of resistance and is in a way the easiest to deal with. For the most part employees do not take this alternative, at least not immediately. Frequently they have limited opportunities for change in employment and desire to maintain a continuing relationship with the organization. If an employee stays with the organization, a negative reaction can take many forms, ranging from open opposition, rebellion and even destruction to apathy and indifference.

The outward manifestations of resistance to change may take many forms which have a direct bearing upon the efficiency of the operation, such as decreased quality or quantity of production, increased absenteeism, tardiness, grievances and strikes. Unfortunately, it is difficult to trace these concrete results of the resistance back to the original change and to the original cause. Frequently, people do not display resistance in a direct fashion, but their behaviour will show its influence in a variety of ways. Nor, in discussing the problem, is it always easy for the superior to determine what really is wrong. People often will disguise their real concern over the impact of change by trying to appear to be rationally motivated in the best interest of the company. It is especially difficult to deal with those who have rationalized their resistance in terms of the organizational benefits. This is one of the chief forms of resistance to change on the white-collar and managerial level. Individuals in this category may resist change in their work environment by rationalizing that this will have a direct and adverse effect upon their performance and consequently organizational effectiveness will deteriorate.

Because of the many ways of displaying resistance to change and the great difficulty of correcting resistance and moving back into a new, effective equilibrium, it is highly desirable for management to make every effort possible to effectuate the change properly and to facilitate adjustments to it. Giving adequate consideration to the problems of change, both technical and social, prior to the change is much more satisfactory than simply making the change and waiting for the chips to fall. Before we look at some of the ways in which management can ease the transition and make the kinds of changes which are necessary in transition to a systems concept, it will be helpful to look at the areas in which the systems approach will have its greatest impact.

IMPACT OF THE SYSTEMS CONCEPT

Where will the application of the systems concept have its impact upon the business firm in the future? Perhaps the two greatest impact areas of the concept will be in the continuation of the trend toward automation of production operations and toward automatic information-decision systems. Information-decision systems require the application of computers, data-processing equipment, and other techniques in a systematic way to help in planning, organizing and controlling the business functions. Both automated production and information-decision systems are adaptations of the systems concept and will have an impact upon people.

Automation and People

Since the beginning of the industrial revolution, with its substitution of mechanical power for human power, there has been an ever-increasing trend toward mechanization. In the early phases of the industrial revolution, this had a traumatic effect upon people. Their life-long skills were lost; unemployment was rampant; there was a wholesale displacement of workers; and women and children who could operate machines as effectively and at a much lower cost than men were utilized. From these early stages of industrialization rapid advances have been made in minimizing the impact of mechanization on employees. We have come to recognize the importance not only of sharing the benefits of technological improvements but also of sharing some of the social costs involved. The economy has developed important social innovations, such as unemployment compensation, protection for the employee through legislation, collective-bargaining contracts and efforts by business organizations to retrain and reorient their workers to new technologies.

In some ways automation can be thought of as a further extension of the trend toward mechanization which has been going on over the past few centuries. However, it is even more dramatic and brings into focus a number of new problems. The introduction of automation creates a dramatic and violent change—people are replaced by machines. This is obviously the kind of change which meets greatest resistance from people, and yet it is also the kind of change which is vitally necessary for our economy in order to increase the general welfare.

Automation is a well-known example of the application of the systems concept. Automation is not just further mechanization—the replacememnt of human power with mechanical power. It is an overall system which integrates all the operations of the business firm—product research and development, manufacturing processes, distribution methods and other facilitating activities—into an operational human-machine system. This broad concept of automation was described by Hurni: 'The true roots of automation lie not in the mechanical feasibility of replacing hand operations but in the logic of an over-all system of operation. And this logic, in turn, is grounded not in manufacturing alone, but in marketing and engineering design as well.'[18] Under this systems concept, automation has an impact upon the entire business organization, all the way from the initial design of the product to final distribution.

Automated equipment is practical only if it displaces labour, reduces per-unit labour cost or makes possible some desirable results that could not be accomplished in any other way. The fact that machines will replace workers must be accepted; the vital question is whether the workers who have been replaced will be unemployed. Wiener was pessimistic about the future impact of automation:

> Let us remember that the automatic machine, whatever we think of any feelings it may or may not have, is the precise economic equivalent of slave labor. Any labor which competes with slave labor must accept the economic conditions of slave labor. It is perfectly clear that this will produce an unemployment situation, in comparison with which the present recession and even the depression of the thirties will seem a pleasant joke. This depression will ruin many industries—possibly even the industries which have taken advantage of the new potentialities.[19]

Certainly this is a most pessimistic view and is not shared by most businessmen/women or even labour leaders. It is pointed out that in the future, productivity must increase tremendously if the growth in our standard of living and national income is to be continued.

Over the long run, technological change in the past has led to increasing rather than decreasing employment. We foresee this same trend in the future, as a result of automation. With a continuation of the growth in population, a rising standard of living, increasing expenditures for education, recreation, retirement and so forth, and increasing competition on the international scene, our nation will need to expand productivity greatly in the next several decades.[20] Automation and advancing technology are the answers for this expansion. No matter how necessary this advancing automation is for our future well-being, however, there will be many short-run results which adversely affect a proportion of individuals.

There is evidence, both over the long run and in the short run, that in some areas automation and increased mechanization have created problems for certain groups of employees. In particular, in the coalmining industry, which has mechanized over the past 20 years, the problems of technological unemployment are severe. Again, with more automation in the automotive industry, the level of unemployment in the Detroit area increased. This technological unemployment seems to be a direct result of automation in the automotive plants. However, the high level of economic activity in recent years has helped absorb workers released through automation.[21]

Often the impact of automation is to change substantially the nature and type of work. James Cross, president of the Bakers Union, said, 'We have 170 000 members in the union as against 113 000 in 1946, but I doubt if 16 000 of them are bakers. . . . But the machines, while eliminating bakers, require great numbers of men to assemble the packaging materials, store and move the product. We've exchanged bakers for bakery workers.'[22]

Frequently, under automation, certain groups of employees bear the brunt of the dislocation. Although unemployment can affect all classes of workers, some employees and groups appear to be more susceptible. Young persons under 25, Negro workers, manual or blue-collar workers, workers attached to construction, mining, and manufacturing and, notably, workers with little or no education are affected most by unemployment.[23]

One of the most disputed questions about the application of the systems concept through automation is whether or not it will increase or decrease the skill level of workers. On the one hand, it is argued that with the advent of automatic equipment, fewer workers will be needed to feed the machines or to carry on the dull routine jobs and that it will be possible to place more workers in the jobs that offer a greater amount of self-satisfaction. Evidence supporting this idea is taken from the past trends which show that the percentage of skilled and semiskilled workers in the total labour force has increased greatly over the past 30 years, whereas the proportion of unskilled workers has declined dramatically. This argument suggests that the whole range of skills from the worker level all the way to the designer of the automatic equipment generally will be upgraded.

There are others who feel that automation will downgrade the skill requirements of the work force. Bright, after an intensive study of a number of firms that had adopted automated operations, stated:

The significant argument arising out of this study is that it is not true that automaticity—automation, advanced mechanization, or whatever we call it— *inevitably* means lack of opportunity for the unskilled worker and/or tremendous retraining problems. On the contrary, automation often reduces the contribution by the individual at the machine. Automated machinery requires less *operator* skill, or at least not any more skill, *after certain levels of mechanization are passed*. It appears as though the average worker can more quickly and easily master new and different jobs where highly automatic machinery provides the skill, effort, and control required. Furthermore, some 'key' skilled jobs, currently requiring long experience and training, are reduced to easily learned machine-tending jobs.[24]

Automation does affect the entire work situation in many other ways. Faunce found that workers believed they were more closely supervised under automation than they had been in regular assembly-line production and that they were less satisfied with their relationships with foremen.[25] He also found that workers had less social interactions because of the need for greater attention to the equipment and the isolation of the work. Walker found similar results in his study of work groups in a semiautomated steel mill.[26] Lipstreu and Reed, in a study of a large baking plant employing 1200 people, concluded that automation increases the amount of supervisory responsibility, increases the interdependence of work between supervisors at the same level, reduces the size of work crews, increases the ratio of supervisors to workers, leads to isolation of workers, reduces the freedom of movement of workers and increases the proportion of indirect labour.[27]

Automation also has major impacts upon company-union relationships in such areas as employee classification, job evaluation, and pay; education, training and retraining; job displacement and seniority rights; and the distribution of gains from greater productivity.[28] It would be impossible to suggest all the possible impacts of automation. The changes in work, satisfaction and group relationships are complex and vary widely in different companies. Generalization as to the total impact, from the present viewpoint, is difficult and perhaps foolhardy.

We can, however, suggest a number of other changes. With automation, the output per man-hour will increase and wage increases v'll probably result. Furthermore, there will be a continuation of the trend of the past century towards the reduction of hours of work per week, and automation will make this feasible without a reduction in overall productivity. Furthermore, the benefit of automation to labour through better working conditions is significant. Generally, plants will be cleaner, less congested, and safer places to work.

Automatic technology, a system concept, has major implications for our society. First, for us as consumers, it will offer greatly increased productivity and output, hence a rising standard of living. For us as producers, there are some difficulties. In this process of change, some workers will inevitably suffer losses as a result of displacement, whereas others will benefit as a result of upgrading.

There is a need for adequate measures to ease the hardships on displaced individuals, to train workers with new skills, and to adjust conflicting interest in the enterprise. These are likely to be important issues during the transition to automation. Labour, management and government agencies responsible for education, vocational training, employment services, unemployment insurance, apprenticeship, wages and hours and industrial relations are likely to be increasingly concerned with the problems created by advancing technology and automation.[29]

Automatic Information-decision Systems

The automation of manufacturing processes is a natural continuation and extension of the industrial revolution. There is an increasing trend toward the substitution of mechanical devices and equipment to replace physical activities in the
factory. Automation also means some replacement of the decision-making and
mental activities of man/woman in the factory. However, it is not just in the factory that the systems concept is being implemented by means of new equipment
and techniques. The clerical jobs and even the front office are feeling the impact
of the new technology. Whereas mechanical operations have undergone a continual transition towards more mechanization, the traditional white-collar and
managerial functions have remained to a major extent humanized. Although
there were typewriters, dictating equipment and other mechanical aids to these
functions, much of the actual work depended directly upon human skills and
applications. There has been a continual increase in the proportion of people in
the white-collar and managerial classes, whereas people engaged in actual direct
production—factory workers, and also farmers—actually have declined. But certainly on the horizon, and some would suggest moving rapidly, are the same kinds
of technical development that led to automation in the factory and that promise
an even more dramatic revolution in large-scale clerical operations. For this
revolution in clerical and managerial functions, we have utilized the concept
automatic information-decision systems. Basically, this concept covers two
primary areas of activity:

1.   The use of automatic-data-processing equipment for the collection, pro-
      cessing and comparison of information
2.   The application of computers to aid directly in the managerial decision-
      making processes

   The most apparent impact is in the first phase, that of the use of electronic-
data-processing equipment for processing vast quantities of information.
However, the second phase, the application of computers to decision-making,
may have the greatest impact in the future.

   Automatic data-processing has had and will have a substantial effect upon
clerical and white-collar employees. With the growing complexities of business
operation and the increases in size, many organizations have found the problem
of record-keeping and storage overwhelming, and clerical costs have increased
disproportionately in relation to total operating costs. In many ways, the process
of replacement of clerical workers with data-processing equipment is similar to
that involved in the replacement of the worker in the factory. The problems of
resistance to change on the part of the white-collar groups will be equal to, or
perhaps even greater than, that involved with blue-collar employees.

   Of even greater importance may be the impact that automatic information-
decision systems have upon management itself. The integrative effects of this
concept, with its emphasis upon systemization and development of rules and procedures and the increase in volume and accuracy of information circulation, can
have a profound impact upon management decision-making. It is quite probable
that many of the routine decision-making functions of lower- and middle-level

management will be 'mechanized'. Programming of decision-making in such areas as production and inventory control has already been accomplished in numerous organizations. In many ways this increased programming of the decision-making processes within the organization is characteristic of the trend established in the early history of the industrial revolution. Scientific management was geared primarily to making decisions for the workers; that is, they were told exactly what to do and how to do it and were given specific directions and control over their efforts. Since that time there has been a gradual extension of these programmed activities towards higher levels of operation.

Simon suggests that new data-processing technology has been utilized to help in making programmed decisions—decisions which are repetitive and routine and have continuity. For this decision-making, the electronic computer has brought a higher level of automation to routine decision-making and data-processing formerly done by clerks; important strides have been made towards programming decision-making formerly regarded as judgemental—primarily in the areas of manufacturing and inventory; the computer has made possible the use of previously unavailable mathematical techniques for the programming of many types of decisions; and companies are now combining mathematical techniques of decision-making with the data-processing capabilities made possible by the computer. Simon foresees, 'The automated factory of the future will operate on the basis of programmed decisions produced in the automated office beside it.'[30]

Even further in the future is the possibility of using analytical techniques and computers for the processes of nonprogrammed decision-making. By nonprogrammed decision-making, we mean those decisions which are new and unstructured and do not have a set pattern for handling. It is this type of problem which is of most importance for middle and higher levels of management. Generally, problems requiring this type of decision-making have not been susceptible to computer and data-processing techniques. A number of people have suggested that through a greater understanding of the human decision-making processes for nonprogrammed decision we can learn and transform these processes into computer programs. Theoretically, with heuristic programming, management could acquire the capacity to automate nonprogrammed decision-making.

There is increasing research in the area of 'artificial intelligence', that is, constructing computer programs which exhibit behaviour similar to human intelligent behaviour. Although there continues to be much discussion on 'whether computers can think', there are indications that computer technology is progressing in the direction of simulating rudimentary human intelligence. 'Comparisons can be made between men and machines in the continuum of thinking. If there is objection to the use of the word "thinking" then "ability to process information" or some similar term can be used. But it must be admitted that there exists some continuum of behavior in which men and machines coexist and in which they can be compared.'[31] While some progress is being made, we do not believe that the evolution of artificial intelligence will be as rapid as Minsky indicates, 'We are on the threshold of an era that will be strongly influenced, and quite possibly dominated, by intelligent problem-solving machines.'[32]

Although it is apparent that many of these projected changes are some distance away in the future, we can already see how data-processing, the computer and management science have made a major impact upon clerical operations and programmed managerial decision-making, particularly at the lower and intermediate levels of management. These changes will have a rather dramatic impact upon the white-collar and management worker. In many ways they will bring changes to this group which are typical of those affecting the blue-collar worker in the early stages of industrialization. Decision-making likely will be more centralized, and work will be more routine and specified by the programming. The problems of motivation and identification of the white-collar worker and lower-level management with the organization will become more difficult. Of great importance is the recognition that the white-collar employees and management, because of their position with the organization, generally have more effective means for resisting changes which affect them adversely. Numerous studies have suggested that the white-collar workers have been even more resistant to technological change than have the blue-collar workers. Furthermore, the new techniques place great demands upon management. Major changes usually increase the skill requirements of the supervisors in many areas: technical, administrative and human relations.[33]

With the dynamic changes that the applications of the systems concept—automation, electronic computers, integrated data-processing and management science—will bring, management must be prepared to deal with resistance and the problems of human adjustment to these changes. How management handles the human problems will have an important bearing on how effective the new systems are in meeting their output potential and will also have an impact upon the social and individual well-being of people in business organizations.

This discussion of applications of the systems concept has centred upon the problems associated with human adjustments to automation and automatic information-decision systems. Another aspect of human-systems relations is in the design of complex systems taking human factors as a major subsystem.

HUMAN FACTORS IN SYSTEMS DESIGN

There is a growing field in the systematic conception of the application of psychological principles to the invention, design, development and use of complex human-machine systems. Melton terms this a theory of psychotechnology of human-machine systems and suggests that 'it achieves integration of what has heretofore been variously called "human engineering", "human factors engineering", or "engineering psychology" on the one hand and "personnel psychology" or "personnel and training research" on the other hand. This union comes easily and naturally once the concept of *system* is examined and once the full implications of the concept of the human being as a *component* of a man-machine system are recognized.'[34]

Research on integrating human factors directly into complex systems was given stimulus by development of the weapon-system concept in the air force, which brought together teams of scientists to deal with the problems of systems and their human and equipment components. This research has significance for many human-machine system developments.

Planning for human components of a system must be thoroughly integrated with planning for machine developments. The first stage is to determine the purposes or 'missions' of the system and to develop an advanced operational design. From these, together with inputs about the current state of technological knowledge, are derived decisions about the major parts of the total system and the way in which they can be connected to fulfil the systems mission. This leads to the assignment of functions to humans and machines. Gagné suggests the diagram shown in Figure 17.1 as a model to use in human-machines system development.

Psychotechnology has important implications. The basic assumption is that people should be considered as one of the major components of a total system rather than merely users of the system once it is developed. It denies that systems development is purely an engineering problem—psychological and social factors must be considered.

> Any reasonably complex system requires a true interaction between man and the other parts of the system, which may be machines, other men, or combinations of these. Some way must therefore be found for thinking about the functions of machines and the functions of men within a framework which makes possible the relations of these two kinds of functions to common goals—that is, to system goals.[35]

In spite of the pioneering work pointed to by Gagné, there is a great deal to be done in the integration of people and equipment into large systems. Yet, the past efforts do point a new direction for psychologists and other behavioural scientists. As Kennedy suggests:

> The major implication of the system development point of view for psychology seems to be that psychological methods and techniques must be expanded to encompass the managerial problems encountered when men and machines are organized into complex systems. The traditional way of dealing with people in systems by means of an externally organized 'personnel subsystem' does not force the psychologist to confront the criteria of total system performance and the developmental processes involved in achieving system goals.[36]

So far, the approach of psychotechnology has been applied mainly in weapon and space systems. We perceive that the systems concept has even broader implications as a basis of human integration into complex social systems.

OPEN-SYSTEMS CONCEPT AS A BASIS OF HUMAN INTEGRATION

The *open-systems concept* offers the basis for more effective management of human and social factors in large organizations. Management does not deal with static structures but with the dynamic inter-relationships of individuals, groups

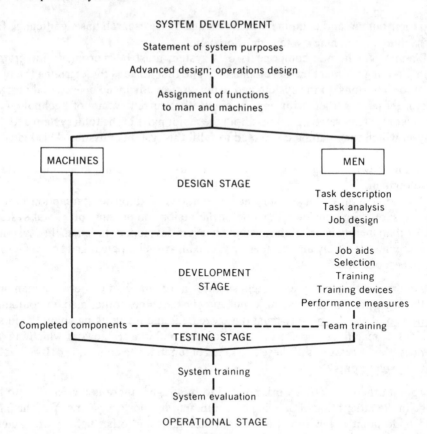

Figure 17.1 Men-machines system development Source: Gagné R.M. (ed.) (1962) *Psychological Principles in System Development*, p 4, figure 0.1. Holt, Reinehart and Winston, Inc., New York

and physical factors—the systems concept provides the basis for understanding and operating in this role. An increasing number of researchers and writers express the view that the 'new' organization and management theory should be based on the open-system approach. For example, the psychologists Katz and Kahn use this concept as a framework for their study of organizations. In their preface they state:

In our attempts to extend the description and explanation of organizational processes we have shifted from an earlier emphasis on traditional concepts of individual psychology and interpersonal relations to system constructs. The interdependent behavior of many people in their supportive and complementary actions takes on a form or structure which needs to be conceptualized at a more appropriate collective level. Classical organization theory we found unsatisfactory because of its implicit assumptions about the closed character of social structures. The development of open-system theory, on the other hand, furnished a much more dynamic and adequate framework. Hence, our effort, in the pages to follow, is directed at the utilization of an open-system point of view for the study of large-scale organizations.[37]

Similarly, Likert uses the systems concept in the development of his 'new theory' of management and Sayles adopts the open-systems view in his study of managerial behaviour.[38] These are just a few examples; across the entire spectrum of academic specialities dealing with management and organizations we find the systems concept emerging as the dominant model. Although the early systems approach was geared to technical and engineering operations, it is now being used increasingly as a basis for the study of human factors in organizations.

Limitations of Traditional Views

The classical assumptions on human behaviour in organizations are based upon the bureaucratic theory of Max Weber, the scientific management approach of Frederick Taylor and the administrative theory of Gulick, Urwick, Mooney and Reiley, and others. This traditional view emphasized the hierarchical structure, legitimate authority, vertical communications patterns, span of control considerations and line and staff relationships. It attempted to structure human behaviour to meet organizational requirements. In contrast, the systems concept views individuals and groups, with their motivations, interactions and values, as vital subsystems of the total organization. The structuring of behaviour under the traditional approach may be somewhat appropriate in highly regularized, routine activities and in organizations which are very stable; it is not feasible for dynamic systems subject to change. Shepard says:

> Bureaucratic structures are designed to do programmable things in a stable predictable environment. More and more, programmable things can be mechanized and automated. More and more, the environment is unstable and rapidly changing. The present need is for modes of organization which permit rapid adaptation to changing circumstances; the search is for ways in which people can organize for innovative, unprogrammable activities. The main point of this chapter is that a more humanistic organization theory than we have known in the past is required, and that it is realizable in practice.[39]

We feel that the systems concept offers opportunity for the 'more humanistic organization theory' which Shepard envisages.

Need for New Relationships

Traditional management theory emphasized the scalar chain of command and vertical relationships to the neglect of horizontal and diagonal networks. Even the line and staff concept provided only a limited means of dealing with communications outside the vertical channel. The systems approach is based on establishing information-decision networks including all relationships—vertical, horizontal and diagonal. Our discussion on programme management indicated the importance of these networks in the management of complex systems.[40] We believe that new organizational requirements will result in a continuing decline in the emphasis on hierarchy and increasing reliance upon horizontal and diagonal information flows.[41] One of the consequences of this transition will be the ability to integrate more completely the goals of individuals and the organization through better motivation, task orientation and reward structures.

Integration of Activities Around Systems and Subsystems

Systems design involves the establishment of project and facilitating subsystems to accomplish certain tasks or programmes. Under this approach the network of human interdependence required to accomplish a given task is based on shared responsibility of the participating members of the subsystem. In contrast, the traditional organization is geared to functional performance and the integrating force is authority. Instead of gearing participant activities to rule obeyance and closely structured behaviour, the systems concept provides a basis for active participation in meeting task requirements. The manager is looked upon as a resource person who can help the group meet its goals as well as a source of authority and control. Thus, the systems approach provides the structure by which the new concepts of motivation, leadership and participation can be applied effectively within the organization.

Interaction-influence System

The systems approach has been used by Likert in the development of a concept of management he calls the 'interaction-influence system'. He suggests the development of highly effective work groups linked to other such groups into the larger organizational system. There is an overlapping of these groups so that a multiple 'linking-pin function' provides additional channels through which information and influence can flow. Basic to the development of his 'interaction-influence' system was research which suggested the need for a newer theory of organization and management that would develop highly coordinated, motivated and cooperative social systems. In describing the organization operating under this new theory he says:

> The organization consists of a tightly knit, effectively functioning social system. This social system is made up of interlocking work groups with a high degree of group loyalty among the members and favorable attitudes and trust between superiors and subordinates. Sensitivity to others and relatively high levels of skill in personal interaction and the functioning of groups are also present. These skills permit effective participation in decisions on common problems. Participation is used, for example, to establish organizational objectives which are a satisfactory integration of the needs and desires of all members of the organization and of persons functionally related to it. High levels of reciprocal influence occur, and high levels of total coordinated influence are achieved in the organization. Communication is efficient and effective. There is a flow from one part of the organization to another of all the relevant information important for each decision and action. The leadership in

the organization has developed what might well be called a highly effective social system for interaction and mutual influence.[42]

Collaborative-consensus Systems

Closely related to Likert's views are those expressed by Shepard. He suggests that organizations can operate under two broad approaches. The 'coercion-compromise' system relies heavily upon an internal system of command, on authority and obedience and on bureaucratic regulation for governing the actions of participants. 'In others, the authority system is rarely appealed to for resolving conflict, solving problems, or making decisions. These organizations approach, in their functioning, systems of collaboration and consensus.[43] There are many adverse consequences of the coercion-compromise system, such as cancelling-out processes where the energies which might be directed to meeting organizational goals are consumed in attempts by individuals and groups to control, counteract or exploit one another. There are also a number of other forces which reduce the effectiveness of this approach. By contrast, he sees the development of a system of collaboration and consensus as a means for more effectively meeting organizational and individual goals. He says:

> The commitment of members of collaboration-consensus systems is to one another's growth, and to superordinate goals on which their growth in part depends. .... Control is achieved through agreement on goals, coupled with a communication system which provides continuous feedback of results, so that members can steer themselves. ...
>
> In consensus-collaboration systems, good management is understood to be the emergent product of adequate working relationships among the organization's members. Improving and perfecting the communication, control, and decision-making networks within the organization is, first of all, a problem of improving work relationships among managers so that they will use the systems they develop.[44]

Likert's interaction-influence system and Shepard's collaboration-consensus system with their humanistic orientation are compatible with our systems concept. They express dissatisfaction with the classical view as a basis of human collaboration in organizations and suggest the need for new theories. Open-system concepts provide a more fruitful avenue for the development of these new approaches.

New Managerial View

The systems concept suggests a new role for management. In the traditional view the manager operated in a highly structured, closed system with well-defined goals, clear-cut relationships, tight controls and hierarchical information flows. In the open-systems view, the organization is not static but is continually changing to meet both external and internal disturbances. The manager's role is one of developing a viable organization, meeting change and helping participants establish a dynamic equilibrium.

> The one enduring objective is the effort to build and maintain a predictable, reciprocating system of relationships, the behavioral patterns of which stay within reasonable physical limits. But this is seeking a moving equilibrium, since the parameters of the system (the division of labor and the controls) are evolving and changing. Thus the manager endeavors to introduce regularity in a world that will never allow him to achieve the ideal.[45]

The systems concept does not provide a prescription for making a manager's difficult and complex job easier. Rather, it helps them to understand and operate more effectively in the reality of complex, open systems. It suggests that operations cannot be neatly departmentalized but must be viewed as overlapping subsystems. Leadership patterns must be modified, particularly when dealing with professionals and highly trained specialists, and motivation must be directed toward active, willing participation rather than forceful subjugation. These and other forces suggest a different role for the manager. Sayles says:

> A systems concept emphasizes that managerial assignments do not have these neat, clearly defined boundaries; rather, the modern manager is placed in a network of mutually dependent relationships. All the strands of the net are not alike; some impose one pattern of initiation and response upon him, some impose very different tempos and rhythms. . . .
>
> Successful managers recognize these dynamics and seek to shift their own behavior, both as a means of detecting changes in the system and responding to the changes that are identified. Rather than becoming frustrated by rules that are always changing, where one is not automatically given the resources needed to do a job (the dimensions of which are in flux), the sophisticated manager recognizes these as hallmarks of the world in which he must live.[46]

Human Factors Predominate in Systems Approach

The earlier applications of the systems concept placed emphasis upon technical aspects. Thus, *systems engineering, systems analysis,* and *systems technology* are all considered technical and economic factors with little interest in the human element. Increasingly, however, applications of the systems approach have been directed towards human subsystems. We see the development of psychotechnology as an approach to integrating human and technical subsystems into total systems. And, of even greater significance, the behavioural scientists increasingly are using the systems concept as a basis of thinking about human organizations. As a result, humanistic and social values are influencing our views about complex human-machine systems. Katz and Kahn suggest a new trend:

> Too often changes in the social arrangements of organizations are lagging and fragmentary adjustments to technical changes already accomplished. We

automate the equipment first and repair the social dislocations afterwards. The same rational considerations, however, that operate within the framework of technology can be utilized to determine social objectives and thus make the technical system the means rather than the master of social organization.[47]

MEETING THE HUMAN AND SOCIAL PROBLEMS

Even though the systems concept provides a more effective basis for motivating and integrating the activities of organizational participants than traditional management approaches, there remain problems in transition from an old to a new system. The application of the systems concept does create change and consequent resistances. We discussed this resistance in relationship to the introduction of automated production and data-processing systems. What can management do to help organizational members make the transition and reach a new and better equilibrium? How can changes be made effectively and efficiently? We agree with Shepard that the coercion-compromise approach is much less effective in initiating and gaining acceptance of change than is the collaboration-consensus approach. In fact, one of the major advantages of this latter method is that it is geared to change rather than stability. However, given a managerial orientation toward the collaboration-consensus approach there still remain questions of specific means for making changes.

Leavitt suggests that there are a number of approaches to organizational change:

> One can view industrial organizations as complex systems in which at least four interacting variables loom especially large: task variables, structural variables, technological variables, and human variables. If one takes such a view, he can go on to categorize major applied approaches to organizational change by using three of the same variables: *structural* approaches to change, *technological* approaches, and *people* approaches.[48]

We have discussed a number of the technical and structural approaches to change in such areas as numerical control, electronic data-processing, programme management, and systems design. The human approach to organizational change has received increasing emphasis in recent years.[49] This view tries to change organizations by first modifying the behaviour of participants. It is suggested that changing human behaviour will result in modifications in the structure and in the development of technical innovations.

In reality, it is quite difficult to categorize separately these several approaches to organizational change. Most efforts to effect change must deal with the interactions among technology, structure and people, and must therefore integrate all three approaches. Katz and Kahn suggest that there is a major error in assuming that the primary method for organizational change is through changing individuals. In discussing the people approach to change and its limitations they say:

Its essential weakness is the psychological fallacy of concentrating upon individuals without regard to the role relationships that constitute the social system of which they are a part. The assumption has been that, since the organization is made up of individuals, we can change the organization by changing its members. This is not so much an illogical proposition as it is an oversimplification which neglects the interrelationships of people in an organizational structure and *fails to point to the aspects of individual behavior which need to be changed.*[50]

In order to initiate organization innovations most effectively, they suggest that consideration be given to changing individual behaviour and also to direct structural or systemic alterations. The following methods are available to bring about organizational change:

The use of information—The supply of additional cognitive inputs to the participants concerning the nature of the change and its impact on them. However, information alone is not a source of motivation and this method is of limited effectiveness unless combined with other approaches.

Individual counselling and therapy—These methods attempt to help the individual gain new insights and changes of attitudes which will alter his behavior.

Influence of the peer group—A third, and often more effective, approach to organizational change is through the influence of the peer group. Peers do exert strong influences on individual behavior and can help in bringing about change.

Sensitivity training—This approach is closely related to the peer-group approach. This method helps the individual to better understand his own attitudes and feelings through processes of group interaction and can help him adapt to change.

Group therapy in organizations—The essence of this approach is to have the organization change itself by means of group processes occurring at every level in the organization. The first step is the improvement of people's understanding of their organizational interrelationships and their own personal motives. A further objective is organizational restructuring by responsible organizational participants.

Feedback and group discussion—This procedure involves the feedback of information from research and surveys to various organizational families, each consisting of a manager and his immediate subordinates. There is integration through linking processes which provide a communications network covering the organizational hierarchy.

Systemic change—This approach is not directed at changing individuals but requires the direct manipulation of organizational variables. One example would be the attempt to change the hierarchical distribution of decision-making power in an organization. Another is the attempt to provide the best fit between the social and technical systems and to introduce into the organization changes needed to attain this fit.[51]

The first four methods listed are directed at altering individual behaviour as a means of effecting organizational change. The last three approaches are directed more towards modifying role and structural relationships. In our view each of the above approaches provides a useful method for achieving organizational change. There is no set pattern which is most effective in all cases. The manager's role is one of recognizing the dynamics of change in complex human-machine systems and of adopting approaches which will minimize the disruptions and enhance the development of a new equilibrium.

SUMMARY

People do not resist systems per se. Rather, normal human beings seek satisfactory systems of personal and interpersonal relationships which guide their activities. The problem arising from the use of systems concepts is not one of requiring us to change our total pattern of living and to adapt for the first time to the systematic organization of our behaviour. Rather, the problem is primarily one of requiring us to change from old systems of work and interpersonal relationships to a new and different systems environment.

A dynamic society must expect and even welcome change; it is through change that better material and social welfare is achieved. Generally, it is not technological change which is resisted; resistance develops primarily because of changing sociological relations and because economic well-being is threatened. Resistance to change can take many forms, ranging from quitting, open opposition and rebellion to apathy and indifference. Frequently, people do not manifest their resistance in a direct fashion, but it may influence their behaviour in a variety of ways.

Two of the most dramatic areas of the impact of the systems concept upon people are in automation of production operations and the development of automatic information-decision systems. Automation is the best-known example of the application of the systems concept and will have its major impact upon factory operations. Automatic information-decision systems will cause a revolution in clerical and managerial functions. It will have two important phases: first, the use of electronic data-processing equipment for processing vast quantities of information, and second, the application of computers to decision-making. The first will affect the clerical worker, and the second, lower and middle management.

The successful administrator can foresee that the disruption and trauma resulting from the rapid application of systems techniques are potential sources of difficulty for both the individual and the organization. Because of the many ways of displaying resistance to change and the great difficulty of correcting resistance and moving back into a new, effective equilibrium, it is highly desirable for management to make every effort possible to effectuate the change properly and to facilitate adjustments to it. Giving adequate consideration to the problem of change, both technical and social, prior to its implementation is essential to long-run success.

Psychologists and other social scientists increasingly are applying their knowledge to the invention, design, development and use of complex human-machine systems. Psychotechnology requires that planning for human components of a system be integrated with planning for machine and technical developments. A person is considered as one of the major components of a total system rather than merely a user of the system once it is developed.

The systems concept offers the basis for more effective management of human and social factors in large organizations. Management must deal with the dynamic interrelationships of individuals, groups and physical factors, and the systems concept provides the basis for understanding and operating in this role. Increasingly, managers and social scientists are adopting the open-systems view. The traditional management theory emphasized highly structured relationships and is not feasible for dynamic organizations subject to change.

Likert's interaction-influence system and Shepard's collaborative-consensus system are related closely to our systems concept. Their views suggest the broadening of the systems approach to include not only technical factors but human and social relationships. Thus, the systems approach provides the structure by which the newer concepts of motivation, leadership and participation can be applied effectively within organizations.

The systems concept suggests a new role for management. In the traditional view the manager operated in a highly structured, closed system with well-defined goals, clear-cut relationships, tight controls and hierarchical information flows. In the open-systems view, the organization is not static but is continually changing to meet both external and internal demands. The manager's role is one of developing a viable organization, meeting change and helping participants establish a dynamic equilibrium.

Over all, we are not pessimistic and do not think that the implementation of the systems concept will have major adverse effects upon indivduals or society. Rather, we view the implementation of this concept as offering greater material rewards and providing more opportunities for gratifying personal and inter-personal relationships.

QUESTIONS

1. What is the relationship between the systemization of human behaviour and organizational participation?
2. Outline the major social groups with which you are identified. How does your 'role' differ in each of these groups?
3. Do you believe the work organization is assuming an increasingly important basis of human identification and need satisfaction?
4. What are the major problems in relating people to systems?
5. How have technological factors affected man's social organizations?
6. Give your evaluation of the various factors causing resistance to change.

7. What are the impacts of automatic information-decision systems on people within organizations? What do you forecast for the future?
8. What is meant by psychotechnology and what is the importance of its development?
9. In what ways can the systems concept provide a basis for meeting human problems in complex organizations? What are its major limitations?
10. Why does the systems concept provide for closer task orientation and identification than the traditional organizational approaches?
11. What is the new role which the systems concept suggests for the manager?

REFERENCES

1. Sherif, M.and Sherif, C. W. (1956) *An Outline of Social Psychology*. Harper & Row, Publishers, Incorporated, New York, p 366
2. Durkheim, E. (1930) *Le Suicide*, Librarie Félix Alcan, Paris
3. Mayo, E.(1945) *The Social Problems of an Industrial Civilization*, Harvard University, Graduate School of Business Administration, Boston, p 8
4. Walker, C. R. (1962) *Modern Technology and Civilization*, McGraw-Hill Book Company, New York, p 1
5. Zaleznik, A. (1965) Interpersonal Relations in Organizations, in James G. March (ed.) *Handbook of Organizations*, Rand McNally & Company, New York, p. 589. For a discussion of role theory see: Erving Goffman, (1961)*Encounters*, The Bobbs–Merrill Company, Inc., New York, and D. J. Levinson, (1959) Role Personality, and Social Structure in the Organizational Setting, *Journal of Abnormal and Social Psychology*, March, pp 170–80
6. Levinson, H. (1965) Reciprocation: The Relationship between Man and Organization, *Administrative Science Quarterly*, March, p 373. He suggests that the individual and the organization integrate their goals through a process of reciprocation.
7. Sayles, L. R. (1963), *Individualism and Big Business*, McGraw–Hill Book Company, New York, p 179
8. Kennedy, J. L. (1962) Psychology and System Development, in Robert M. Gagné *Psychological Principles in System Development*, Holt, Reinehart and Winston, Inc., New York, p 16
9. Drucker, P.F. (1959) *Landmarks of Tomorrow*, Harper & Row, Publishers, Incorporated, New York, p 21
10. Bennis, W. G., Benne, K. D., and Chin, R. (eds.) (1962) *The Planning of Change*, Holt, Reinehart and Winston, Inc., New York, p 9
11. *Ibid.*
12. Austin, R. W. (1965) Responsibility for Social Change , *Harvard Business Review*, July–August, p 52
13. Ronken, H. O. and Lawrence, P. R. (1952) *Administering Changes*, Harvard University, Graduate School of Business, Boston, p 292
14. Roethlisberger, F. J. (1941) *Management and Morale*, Harvard University Press, Cambridge, MA, pp 61–62
15. Haire, M. (1956) *Psychology in Management*, McGraw-Hill, New York, p 62
16. Strauss, G. and Sayles, L. R. *Personnel: The Human Problems of Management*, Prentice-Hall, Englewood Cliffs, NJ, p 266
17. Sherif and Sherif, *op cit.*, p 687
18. Hurni, M. L. (1955) Decision Making in the Age of Automation, *Harvard Business Review*, September–October, p 53

19.   Wiener, N. (1950) *The Human Use of Human Beings*, Houghton Mifflin, Boston, p 189

20.   *Automation and Technological Change, Hearings before the Subcommittee on Economic Stabilization of the Joint Committee on the Economic Report*, 84th Cong., 1st Sess., 1955, p. 182

21.   The findings of the Congressional Committee on Automation and Technological Change indicated that the past shifts to automation and the accelerating pace of technology took place in a background of relatively high employment in a generally prosperous economy, most of the post-Second World War period. Under these conditions, dislocation and adjustment tend to be less painful. The committee pointed out, however, that any significant recession in levels of employment might create new problems, as it magnified the difficulty of adjustment. *Ibid.*, pp. 262–79

22.   'Automation: What the Unions Will Demand', *Fortune*, May, 1955, p 59

23.   U.S. Bureau of Census (1957) 'Educational Attainment of Workers, March, 1957', *Current Population Reports*, series P-50, no. 78, p 8

24.   Bright, J. R. (1958) *Automation and Management*, Harvard University, Graduate School of Business Administration, Boston, pp 176–7

25.   Faunce, W. A. (1958) 'Automation in the Automobile Industry', *American Sociological Review*, August, pp 406–7

26.   Walker, C. R. (1957) *Toward the Automatic Factory*, Yale University Press, New Haven, CT.

27.   Lipstreu, O. and Reed, K. (1965) 'A New Look at the Organizational Implications of Automation', *Academy of Management Journal*, March, pp. 24–31

28.   For a discussion of the impact of automation on industrial relations see: Edward B. Shils (1963) *Automation and Industrial Relations*, Holt, Reinehart and Winston, New York

29.   For a more complete discussion of the possible impacts of automation see U.S. Department of Labor, 'Impact of Automation', *Bulletin* 1287, and Richard A. Johnson (1961) *Employees—Automation—Management*, Bureau of Business Research, University of Washington, Seattle

30.   Simon, H. A. (1960) *The New Science of Management Decisions*, Harper & Row, New York, p. 20

31.   Armer, P. (1963) 'Attitudes toward Intelligent Machines', in Edward A. Feigenbaum and Julian Feldman (eds.), *Computers and Thought*, McGraw–Hill, New York, p. 391

32.   Minsky, M. 'Steps toward Artificial Intelligence', in *ibid.*, p. 406

33.   For a case study of the impact of the introduction of electronic-data-processing equipment and the changing managerial requirements as a result of this introduction, see: Mann, F. C. and Williams, L. K. (1960), 'Observations on the Dynamics of a Change to Electronic Data-processing Equipment', *Administrative Science Quarterly*, September, pp 217–56

34.   Melton, A. W. (1962) in Robert M. Gagné (ed.), *Psychological Principles in System Development*, Holt, Reinehart and Winston, New York, p. v.

35.   Gagné, R. M. 'Human Functions in Systems', *ibid.*, p. 35

36.   Kennedy, J. L. 'Psychology and System Development', *ibid.*, p. 29

37.   Katz, D. and Kahn, R. L. (1966) *The Social Psychology of Organizations*, John Wiley, New York, p. vii

38.   Likert, R. (1961) *New Patterns of Management*, McGraw–Hill, New York, and Sayles, L. R. (1964) *Management Behavior*, McGraw–Hill, New York

39.   Shepard, H. A. (1965) 'Changing Relationships in Organizations', in James G. March (ed.), *Handbook of Organizations*, Rand McNally, Chicago, pp 1141–2

40.   Johnston, R. A., Kast, F. E. and Rosenweig, J. E. (1967) *The Theory and Management of Systems*, McGraw–Hill, New York, chap. 7

41.   This view is presented more completely in Read, W. H. (1965) 'The Decline of Hierarchy in Industrial Organizations', *Business Horizons*, Fall. pp 71–5
42.   Likert, *op. cit.*, p. 99
43.   Shepard, *op. cit.*, p. 1128
44.   *Ibid.*, pp 1128–9
45.   Sayles, *op. cit.*, pp 258–9
46.   *Ibid.*, p. 258
47.   Katz and Kahn, *op. cit.*, p. 471
48.   Leavitt, H. J. (1965) 'Applied Organizational Change in Industry: Structural, Technological and Humanistic Approaches', in James G. March (ed.), *Handbook of Organizations*, Rand McNally, Chicago, p 1144
49.   Some examples of this approach are seen in: Lawrence, P. R. (1958) *The Changing of Organizational Behavior Patterns*, Division of Research, Harvard Business School, Boston; Guest, R. H. (1962) *Organization Change: the Effect of Successful Leadership*, Richard D. Irwin, Homewood, IL; Ginzberg, E. and Reilly, E. (1957) *Effecting Change in Large Organizations*, Columbia University Press, New York; and Bennis, W. G., Benne, K. D. and Chin, R. (1961) *The Planning of Change*, Holt, Reinehart and Winston, New York
50.   Katz and Kahn, *op. cit.*, p. 391
51.   Katz and Kahn, *op. cit.*, pp. 392–451

PART 4
IMPLEMENTATION

The material in this final part addresses an area of change-management which is frequently overlooked or mishandled. In the Open University course on change it is argued that the implementation phase of activity has to be managed with just the same care and attention as is usually given to the proposed package of changes. Implementation must therefore be taken into account at a very early stage in the change process and cannot be left to chance.

The lessons emerging from the crises which have been generated in some organizations by the adoption of new technology all point to the importance of this stage. The technology itself is simple compared to the processes of consultation, of training and of generating motivation which must be managed simultaneously if the new systems are to improve on the old.

The chapters in this part include a study by Nanton of the problems of implementing changes in the area of local government and race relations. He stresses the importance of motivation and appropriate training.

Some of the same lessons emerge in Dorothy Leonard-Barton and William Kraus's writings on new technology in North America, whilst Alexander's survey of implementation problems provides a clear indication of the pitfalls to avoid.

At the level of strategic change Owen provides some clear advice, including the all-important senior management support that ensures that decisions are taken, necessary resources provided and experiments protected.

The cyclical nature of the change process means that change almost inevitably generates change and reminds us of the opportunity provided for improving the capacity to manage change by evaluating previous exercises and upheavals. Product launches, new structures, new processes, all bear examination with the benefit of hindsight. But the real art or craft of change-management is to be able to incorporate these lessons into the institutional memory.

18 HOW TO IMPLEMENT STRATEGY
Arthur A. Owen

Senior managers today are mostly familiar with the jargon of strategic planning, and systematic approaches to the planning of business strategies are now being used by many professionally managed corporations. Terms such as 'business unit', 'competitive position', 'industry maturity' and 'experience curve', all of which evolved during the 1970s, are an accepted part of management language, and the techniques of planning have been sufficiently well-developed, in one form or another, to produce strategies for most corporations. But even top-class strategies are worth nothing if they cannot be implemented—and in the 1980s more and more attention is being given to ways of improving the rate of success in implementation: better a first-class implementation procedure for a second-class strategy than *vice versa*.

In real life, all too many strategic plans have ended up as mere documents on the chief executive's shelf, while the corporation plods on in its old familiar ways. The value of strategic planning, and the positions of those who use it, will be called into grave question unless more effective approaches are developed to ensure the success of strategies. These can be defined as the key intentions of top management, towards which corporate resources must be directed so as to achieve specific objectives relevant to the competitive environment; such as broadening the product line, moving into embryonic technologies or increasing manufacturing efficiency.

'Intentions' do not exist as strategies unless the management has thought through what needs to be done, by when and by whom, using which resources, to achieve what objectives. Strategies are specified in relation to the market place or in relation to internal organization and efficiency. The strategic plan involves specifying the implications of strategies: and, to be meaningful, strategies must be communicated to, agreed to and supported by management.

Problems of successful implementation centre on how well or badly the existing organization responds and how adequate or otherwise its reporting

Owen, A. (1982) How to implement strategy, *Management Today*, July, pp 51–53 proves to be. In practice, the problems fall into four main categories. The first difficulty is that, although strategies need to be developed around the 'business units' of the corporation, these units often (alas) do not correspond to parts of the organization structure. Business units have an external market place for goods and services, and their managements can plan and execute strategies independent of other pieces of the company. On the other hand, the organization structure— and how that functions—derives from its history of takeovers, tax considerations, shareholder considerations, economies of scale, personnel strengths and weaknesses, personal relationships, ambitions, national legal requirements and so on. Strategic planners must attempt to cut through this 'culture' and to plan in relation to the various competitive environments by identifying the strategic business units (SBUs) and developing strategies for them. The catch is that the strategies still have to be implemented by the organization as a whole.

As an example of the mismatch between business units and organization, one highly diversified corporation in Europe consisted of about 140 operating companies. We identified within the corporation about 85 SBUs. But only 30 of these consisted of complete operating companies. The remaining 55 all contained bits of the latter. While half the operating companies fell clearly into SBUs, the other 70 or so had their activities split across units.

In addition, the corporation had grouped its companies into four divisions by broad category of activity, while SBUs often incorporated companies from more than one division. Naturally, top management is not keen to reorganize the whole corporation drastically in order to implement strategies—thus, unless responsibility for strategies is clearly defined, nothing will happen. In the above case, getting business-unit strategies implemented through the divisions and operating companies demanded the development of new techniques to improve strategy control and communication.

A second problem area is that traditional management reports are not sensitive enough to monitor the implementation of strategies. Such reports are designed to help manage operations, working through the organization structure represented by 'profit centres', 'cost centres' or other forms of responsibility or reporting centre. These reports should reflect the detail of all planning (but often do not); and therefore cannot be used to monitor individual strategies. Even if performance turned out as planned, it would not be clear which strategies had worked out as intended; a better than expected performance of strategy A could have compensated for underperformance of strategy B. For example, did the stock reductions take place because of the new material-requirements-planning system, or as a result of the product rationalization programme?

Since responsibility centres frequently do not coincide with SBUs, the effects of strategies can only be noted, if at all, by looking at several of the traditional reports. As the latter are required for regular periodic control, they are 'calendar-driven' and cover a different time-frame from strategy implementation controls, which are 'event-driven'. Often, implementation will cover several cycles of traditional reporting, whose mechanisms, anyway, contain far too much detail and swamp the key measures required to monitor particular strategies. There are many examples of reporting systems which are inappropriate for this purpose; indeed, very few serve it well.

WHY STRATEGIES DON'T MATERIALIZE

Companies face many problems in introducing change. They find that:

1. Implementation of their chosen strategies cuts across traditional organization units
2. Information available for monitoring implementation is not adequate
3. The organization resists change
4. Payment systems are geared to past achievements, rather than future goals.

STRATEGIES MUST BE MONITORED

Once again, top management, naturally enough, will not want to make drastic changes to the traditional reporting systems just to control strategies over a specific time-period of a year or two or three. But unless strategies can be monitored, the success of the strategic plan cannot be evaluated—and the planning process is further diminished if lessons cannot be learned for future planning.

Implementing strategies involves change, and change involves uncertainty and risk. Managers will happily agree to change in the cosy confines of the planning meeting; but when the crunch comes, there are always excuses, relating to the pressures of day-to-day operations, that justify putting off the process. Unless the corporation ensures that management is committed at the most senior levels, change will not take place. Any system for implementing strategy must maintain the motivation that is often generated during the planning process itself.

Finally, management systems are seldom adapted to ensure the success of strategies. Management systems involve review and reward processes, communication channels, management and personnel development and so on. These systems are often in place as a result of past strategies; they are rarely tuned or revised to meet the needs of new ones.

So how can successful implementation of strategies be ensured? How can management be sure that the assumptions underlying its strategy remain valid, that planned progress is maintained, that specific intermediate goals are being met, that variances from plan are dealt with effectively? The implementation process, as used by Arthur D. Little, recognizes that strategies are similar in nature to projects, that is, an objective has to be realized, with a given set of resources, within a given time-scale. The techniques of project management can therefore be applied to assist the successful implementation of strategies by focusing management's attention on achieving strategic objectives. Project-management techniques does not mean complex computer-based critical path analyses (although these have their place in helping to implement extremely complex strategies); but they do include five basic principles:

1. Allocation of clear responsibility and accountability for the successful outcome of the overall strategy project
2. Limiting the number of strategies pursued at any one time
3. Identifying actions to be taken to achieve the strategic objective, allocating and getting agreement to the detailed responsibilities for the actions
4. Identifying a list of 'milestones' or major intermediate progress points
5. Identifying key performance measures to be monitored throughout the life of the strategy project, and creating an information system to record progress.

Since the organization cannot be changed significantly in the short term, and many of its aspects and its reporting system need to be retained, these five basic principles should be superimposed on the existing organization. The techniques of project management can then be tailored to suit the strategy being implemented. A material-requirements-planning system to reduce manufacturing costs and inventory will need different management from a strategy to diversify into related, but different industries; the management and controls for implementing various strategies can then come and go with the strategies themselves. However, our experience has shown that several general organization and control steps, derived from project-management techniques, can be systematically followed to promote successful implementation.

First, what are the implications of the strategies for the existing responsibility centres in the traditional budgets—what is the impact on revenue, costs, capital, personnel and so on? These basic mechanisms for controlling the organization must take into account what resources are required to implement each responsibility centre's contribution to strategies. Planners and management accountants must look for a fit between what the strategic plan requires and what revenue and resource assumptions are contained in the traditional budgets. Minor changes or 'revectoring' of one or the other may well be required to pull them into line. A manager is then given responsibility for the success of the strategy.

As mentioned, implementing strategy cuts across organizational boundaries. Thus, one client who was following a rationalization strategy found, while attempting to prune a major product line, that the strategy had implications for its marketing division, manufacturing side and the central raw materials purchasing department. Another client, a Dutch construction group, has domestic divisions for civil engineering, road-building, pipe-laying and house-building; while pursuing a strategy of overseas penetration, it has had difficulty in developing foreign markets as a full-line contractor and in promoting its activities as a homogeneous group—all because of the divisionalized profit centres in its national market.

The chief executive or the corporate management team must make one manager responsible for the successful outcome of the strategy. The 'strategy manager' takes on this responsibility in addition to his/her normal executive role. He/she will be the person most concerned with the successful outcome of the strategy, even though some of the resources to implement it may lie outside his/

her organizational jurisdiction. As an added incentive, it may be necessary to provide new financial rewards for the management and other staff closely associated with a strategy's success.

The strategy manager draws on the help of the corporate planners, management accountants and other managers of responsibility centres associated with the plan. He/she starts with the agreed strategic objectives, resources and financial implications agreed upon and prepares a detailed implementation plan. It will include:

1. Specific activities and actions to be performed, allocation of responsibility for achieving these actions and time-scales within which they must be achieved
2. Physical resources to be consumed or made available
3. Manpower level requirements, manpower development programmes and compensation systems and incentives appropriate to achieve success
4. Levels of investment required to implement the strategy
5. Revised effects on responsibility centre budgets
6. Performance factors to be monitored continuously to ensure successful implementation of the strategy, including assumptions made about aspects of the external environment that can affect the outcome of the strategy— national economic considerations, responses of the competition, external raw material costs and so on
7. Milestones to be recognized as progress points or checkpoints to ensure that the strategy proceeds within the planned time-scale, and that the effects on the business can be measured.

These benchmarks also provide opportunities to reassess the plan and make any adjustments as a result of variances.

HOW TO MAKE STRATEGIES WORK

Project-management techniques can be used which involve:

1. Allocating clear responsibility and accountability for the success of the overall strategy project
2. Limiting the number of strategies pursued at any one time
3. Identifying actions to be taken to achieve the strategic objective, allocating detailed responsibilities for the actions—and getting agreement to them
4. Identifying a list of 'milestones', or major intermediate progress points
5. Identifying key performance measures to be monitored throughout the life of the strategy project, and creating an information system to record progress.

FINAL TOP APPROVAL AND GO-AHEAD

The plan is submitted for final approval and go-ahead to the top management, which will already have made the initial broad decisions to allocate resources, and will be kept informed throughout the development of the plan—so there should be no major surprises. Nevertheless, detailed planning of strategic projects may have implications for other projects, and corporate management may require some final changes—for example, if less money is available for investment than was expected.

The successful implementation of the approved project is then monitored—as the overall strategy manager watches the performance factors and reports on milestone achievements to top corporate management. He/she may need to set up a temporary information system, and the data-processing department may be able to help by abstracting results from the traditional operating reports. Data-processing departments which have successfully promoted data-base techniques will be better able to respond quickly to short-term needs than others. (A 'data base' is a file or collection of files designed for sharing by several users.) Indeed, one US client was advised to structure its data base around the 'planning model' of SBUs as the 'fundamental building blocks' of the corporation. Reports by responsibility centres and by planning units can then be produced from the same statistical base.

There is no general rule about which measures of performance should be used to monitor success—they depend on the strategy. However, the choice of the appropriate measures should be carefully considered by the strategy manager, planners and management accountants. Often, the best approach is to monitor physical measures separately from external factors such as inflation, energy costs and financing. The latter are subject to different influences and fall less easily within the corporation's control. By separation, the true causes of variance from plan can be measured and acted on. Progress reviews at milestone points may lead to a review of initial assumptions and of changes in the environment, and thus to some replanning.

Communications may well have to be improved to ensure the success of the strategy—especially if the strategy manager depends on other managers outside his/her control. All corporations have their means of communication, both formal and informal, but these may not suit the specific purposes of the strategy which is being implemented. It may be necessary to set up a project committee (initiated by the strategy manager) to coordinate activities during strategy implementation or key phases of it. Any conflicts that arise between a manager's implementing responsibility and his/her other priorities should normally be resolved by the strategy manager and department head concerned. Higher management should be called in to arbitrate if they fail.

THE CHIEF EXECUTIVE AS LYNCHPIN

The chief executive remains the lynchpin of both strategic planning and strategy implementation. His/her role is to ensure that the corporation will be servicing market needs in three, five or 10 years time—or whatever time-scale is appropriate to the industry. Without his/her full commitment to the strategic development of the corporation, the planning and implementation processes will not work: he/she and corporate management must ensure that managers are brought out of their day-to-day tasks to take part in developing the business unit plans. Obviously, the chief executive and corporate management are deeply involved in the development of the corporate plans. The chief executive appoints the strategy project managers and reviews and authorizes the project plans, and then reviews strategic progress at milestones and coordinates reactions to variances.

The planner administers the planning process and acts as an 'information broker', passing information between managers and the chief executive and *vice versa*, acting as an adviser to both and as a strategy evaluator looking for realism, consistency and desirability from the corporate point of view. He/she also assists strategy managers to prepare their plans, identifies performance measures and advises on an appropriate project information system. During strategy implementation, the planners act as the eyes and ears of the chief executive.

HOW TO IMPLEMENT STRATEGY

Management accountants must be prepared to adopt a flexible approach to providing information for planning meetings and subsequently in assisting strategy managers to track the key factors for controlling implementation. In this, management accountants are likely to work very closely with the data-processing department. The planning process revolves round the profit centre managers; they contribute their market knowledge, ideas and experience. They then take on the strategic development role as discussed and agreed at the planning meetings.

How does the complete process work in practice? One European client recognized that a major profit-improvement strategy—indeed, one that was crucial for survival—was to improve manufacturing efficiency by reducing stocks and costs. The method was to introduce an integrated materials requirements planning and production control system. The chief executive realized that implementing the strategy would cut across several divisions and change established work practices. He made the manufacturing manager responsible for its successful outcome. A detailed plan along the lines outlined above was prepared as a basis for implementation. The activities of marketing, sales forecasting, data-processing, manufacturing, accounts and purchasing departments were clearly specified and agreed.

The amounts of capital to be invested in computers, shop-floor recording service, stores recording and the like were quantified, agreed to by top management and carried through into departmental budgets. Performance factors such as levels of project expenditure, raw material purchases and stock and shop-floor turnaround were chosen to monitor the success of the strategy and several milestones were agreed for monitoring implementation—availability of key computer program, completion of training schedules, achieving an agreed level of stock improvement. This approach paid off, and the strategy has worked. Many companies would have taken the easy way out and left it to the data-processing department: but other clients which did indeed adopt the latter approach paid for it by spending considerable sums without achieving their objective.

Adopting a systematic project management approach to strategy implementation has a number of significant advantages:

1. It allocates clear responsibility for the strategy. Someone has responsibility to cut across the organization boundaries, pull the pieces together and make sure it happens.
2. A more formal and impersonal reporting procedure tracks progress both for the benefit of the strategy manager and, more important, for the chief executive. Without such a procedure, management is dependent on informal comment, which is often inaccurate reflecting the reluctance of managers to identify problems early because this may be seen as reflecting on their personal abilities.
3. The system redresses the organization's desire to keep going in the same direction and to resist change. It overcomes the need to make dramatic changes in organization, traditional reporting or managerial behaviour, all of which take time and money. The process is added to the normal behaviour pattern and provides a timely control mechanism. As implementation proceeds, more fundamental changes to the organization and management processes can be made in the confidence that the strategy is on course and that the risks associated with change are minimized.
4. Manpower development and compensation can be planned to achieve strategic goals.

All of these benefits lead to greater confidence by the chief executive in his/her ability to control and monitor the implementation of strategy. This in turn will make possible the most aggressive initiatives which the 1980s surely demand.

19 IMPLEMENTING NEW TECHNOLOGY
Dorothy Leonard-Barton and William A. Kraus

Introducing technological change into an organization presents a different set of challenges to management than does the work of competent project administration. Frequently, however, the managers responsible for shepherding a technical innovation into routine use are much better equipped by education and experience to guide that innovation's development than to manage its implementation.

In the following pages, we describe some of the challenges managers must overcome if companies are to absorb new technologies efficiently. We also suggest strategies managers can use to address these difficulties. Although the examples we cite are all computer-related and come from the experience of large manufacturers, the issues raised and strategies proposed apply every bit as well to small businesses, to service operations—in fact, to any organization where technological innovation flourishes.

Our findings derive from our combined research and consulting experience with more than 20 large multinational corporations and with some 70 organizations within General Electric. Our focus is on internally developed technologies; but as vendors of advanced manufacturing equipment have found in their efforts to help implement the systems they market, new technologies, no matter what their origin, confront managers with a distinctive set of challenges.

A DUAL ROLE

Those who manage technological change must often serve as both technical developers and implementers. As a rule, one organization develops the technology and then hands it off to users, who are less technically skilled but quite knowledgeable about their own areas of application. In practice, however, the user organization is often not willing—or able—to take on responsibility for the technology at the point in its evolution at which the development group wants to hand it over. The person responsible for implementation—whether located in the developing organization, the user organization or in some intermediary position—has to design the hand-off so that it is almost invisible. That is, before the baton changes hands, the runners should have been running in parallel for a long time. The implementation manager has to integrate the perspectives and the needs of both developers and users.

Perhaps the easiest way to accomplish this task is to think of implementation as an internal marketing, not selling, job. This distinction is important because selling starts with a finished product, marketing, with research on user needs and preferences. Marketing executives worry about how to position their product in relation to all competitive products and are concerned with distribution channels and the infrastructure needed to support product use.

Adoption of a marketing perspective encourages implementation managers to seek user involvement in the: early identification and enhancement of the fit between a product and user needs; preparation of the user organization to receive the innovation; and shifting of ownership of the innovation to users. We discuss the first two of these issues in this section of the chapter; the third we cover later.

Marketing Perspective

That involving users in a new technology's design phase boosts user satisfaction is quite well-known, but the proper extent, timing and type of user involvement will vary greatly from company to company. For example, software developers in an electronic office equipment company established a user design group to work with developers on a strategically important piece of applications software when the program was still in the prototype stage. Prospective users could try out the software on the same computer employed by the program's developers. The extremely tight communication loop that resulted allowed daily feedback from users to designers on their preferences and problems. This degree of immediacy may be unusual, but managers can almost always get some information from potential users that will improve product design.

A marketing perspective also helps prepare an organization to receive new technology. Many implementation efforts fail because someone underestimated the scope or importance of such preparation. Indeed, the organizational hills are full of managers who believe that an innovation's technical superiority and strategic importance will guarantee acceptance. Therefore, they pour abundanat resources into the purchase or development of the technology but very little into its implementation. Experience suggests, however, that successful implementation requires not only heavy investment by developers early in the project but also a sustained level of investment in the resources of user organizations.

A very promising implementation effort in a large communications and computer company went off the rails for many months because of inadequate infrastructure in the user organization. New computerized processing control equipment was ready for shipment to prospective users enthusiastically awaiting its arrival, but a piece of linking software was not in place. Arguments erupted over who should pay for this small but critical piece of the system. Equally troubling, there were no resources for training because the developers did not see providing these resources as part of their normal responsibilities. No-one in the user organization had prepared the way for the innovation, so there was no-one to whom developers could hand it off.

Framework for Information

Just as marketing managers carefully plan the research through which they will gather critical product information, so implementation managers must develop an iterative, almost accordion-like framework to guide decisions about when and how to collect needed information from all groups affected by an innovation. We say 'accordion-like' because the process necessarily involves a search for information, a pause to digest it, and then another active period of search—cycle after cycle. What information is important—and who has it—may vary at different stages of the implementation process, but someone must coordinate the iterative work of gathering it—and that someone is the implementation manager.

When, for example, a turbine manufacturer designed a CNC system for shop-floor control in one of its small parts operations, project managers were careful to:

Observe the current job routine. System designers visited the factory floor several times and each time interviewed 8–10 operators about their work procedures.

Pay special attention to those parts of the work that required users to make decisions or seek information about which tools or materials to use, which sequence of steps to follow in machining, and which jobs operators ought to run first.

Discuss with workers what they found especially frustrating or rewarding about their work. In this case, it turned out that they liked some flexibility in the sequencing of jobs, felt that the choice of materials should be theirs, and were often frustrated by the difficulty of finding tools.

Examine how this manufacturing process related to others. The machine operators were extremely dependent on materials personnel, maintenance, the tool room, and order expediters.

From their discussions with operators, the system designers could understand the important variables as the operators saw them and, therefore, could design a system that solved problems the operators really faced without creating new ones. These discussions also facilitated a transmission of information back to the users through education and hands-on practice sessions with the users and their supervisors.

MULTIPLE INTERNAL MARKETS

The higher the organizational level at which managers define a problem or a need, the greater the probability of successful implementation. At the same time, however, the closer the definition and solution of problems or needs are to end-users, the greater the probability of success. Implementation managers must draw up their internal marketing plans in light of this apparent paradox.

As these managers identify the individuals or groups whose acceptance is essential to an innovation's success, they must also determine whom to approach, when, and with which arguments. Top management and ultimate users have to buy into the innovation to make it succeed, but marketing an idea to these two groups requires very different approaches. How, then, can an implementation manager foster general acceptance of an innovation from such a range of constituencies? We believe this executive must view the new technology from the perspective of each group and plan an approach to each accordingly.

Top management, most concerned with an innovation's likely effect on the bottom line, is accustomed to receiving proposals that specify return on investment and paybacks. Many of today's computerized technologies, however, do not lend themselves to justification in traditional financial terms, yet they may be essential to a company's future. Amid growing calls for the accounting profession to provide better means to assess the value of robots, CAD and computer-integrated manufacturing, some companies are beginning to realize the limitations of traditional capital budgeting models.

When GE set up its state-of-the-art automated dishwasher plant, it originally justified the costs on the basis of savings over time, but the plan has experienced payoffs from the investment in unanticipated ways. The quality of the product improved, lower manufacturing costs led to an expansion of market share, and the plan proved able to serve as a manufacturing site for other products. Each time managers document such nontraditional benefits, they make it easier to justify similar investments later.

Top executives may also be swayed by strategic considerations. When large-scale automation was introduced into GE's large steam-turbine generator business, the innovation was sold to top management on the basis of changing business needs: a shift from the manufacture of large, one-of-a-kind products to the manufacture of small parts. The new systems also helped drive the continual quality improvements needed to keep operations competitive when the currently sluggish market revived.

Selling top management on the case for new technology—without simultaneous involvement of user organizations in the decision-making process—is not enough. It is equally important for users of an innovation to develop 'ownership' of the technology. The meaning of this term depends largely on the scope of the project. Although it is patently impossible to involve all users in the choice and/or development of an innovation, that is no excuse not to involve their representatives.

Perhaps even more important is to plan for the transfer of knowledge from the old operation, in which people knew the materials and the product very well, to the new process, which outsiders may initially design and run. The developers of the new process (especially when it is computer software) often know their tools very well, but rarely do they understand the materials and processes to which their software is applied as well as the people on the plant floor who have been working with both for years. At the very least, managers should provide some mechanism and time for such knowledge to flow from experienced worker to developer.

An example of well-developed ownership is the case of a marketing organization about to switch from manual files to an electronic filing, messaging and data-retrieval system used by both account officers and secretaries. Managers decided to take the time to do it right the first time instead of doing it over. The project manager set up a committee of elected representatives from all groups affected. This committee met regularly, first to select the right software package and then, when it became apparent that they would have to build their own system to get all the features they wanted, to give advice on its structure and content.

The result was an inventive, well-accepted and widely used system. Moreover, users regarded the minor problems that did arise as bugs to be worked out of *our* system. As one manager told us, 'The users wanted it, so they built it.'

Critical to the success of this project was the choice of opinion leaders among users for involvement. Managers who have wrought change have known for a long time that the opinions of a few leaders profoundly influence the speed and extent of an innovation's diffusion. The basis for leadership differs from organization to organization, but these leaders are not usually hard to identify. Frequently, they occupy their place of influence as a result of technical proficiency, not formal position.

Opinion leaders, however, are not necessarily the *most* skilled operators. Behavioural science studies have shown that people commonly seek two kinds of credibility in such leaders: 'safety' credibility (this person is enough like me for his opinions to be trusted) and 'technical' credibility (this person knows what she is talking about). Someone whose technical skills are so superior that followers can have no hope of emulation may fall too far outside the norms of a group to be a real opinion leader.

In the marketing organization just described, one senior account manager refused to use the new electronic system. The system implementers were at first alarmed but then realized that this individual was not an opinion leader. Their efforts flowed around him, unimpeded by his opposition. Six months after everyone else went on the system, he capitulated, convinced at last of its utility.

PROMOTION VS HYPE

Many a technology developer will confess bewilderment that innovations do not win automatic acceptance. It may be overly optimistic to believe that an innovation will sell itself, but it is equally dangerous to oversell the new system. Novel and exotic technologies are especially vulnerable to hype.

Articles in the media about robots and artificial intelligence, for example, have raised expectations far higher than the actual performance of current technologies warrants. Potential users quickly grow disillusioned when much touted innovations perform below expectations. When one computer maker developed artificial intelligence software to be used in manufacturing, the outside world thought it was a finished product long before it was out of the 'vaporware' stage. Months before they had their hands on the software, intended users faced questions from their customers about how they liked it.

The gap between perception and reality was traceable to the energetic efforts of one project manager early on. Knowing the importance of selling the concept to management, this enthusiast had extended his campaign to virtually anyone who would listen. Since it was a sexy topic, the new artificial intelligence system received wide attention in the media as well as in organizational newsletters. This oversell presented a problem to implementation managers, who had to fight the perception that their project was way behind schedule and that their product delivered less than promised.

RISKY SITE, SAFE INNOVATION

There are two reasons for conducting a pilot operation before introducing an innovation across the board in a large organization: first, to serve as an experiment and prove technical feasibility to top management and, second, to serve as a credible demonstration model for other units in the organization. These two purposes are not always compatible.

If the innovation must succeed at the pilot site in order to survive politically, the implementation manager may choose a site that poses virtually no risk but that neither offers real benefit to the organization nor establishes a model for other units. At the same time, however, if the trial is to be a credible test, it cannot take place among the most innovative people in the corporation. Success at this kind of site is vulnerable to the criticism that these users are far from typical.

Testing the new technology at the worst performing unit, even though it may be where the innovation is most needed and would show the most spectacular results, is no better a choice. If the project fizzles, the implementation manager will not know how much of the failure was caused by extraordinary problems with the site and how much by the inherent properties of the technology. If the project succeeds, critics will be quick to note that anything would have helped operations at that site.

The solution, therefore, is to be clear about the purpose of the test—experimental or demonstration—and then to choose the site that best matches the need. The customized end of one large computer manufacturer's business suffered from a problem. If customers cancelled orders, the partially built systems were either totally scrapped—that is, broken down into components and sent back to the warehouse—or matched with incoming orders to determine if the fit was close enough to warrant retrofitting. When this matching process, which had been done manually, was computerized, the first applications site was an operation with an enthusiastic champion, but it was to be phased out in a matter of months. The site was politically risk-free but not useful for a demonstration. Although the first application was successful, the operation closed down before the site could serve as a demonstration for other plants, and the implementation manager in charge of the next site had to start all over.

Consider a different example: a papermaker that chose one of its high-visibility mills as the first site for an expensive, large-scale computerized control system. Although the system was needed to boost sagging profit margins, the mill was neither the company's best nor worst operation in financial terms. Local management was determined to see the system succeed for the sake of the mill; corporate management viewed it as an experiment. The site was promising but not risk-free.

Even if managers realize that the trial of a new technology is a critical demonstration, they do not always ask the next question: a demonstration for whom? The physical and organizational position of the first site will heavily influence who the next wave of users will be.

Over the years, many studies have shown a strong inverse relationship between proximity to facilities and use of them. This result is not surprising if the distance is measured in miles. What is surprising is that out of sight—no matter by how much—generally means out of mind. The difference in the use of a library by engineers on a college campus depended on how many more feet, not miles, nonusers were from the library than users. Similarly, new computer terminals in a large oil company were used first by people with adjoining offices and only reluctantly people even a few more feet down the hall. Distance is a relative, not absolute, measure to be weighed against current routine rather than against any objective standard.

Obviously, it is not always possible to site new equipment for everyone's convenience. Even so, the placement of an innovation frequently determines who uses the new technology first and most. If the equipment is located farther away from older or more reluctant potential users, they have a ready excuse for avoiding it. Consequently, managers who do not consider physical layout in their implementation strategies may, by default, select as first users people with little or no influence in the organization.

As noted earlier, involving opinion leaders in the planning process helps to smooth the path of implementation. If the first users of a new technology are credible role models (neither extraordinarily adept nor very poorly skilled), their demonstration has heightened meaning for a wide audience. Sometimes these opinion leaders strongly resist the technology, and getting even one of them to use it can create the necessary crack in the dam. Getting them to try the innovation may require nothing more elaborate than a well-paced and tactfully presented training session.

Often, however, an implementation manager has to create new role models by siting the innovation where the workers most open to change can demystify the technology for others by using it themselves. Although it is definitely a mistake to correlate resistance with age per se, it remains true that people with a long-term investment in certain routines and skills often hesitate to give up the security of those habits. Again, it is best to avoid extremes and to site new technology near workers who are fairly open to change but not so different from those whose resistance makes them poor models.

When a large warehouse installed a materials-handling system, it relied on its so-called 'hippy' crane operators instead of workers on the loading platform. Once the crane operators had worked out the wrinkles, management could progressively install the system throughout the plant. The crane operators were not opinion leaders at first because of their relative youth and different backgrounds, but they were both receptive to innovation and not so very different as to be unacceptable role models.

THE MANY AND THE ONE

If an innovation is to succeed, the implementation team must include: a sponsor, usually a fairly high-level person who makes sure that the project receives financial and manpower resources and who is wise about the politics of the organization; a champion, who is salesperson, diplomat, and problem solver for the innovation; a project manager, who oversees administrative details; and an integrator, who manages conflicting priorities and moulds the group through communication skills. Since these are roles, not people, more than one person can fulfill a given function, and one individual can take on more than a single role.

Even if all these roles are filled, however, the project can still stall if the organization does not vest sufficient authority in one person to make things happen. One of these individuals—usually the sponsor or the champion—must have enough organizational power to mobilize the necessary resources, and that power base must encompass both technology developers and users.

There are, of course, many ways to mobilize supplies and people. By encouraging ownership of an innovation in a user organization, for example, skilful advocates can create a power base to pull (rather than push) the innovation along. But enthusiasm for a new technology is not enough. New technology usually requires a supportive infrastructure and the allocation of scarce resources for preparing the implementation site. A champion based in the development group with no authority among the receivers must rely on time-consuming individual persuasion to garner the necessary resources. Further, even if prospective users believe in an innovation's worth, they may have to convince their superiors to free up those resources.

A short case will illustrate the point. A manufacturer of engineering test-equipment was in trouble because many orders for its customized products reached the plant floor missing vital components. Technical experts were able to catch omissions and incorrect selection of parts before the orders went into production, but the mechanics of checking orders and cycling them back through the purchase-order process cost enormous amounts of time, money and customer good will. Customers were angry at the delay of orders for weeks when manufacturing bounced them back to the initial salespeople and were even more dismayed when price quotations had to be revised upward because of a part forgotten in the first go-around.

An internally developed technology offered a partial solution: a computer program could automatically check the orders before salespeople issued quotations. Although the people who placed the orders were enthusiastic about the concept, the work of implementing the system was fraught with problems. No sales manager was willing to function as either sponsor or champion for the innovation. Although a user group funded its development, the appointed champion in that organization was too low in the hierarchy to control the resources necessary to install the system. Moreover, he lacked a clear endorsement for the project from his superiors and had mixed feelings toward the innovation. He believed in its purpose but was not certain it was being developed correctly and was afraid to stand behind it wholeheartedly lest it fail in the field. He was, therefore, slow to seek the resources and upper management support that would have moved the project forward quickly. Ultimately, an innovation has to be one person's responsibility.

LEGITIMATE RESISTANCE TO CHANGE

Overt resistance to an innovation often grows out of mistakes or overlooked issues in an implementation plan. Tacit resistance does not disappear but ferments, grows into sabotage, or surfaces later when resources are depleted. Because the advocates of change have such a clear view of an innovation's benefits, resistance often catches them by surprise. The worst thing a manager can do is shrug such resistance aside on the dual assumption that it is an irrational clinging to the status quo and that there is nothing to be done about it. Clinging to the status quo it may indeed be—but irrational, rarely. And managers can do something about it.

Thus the beginning of wisdom is to anticipate opposition. An innovation needs a champion to nurture it, and any new technology capable of inspiring strong advocacy will also provoke opposition. Where there are product champions, there will also be innovation assassins. Assassins, moreover, can fell a project with just one well-aimed bullet, but champions need to marshal forces and nurture support to implement new technology in the face of resistance. The most common reasons for opposition to a new technology are fear of the loss of skills or power and absence of an apparent personal benefit.

Fear of Loss

As talk about the deskilling potential of new computerized technologies has grown, unions are seeking retraining for their members whom automation would otherwise displace. Many companies are upgrading the status of their workers who are forced to trade hard-earned manual skills for the often dreary routine of button pushing. Although the problem is far from being resolved, it has at least merited recognition.

There is, however, another aspect of deskilling that has been much less obvious to implementers: the simple necessity of extending concern about deskilling to foremen and supervisors. They do not, of course, actually have to run the new machinery or to possess the intimate knowledge of the system that daily operators do. Even so, giving subordinates knowledge that supervisors and foremen do not have undermines their credibility. If the foremen or supervisors worked their way up through the ranks, they will know the old machinery well. They served as problem solvers when it broke down and derived no small part of their authority from their experience with it. To train their subordinates and leave them out is to invite hostility.

When a pulp mill introduced a new computerized control room, vendor representatives trained the operators and their assistants. No similar effort was made for the foremen, who thought (with some justification) that they had lost control over the mill's operation. Some of the operators relinquished their novel power by tactfully educating their foremen, but others felt they had earned the right to more autonomy because the foremen's knowledge was obsolete.

One way to deal with this kind of situation is to teach supervisors how to instruct hourly workers about the new technology. These sessions should transmit details of the information hourly workers require, instructions on how best to present it, guides to practice sessions and audiovisual aids.

Another reason for resistance is fear that the innovation will be politically enfeebling and that supervisors and even operators will lose some control by adopting it. A good implementation plan should try to identify where a loss of power may occur so that managers can anticipate and possibly avert any problems arising from that loss.

In one large manufacturing plant, corporate research developed a computerized system for scheduling the production—in small batches—of customized health-care products. Although the manufacturing manager outwardly supported the idea, he never made any of the decisions or appointments necessary to put the new technology into effect. The implementation team finally realized what he had seen at the outset: using the software removed from his hands control over a key piece of his operation. The programmers working on the project reported to management information systems (MIS), not manufacturing. The manager never voiced his opposition since there was little rational basis for it, but his resistance effectively stalled the project. In this case, the programmers were quite willing, as was MIS, to report for the duration of the project to manufacturing, a change that allowed the project to swing into place.

Personal Benefit

An innovation must offer an obvious advantage over whatever it replaces, or potential users will have little incentive to use it. The more visible the costs of an innovation (financial, convenience, the need to learn new skills), the greater the importance of making potential benefits and rewards apparent. These benefits include expanded influence over work (stopping a production line), increased value of work (no in-process inventory), greater recognition (being part of a valued implementation team), solution of a long-standing problem (a shop-floor control system that gives up-to-the-minute production reports), and preservation of jobs.

It is easy for managers to forget that benefits buried in the system, which they can see because of their position, may be totally invisible to the operators on whom the success of the innovation depends. A new technology may pay off for an organization as a whole but not for individuals in any form they can recognize. That is why it is so important to make these benefits visible through encouragement from supervisors as well as through explicit and timely feedback on how the innovation is affecting workers' output. In general, the faster the positive feedback to users, the more visible the benefits will be.

A very large natural resources company ran into difficulties with introduction of a methodology for constructing software. This approach required programmer-analysts to sit down with their clients and, following a regimented procedure with standardized notations, analyze the client's business. A structured approach was expected to identify more potential problems at the design stage and facilitate communication between client and designer. Moreover, the company hoped that a standardized notation would facilitate the transfer of project work between programmers and cut the time spent on programme maintenance.

In retrospect, it is clear that all the benefits of the new technology accrued to the organization, not to the individuals who used it. In fact, many potential users thought they would be penalized for using the new methodology, since managers judged their performance on speed and low cost, not on the quality of their output. The organization's rhetoric supported, indeed mandated, use of the new technology, but the reward structure militated against it.

Now, contrast this situation with one in which managers gave some thought to the challenge of translating organizational benefits into individual rewards. Before installing a shop-floor control system, a major appliance manufacturer conducted informal research into the problems of the hourly work force. They discovered that the current voucher system never permitted workers to know how much their pay would be in a given week. A small modification of the control system's design made it possible for employees to receive a report on cumulative salary with each job they entered. Although this piece of information was not central to the needs of the organization, adding it to the system's design was a low-cost way to boost the innovation's benefits to workers. This small feature more than compensated them for the pain of developing new skills and habits, and the advantage of the new system over the old was apparent every time they used it.

A WORD ABOUT HEDGERS

Besides the champions and assassins in an organization, there will always be some 'hedgers', individuals who refuse to take a stand against an innovation so that others can address their objections but who also refuse to support the new technology. They straddle the fence, ready to leap down on either side to declare that they had foreseen the value of the innovation all along or that they had known it would fail from the start. These risk-averse managers can affect the future of a new technology when they are a key link in the implementation plan. Because these hedgers are usually waiting for signals to tell them which way to leap, astute implementation managers will see to it that they receive the appropriate signals from those higher up in the organization.

Like product assassins, hedgers can be found at any level in an organization and dealing with them effectively requires a sequence of actions. The first, and the easiest, is to persuade top management to take some kind of quick symbolic action in support of the innovation. Whether the action takes the form of a memo, a speech or a minor policy change, it must send a signal that top management will stand behind this technology even in a budget crisis.

The second step, which is harder, is to help managers at all levels send out the right signals. If, for instance, the first step was an announcement of a new drive for quality, the second should be to increase the emphasis on quality throughout the company. If workers hear an announcement about a new quality program but continue with impunity to ship products that they know are inferior, the initial symbolic gesture loses potency. Worse, all future gestures lose credibility too.

The third step is the hardest—and the most necessary. Managers must bring the criteria used to judge the performance of innovation users into conformance with the demands of the new technology. New technologies often require new measures. If, for example, a new, structured software technique requires more time than did the old, managers must evaluate programmer-analysts less on the basis of the quantity of output than on the basis of its quality.

Further, because productivity commonly declines whenever a new technology is introduced, more accurate measurements of productivity in the old sense may lead supervisors to fear that their performance will look worse—not least because, with a fully automated system, direct labour drops but indirect labour grows.

Other adjustments might include a phase-in period for the new technology during which the usual output measurements do not apply. It might also make sense to reward people for preventing rather than just solving problems and for developing work behaviour identified with the new technology. Although operators do not respond well when they view technological systems as controlling their behaviour, they respond quite well when a system gives them feedback on their performance and the performance of their machines. Information increases the amount of control people have over their environment.

Converting hedgers into believers is not a simple task, but it is one more of the inescapable challenges managers face as they try to implement new technology. Indeed, as the competitive environment changes and as the systematic effects of new technologies become even more pronounced, the work of implementing those technologies will increasingly pose for managers a distinctive set of challenges— not least, the task of creating organizations flexible enough to adjust, adapt and learn continuously.

20 STRATEGY AND TACTICS IN ORGANIZATIONAL CHANGE: RACE RELATIONS AND LOCAL GOVERNMENT
Philip Nanton

Strategies to attain racial equality by exerting internal influence on the system of local government are developing common features. This orthodoxy contains major limitations, both in theory and practice, which have failed to be adequately examined. The characteristics of this orthodox approach consist of the application of strategies based on the following assumptions.

1. That necessary change will flow smoothly from decrees issued at the centre of power for implementation at the periphery given sufficient legislative authority and the commitment of those highest placed in local government.
2. Racial equality will be enhanced by the introduction of a process of training of various types and duration for those at important strategic levels in the organization. Training can range from racism awareness to gaining knowledge of the Race Relations Act 1976 or the Code of Practice.
3. Racial equality will be enhanced by the mechanism of an innovator who, either as an individual or with a unit of a small number of like minded committed individuals, intervenes from the centre to confront directly the local government institution perceived to be racist.

WEAKNESSES IN THE ORTHODOX APPROACH

Legislation as a Change Strategy

There is a substantial evidence, both historical and contemporary, to indicate that legislation is a necessary but by itself an inadequate basis on which to build a strategy to attain racial equality. The tendency for the law to be used as a 'declaratory gesture rather than as an effective instrument of individual justice' was shown by Lester and Bindman to date back as far as the first (ineffective) attempts to implement antidiscrimination law in the Indian Civil Service during

Nanton, P. 1984) Strategy, tactics in organizational change, *Local Government Studies*, Sept/Oct, pp 51–60 the time of the British Raj.[1] Other specific limitations on antidiscrimination legislation are outlined in their study *Race and Law*.[2] The Commission for Racial Equality's (CRE) recent experience of the Race Relations Act 1976, in particular section 71 which applies to local government, has led it to conclude that there exists 'a good deal of frustration' due to the vagueness of the duty imposed on local authorities.[3]

Centre Periphery or 'Top-down' Strategy

Official guidelines and informed advice on the attainment of racial equality have been careful to recognize that internal variations within local authorities inhibit the development of a 'standard model'.[4] Similarly, Young and Connelly claim 'no top-down strategy of racial equality can hope to be entirely successful'.[5]

Despite these warnings there has developed in practice a pattern of race policies characterized by just such top-down strategies. Ironically, some of the major proponents of this approach are among those warning against it. For example, the CRE argues the need for a central committee responsibility for race matters and at officer level for the chief executive to have overall responsibilities for taking positive measures to implement legislation.[6] Young and Connelly outline the importance of an effective review of policy and observe 'the role of political and professional leadership is crucial to initiating and sustaining policy review'.[7] The recent Bichard Report assumed that 'responsibilities for coordination and providing the momentum for action lie properly with the chief executive'.[8]

Three major weaknesses can be discerned in this strategy. A fundamental assumption of the top-down strategy as applied to local government is that commitment from the top, at either officer or member level, is both a necessary requirement and can be attained. However, neither official reports nor the recommendations of analysts take into account the situation where commitment is not forthcoming. Alternatively, there may be no more than indifference or merely a willingness at the top not to impede. These are more likely to be common experience among many local authorities. The commitment and practice of acknowledged leaders, for example, Bradford, Camden and the Greater London Council (GLC) was probably a rarity. This has been implicitly acknowledged by the CRE in its review of the implementation of equal employment opportunity programmes: it stated 'the evidence suggests that a great many more [public and private employers] have not yet taken any positive steps towards ensuring that racial discrimination and disadvantage are not occurring within their establishments'.[9] A likely sign of a lack of commitment at the top in many local authorities.

Another limitation of the top-down strategy is that it presents a simplistic view of how power is exercised and policy implemented in large organizations. Such a strategy essentially ignores the implications of a range of peripheral points of power which are significant in the operation of a local authority service. For example, the discretion available to head teachers and heads of residential homes can be sufficient to distort the most explicit of centralized requirements in appointments procedures. In this way the local managers effectively become the policy makers within their limited area of control. The centre's willingness or ability to challenge these local points of power is doubtful given that race issues are both contentious and may retain only lukewarm support at the centre.

Research in the Midlands into the extent to which interviewers rely on nonspecific criteria illustrates another aspect of the scale of the task facing a top-down strategy. Jenkin's investigation into the attitudes of managers in the selection of black people for jobs shows how stated concepts of suitability for various jobs shaded into vague concepts of acceptability with recruiters relying on criteria such as 'gut feeling', 'general manner' and 'attitude, appearance and presentation' when they were choosing candidates.[10] Exhortation is unlikely to help, but what of training?

Training as a Change Strategy

There is a touching faith in the merits of the training process and its applicability to effecting valuable change in race relations in local government in Britain. For example, Peppard's review of the range of training available appears to commend all the various types along with the growing professionalism involved, with scant attention to the issue of the relevance or effectiveness of the new trends being developed.[11]

A 1984 report on race relations training and the police—Report of the Police Training Council Working Party—similarly appears at first glance to hold a strong faith in the benefits of training. It recommends a range of training programmes, including interpersonal and behavioural skills, racism awareness training and community contact among various methods, again with no evidence of their relative merits.[12] At the same time, however, the appendix of the report notes that there is a lack of evidence of the effect of training given to police officers and the existence of ambiguity and confusion as to whether attitudes or skills should be taught and whether human-relations and race-relations issues are distinct. Thus the report managed to look in opposite directions at the same time.

While there is little or no research evidence of the effectiveness of training as a change strategy in the field of race relations in Britain, there is substantial evidence of the doubtful benefit of certain methods of training which are common in local government as a strategy of change. In a seminal paper analyzing the value of training as a change strategy, Georgiades and Phillimore[13] cite evidence from a variety of sources to indicate that the process of changing an organization by extracting individuals from their work environment for training, then returning them to the same environment, is ineffective. Among teachers, changes in expressed attitudes during training were found to be reversed during the first year of teaching.[14] In industry the greatest influence on supervising personnel was found to be not their training but their immediate superior in their place of work.[15] Thus Georgiades and Phillimore state:

> The assumptions behind training as a strategy for inducing organizational change are based upon the psychological fallacy that since work organizations

are made up of individuals, we can change the organization by changing its individual members. There is a plethora of evidence to refute this proposition; not only the generalized psychological research relating to the nature of resistance to change at the workplace ... but also specific research into the evaluation of training programmes.[16]

The Agent of Change—The Race Relations Adviser and the Race Relations Unit

The appointment of Race Relations Advisers or Race Relations Units within the central administration of local government (UK) is becoming increasingly common in urban, shire and borough areas. These post holders daily confront the contradiction that they are given responsibility to act as agents of change within the organization of local government, an organization which is itself structured for stability and to maintain a range of standardized services. Among race advisers an established approach has developed, strongly influenced by the work of Ouseley which is outlined in their study of Lambeth (*The System*).

Ouseley outlines a strategy to attain racial equality dependent on a corporate structure and practice involving the appointment of advisers to all service departments and a principal adviser in charge of a central unit which has 'the initial thrust to sensitize the whole Council apparatus to the new climate in which positive action on race equality could thrive'.[17] He commends a direct combative approach which is summarized in the four key areas of race policy pursued by the unit in Lambeth:

1. Developing and implementing specific policies on race covering employment and training, service provision, community development, public relations, information communication and promotional activities.
2. Involving the black communities in the identification and analysis of their needs, through increased consultations with the specific aim of responding to their demands.
3. Identifying racism, the discrimination it sustains and underwriting explicit commitments to redress imbalances. Creating equal access for black people to all job appointments. Recruiting black people at all job levels and providing them with the career training opportunities so they would be equipped to compete as equals for job opportunities.
4. Confronting racism through comprehensive training programmes for members, officers and staff, to bring about positive changes in attitudes and behaviour and to accelerate changes in procedures and practices.[18]

This confrontational strategy when applied elsewhere has to face a number of problems which detract from its application. First, such a strategy may not be relevant or effective in all local authorities. It is worth noting that Ouseley recognizes the importance of management support: 'effective changes were very dependent on the goodwill of management'.[19] I have argued that this situation will not necessarily be common. Where hostility or indifference are apparent, the strategy will need revision. Revision will be necessary for two reasons: the limited resources available to the race adviser and, in situations where the black communities are dispersed and in relatively small proportions, the ability to exert sustained external pressure on officers and members is limited.

Second, Ouseley's strategy tends to ignore the existing relationships and climate of officer, interdepartment and officer-member relationships into which the adviser is required to intervene. These situations are ignored at the peril of the adviser and his or her recommended policies in an indifferent or hostile climate.

Third, there has been an implicit admission of the problems of confrontation strategy from another adviser. In an unpublished review of the role of the adviser the former principal of the Leicester unit, Graham Mahoney, argues that advisers have limited impact because they lack credibility as professionals among other officers in local government.[20] His solution is to suggest that to be effective advisers should avoid the corporate approach and instead be responsible direct to a member committee and the local community.[21] He also argues that the adviser would be more effective in a form of police role or auditor with overview of all departments. Such a solution, however, appears to be more an attempt to avoid the interofficer issues and relationships rather than a method of coming to terms with them. Furthermore, as officers will have to carry out the imposed strategies, without a direct relationship between adviser and officer, the possible practice of avoidance of race issues again becomes a likely possibility. In my opinion another option is necessary.

I consider that to be effective the race-relations adviser has to overcome three problems: indifference; attaining influence and credibility at both officer and member level; and, when there is a unit or grouping of supportive like-minded individuals there is a need to establish methods of maintaining cohesion when under pressure of opposition from the organization. The strategy to do this which I have adopted has partly coincided and been partly based on the recommended strategy for organizational change developed by Georgiades and Phillimore. What follows is a brief outline of the strategy they recommend and some points as to how elements of it have been adopted in a conservative shire county in the East Midlands. The strategy is offered not as a blueprint but as an alternative. It is founded on the assumptions that racism is widespread, particularly in its institutionalized form, and that to be effective it is first necessary to establish the specific form which racism takes in the particular environment and locality in which one works. As Hall argues, 'It is not helpful to define racism as a "natural" and permanent feature—either of all societies or indeed of a sort of universal "human nature" ... it always assumes specific forms which arise out of present—not the past—conditions and organization of society.'[22] An important implication in Hall's argument, I feel, is that it is first necessary to establish the local form of racism.

GEORGIADES AND PHILLIMORE'S GUIDELINES

Georgiades and Phillimore provide two general points and six guidelines more in the nature of a tactical checklist than a formal anaylsis. They recommend, first, the cultivation of the environment of the organization, that is, the need to establish respect and rapport using demonstrable expertise rather than threats, and, second, they suggest a reappraisal of the time-scale of the change programme. They note, for example, genuine and permanent change takes from three to five years in commercial or industrial organizations. In stable, traditional organizations the period is then likely to be somewhat longer. They also suggest that 'preparation of the environment' can take up to 12 months. The guidelines they suggest are:

1. Work with those who support change and not directly against those resisting change. Thus mass training, mass public-relations exercises are assumed to be unproductive.
2. Establish a team of workers for mutual support.
3. Avoid working with lost causes, that is, those lacking the will or resources to improve.
4. While the agreement of those at the top is needed to proceed, it is more effective to work with those just below the top of the organization. This is based on the assumption that those near the top are less likely to support the status quo and will be more receptive to change.
5. It is useful in large organizations to work with those who in their sphere of control have the authority to carry out change and so can exercise freedom and discretion in managing their own resources and operations.
6. A supportive team is essential with the opportunity for frequent meetings to air doubts, anxieties and new ideas.

ORGANIZATIONAL CHANGE IN PRACTICE: THE RACE ADVISER IN A SHIRE COUNTY

The 1981 Census revealed for Northamptonshire a total of 15 367 people living in New Commonwealth and Pakistan (NC&P) households from a total county population of 524 967; thus the NC&P proportion was 2.9 per cent of the total. This population is concentrated mainly in the towns of Northampton and Wellingborough with 5 and 10 per cent NC&P population respectively, while the two other major towns, Kettering and Corby, contain proportions of 3 and 1 per cent respectively. A 1983 estimate of the proportion of school children in the county indicated a similar small total of ethnic minority children countywide. From a total of 97 000 school children in the country, 4600 or 4.5 per cent belonged to a range of minority groups, European, East Asian, South Asian and Afro Caribbean. Thus, the minority communities in the county are diverse and relatively widely distributed.

The fact that sections of the county police force were sent to Toxteth during the 1981 riots gives one indication of the low level of local urban racial tension at the time of the urban inner-city riots. Ironically, the local police are more active than most departments in promoting black self-help projects in urban areas.

There are important contrasts to this apparent idyll. Unemployment levels of young black people are substantially above their age cohorts in the two main towns. In urban areas Asian and West Indian households live in substantially poorer accommodation and the former are subject to intermittent racial harassment. Levels of attainment of black children in school are no better than in other parts of the country. There is also evidence that the employment of black people within the county council is low with a maximum of 80 employees out of a total part- and full-time work force of 20 537. This is significant because the NC&P population in the county comprise 2.6 per cent of the working population but form only 0.4 per cent of the county council work force. The tendency has been in the past for the county authority to distance itself from race issues. For example, the job description of the 'ethnic minorities coordinator' (later changed to 'race relations adviser') initially emphasized contact with black groups in the county rather than the need to initiate internal changes in policy and practice.

In general, attitudes to race relations in the county council are characterized by complacency and ignorance. There is little understanding of the different characteristics of the various minority populations or the different ways in which they express their demands. The level of suspicion between minority communities and the wider community is substantial, founded on the experience of intermittent petty racial harassment, poor employment opportunities and a lack of English amongst certain of the poorer Asian communities. These features have further encouraged disengagement and a general indifference to many public services.

County services with implications for race relations have tended to be provided on a piecemeal department basis when particular problems have been recognized. However, very often the major issue has been the unwillingness to recognize that race-related problems may have distinct implications for practice or that such issues as discrimination and disadvantage need to be countered in a coordinated, purposeful way.

A complicating feature inhibiting corporate policies in race as in other areas is that department independence is strongly guarded, and there are massive department imbalances in size of work force and funds available as well as significant interpersonal differences at the top of the corporate structure. One experience of this milieu has shown that a corporate approach to establishing an equal-opportunity-employment policy achieved agreement to proceed based on consensus which produced, in effect, the lowest common denominator of agreed recommendations in the policy.

This sketch of the local features affecting the management of race issues and relationships formed the background to my intervention. In my estimation, officer power in this locality is significant, the willingness to avoid race issues is substantial, employment and service delivery, especially in education, social services, police and probation, are major areas requiring intervention.

The structure within the authority which was developed to examine race issues is as follows: two linked officer groups were established to discuss race-relations matters. One, an informal interdepartment group, meets once every two months. It was established just prior to my arrival. The group consists of principal officers from education and social services—the inspector for multicultural education, the head of community involvement with the police department and a representative of health education. Involvement of the local community-relations officers in this structure had not as yet found sufficient support for them to be easily incorporated. The meetings provide an opportunity to exchange information and discuss areas of concern which arise from involvement with the various communities and their organizations. As race adviser I act as chairman of the group and provide a link with the senior officer grouping the deputies race-relations policy group which I service. The regular membership consists of deputy chief officers from education (the chairman), police, social services, probation and chief executive.

Given the present political structure of interdepartment and interoffice relationships the deputies group appears to provide the most leverage, both across departments and to the chief officers as a corporate decision-making group. The informal liaison group fulfils the function of an interdepartment team. Both these groups have proved more effective in service delivery rather than employment issues.

The strategy to establish equal opportunities in employment has developed in a different way. A head count of employees who are not white was requested from each department at an early stage. Next a report on the changes needed to establish an effective equal opportunity policy was carried out with the employee-relations officer (of the central personnel unit), and a number of draft reports submitted to chief officer meetings. The strategy then being followed was the orthodox one of attempting to obtain commitment at the top on a range of employment policies and procedures to change poor representation of blacks in local authority employment. After some months what was finally established locally was a tentative, piecemeal agreement to proceed in three ways. A commitment was made 'to attempt to ensure' fair treatment in employment, concurrent advertising was to be adopted and a pilot monitoring programme was agreed to analyze the implications of a full monitoring programme. The options then available to me as adviser were either to abandon the work or change the strategy to build on the small foothold of agreement which had been attained.

The strategy, developed in conjunction with the employee relations officer, is to intervene to encourage peripheral centres of power to develop their own positive action programmes, to review with them who they employ, what methods they adopt, why and what if anything can be done about it. With no more than the agreement to proceed from the top within the relevant departments this approach started with head teachers, managers of the school meals service and managers of old people's homes, and will be extended to two other areas, smaller departments which recruit centrally and the Department of Highways and Transportation.

The strategy is a less glamorous approach to implementing equal opportunity in employment than those currently available; its effectiveness remained to be tested.

CONCLUSION

The dominant strategy in the development of race-relations work within local government was drawn from the experience of London and other cities. This strategy relied on the underlying assumption of commitment among senior officers and politicians. This assumption is often allied to the race adviser's strategy of direct confrontation with perceived opponents. Where the underlying climate of opinion at the higher echelon of the organization is hostile or indifferent, other strategies need to be developed. One such strategy has been outlined which is applicable to the latter environment. The strategy illustrates that race issues can be subsumed under existing concepts of organizational change, although the strategy needs to reflect a response to the local form in which racism is expressed.

ACKNOWLEDGEMENT

The author wishes to thank Andrew Sutton for the comments and suggestions he made during the preparation of this article.

REFERENCES

1. A. Lester and G. Bindman (1972) Race and Law, *Appendix 1, The first British anti-discrimination law: a cautionary tale*, Harmondsworth Penguin, p 418
2. *Ibid.* pp 88–89
3. A consultative paper (1983) The race relations Act 1976—time for a change? *CRE*, p 40
4. Local Government and Racial Equality, *CRE* (1982)
5 K. Young and N. Connelly (1984) After the Act—local authority policy reviews under the Race Relation Act 1976. *Local Government Studies*, Vol. 10, No.1 (January/February), p 23
6. CRE (1982) *op. cit.* p 11
7. K. Young and N. Connelly, *op. cit.*, p 23
8. (1983) *Local Authorities and Racial Disadvantage: Report of a Joint Government/ Local Authority Association Working Group*, Department of the Environment, p 15
9. (1983) *Implementing Equal Employment Opportunity Policies, CRE*, p 71
10. R. Jenkin (1982) Managing Recruitment Procedures and Black Workers, University of Aston, Birmingham, Working papers on Ethnic Relations, No. 18, p 27
11. N. Peppard (1983) Race relations training: the state of the art, *New Community* (Journal of the Commission for Racial Equality), Vol. XI, Nos. 1/2 (Autumn/ Winter) pp 150–9
12. *Community and Race Relations Training for the Police: Report of the Police Training Council Working Party*, and Appendix 2, Police Training in Race Relations: Some Research Evidence
13. N. J. Georgiades, and L. Phillimore (1975) *The myth of the hero-innovator and alternative strategies for organizational change.* In C. Kiernan and P. Woodford (Eds), Behaviour Modification with the Severely Retarded, Associated Scientific Publishers, Amsterdam

14. A. Morrison and D. McIntyre (1967) Changes in opinion about education during the first year of teaching, *Br. J. Soc. Clin. Psychol*, Vol. 6, pp 161–3
15. E. A. Fleishman (1953) Leadership climate, human relations training and supervisory behaviour, *Personnel Psychol*, Vol. 6, pp 205–22
16. N. J. Georgiades and L. Phillimore, *op. cit.*
17. H. Ouseley with D. Silverstone and U. Prashar, *The System: The Runnymede Trust and The South London Equal Rights Consultancy*, p 24
18. *Ibid.*, p 172
19. *Ibid.*, p 179
20. G. Mahoney, (1983) Discussion of policy implementation, Unpublished paper p 3
21. *Ibid.*, rb. p 17
22. (1978) *Racism and reaction.* In S. Hall, Five Views of Multi-Racial Britain, CRE, p 26

21 SUCCESSFULLY IMPLEMENTING STRATEGIC DECISIONS
Larry D. Alexander

Although strategy implementation is viewed as an integral part of the strategic management process, little has been written or researched on it. The overwhelming majority of the literature so far has been on the long-range planning process itself or the actual content of the strategy being formulated. We have so far been giving lip service to the other side of the coin, namely, strategy implementation. Consequently, it is not surprising that after a comprehensive strategy or single strategic decision has been formulated, significant difficulties are often encountered during the subsequent implementation process.

This study surveyed 93 private sector firms through a questionnaire to determine which implementation problems occurred most frequently as they tried to put strategic decisions into effect. Later on, in-depth telephone interviews with chief executive officers of 21 of these firms were conducted to comprehend these problems more fully. These interviews, combined later on with another 25 interviews with governmental agency heads in another study of implementation in the public sector by this researcher, help to identify factors which promote successful implementation.

Review of the Literature

The available literature on strategy implementation was reviewed in order to identify potential strategy implementation problems. Most of the 22 potential problems were identified from such helpful works as Alexander,[1] Andrews,[2] Galbraith and Nathanson,[3] Hobbs and Heany,[4] Kotter and Schlesinger,[5] Le Breton,[6] McCarthy et al.,[7] Quinn,[8] Steiner and Miner,[9] and Thompson and Strickland.[10] In addition, several in-depth case studies on strategy implementation by Pressman and Wildavsky,[11] Murphy,[12] Quinn[13] and Alexander[14] also helped to identify more potential problems. Finally, a few of the 22 implementation problems were suggested by chief executive officers in earlier interviews conducted by this writer.

Alexander, L.D. (1985) Successfully implementing strategic decisions, *Long Range Planning*, Vol. 18, No. 3, pp 91–97. Reprinted with permission from Pergamon Journals

Companies Surveyed

The 93 firms participating in this survey were strategic business units of medium- and large-sized firms. Some 72 firms (77 per cent) were listed in the *Fortune* 500 list of leading industrials. If *Fortune's* second 500 list of industrials is included along with *Fortune's* top 50 listings for utilities, retailing and services, then 89 firms (96 per cent) responding were included on one *Fortune* list or another.

The firms' SBUs (strategic business units) sampled differed with respect to their size, industry and geographical location within the United States. For example, 26 (28 per cent) of the SBUs had less than 400 employees; 23 (25 per cent) had 400–999 employees; 29 (31 per cent) had 1000–1999 employees; 13 (14 per cent) had over 5000 employees; and 2 (2 per cent) were unidentified. While most of the corporations operated within a number of different businesses, this study was focused on implementing strategic decisions within individual SBUs.

The Strategic Decisions Evaluated

In the questionnaire, each responding company president (or division general manager) was asked to select one recent strategic decision that had been implemented in his SBU. He was asked to select one in which he had a great deal of personal knowledge about its subsequent implementation. Table 21.1 shows the types of strategic decision that were evaluated. The main part of the questionnaire then asked the participants to evaluate the extent to which some 22 possible implementation problems actually were a problem in its subsequent implementation using a five-point Likert-type response scale. Finally, questions were asked to evaluate the overall success of the strategy implementation effort itself.

MOST FREQUENTLY OCCURRING PROBLEMS

The 10 most commonly occurring strategy implementation problems are shown in Table 21.2 in descending order according to mean ratings. Two adjacent pairs of numbers on the five-point Likert response scale are combined for display purposes only as follows: minor and moderate problems (points 2 and 3), and substantial and major problems (points 4 and 5). The 10 listed items are the only ones rated as problems by over half of the sample group.

The first seven listed implementation problems occurred to at least 60 per cent of the firms. They are:

1. Implementation took more time than originally allocated by 76 per cent
2. Major problems surface during implementation that had not been identified beforehand by 74 per cent
3. Coordination of implementation activities (for example, by task force, committees, superiors) was not effective enough by 66 per cent
4. Competing activities and crises distracted attention from implementing this strategic decision by 64 per cent

Table 21.1 Types of strategic decision implemented

Type of strategic decision	Numbers	Per cent
Introducing a new product or service	29	31
Opening and starting up a new plant or facility	17	18
Expanding operations to enter a new market	15	16
Discontinuing a product or withdrawing from a market	11	12
Acquiring or merging with another firm	10	11
Changing the strategy in functional departments	6	7
Other	5	5
	93	100

5. Capabilities (skills and abilities) of employees involved with the implementation were not sufficient by 63 per cent
6. Training and instruction given to lower level employees were not adequate by 62 per cent
7. Uncontrollable factors in the external environment (for example, competitive, economic, governmental) had an adverse impact on implementation by 60 per cent.

Three additional implementation problems listed in Table 21.2 occurred to somewhat fewer firms but still experienced by over 50 per cent of the sample firms.

Three quarters (76 per cent) of the sampled firms found that their implementation efforts took more time than originally allocated. A number of explanations were given by CEOs in the follow-up telephone interviews. As one executive put it, 'In retrospect, we were overly optimistic in thinking how much time it would take to implement a new strategic decision. We though that everything would work fine which it never does.' From the interviews, this problem seems to occur because top management:

1. Understates how long various implementation tasks will take to complete
2. Downplays the likelihood of potential problems that may or may not occur
3. Is blind to other problems occurring altogether

Obviously, when all three of these occur during implementation, it can greatly lengthen the time it will take to implement the decision effectively.

Solutions to the problem of taking too much time are numerous. More time should initially be allocated from the start to handle unexpected problems and, in general, the unknown. More manpower initially can be put on important strategic decisions, and particularly later on when unexpected problems emerged. In addition, rewards and penalties can also be used to bring about the desired results.

Table 21.2 Ten most frequent strategy-implementation problems

Potential strategy-implementation problem	Mean	Frequency of any degree of problem	=	Frequency of minor moderate problems	+	Frequency of substantial major problems
Implementation took more time than originally allocated	2.71	71 (76%)		45 (48%)		26 (28%)
Major problems surfaced during implementation that had not been identified beforehand	2.63	69 (74%)		45 (48%)		24 (26%)
Coordination of implementation activities was not effective enough	2.34	62 (66%)		45 (48%)		17 (18%)
Competing activities and crises distracted attention from implementing this decision	2.29	60 (64%)		41 (44%)		19 (20%)
Capabilities of employees involved were not sufficient	2.28	59 (63%)		40 (43%)		19 (20%)
Training and instruction given to lower level employees were not adequate	2.14	58 (62%)		47 (50%)		11 (12%)
Uncontrollable factors in the external environment had an adverse impact on implementation	2.28	56 (60%)		40 (43%)		16 (17%)
Leadership and direction provided by departmental managers were not adequate enough	2.23	55 (59%)		39 (42%)		16 (17%)
Key implementation tasks and activities were not defined in enough detail	2.09	52 (56%)		36 (39%)		16 (17%)
Information systems used to monitor implementation were not adequate	1.94	52 (56%)		43 (46%)		9 (10%)

The last suggestion is exactly how one CEO handled a strategic decision that had been dragging on and on. As he put it,

> Even though we wanted to withdraw from this particular line of fashion clothes, we kept coming up with new ideas. For every two items we'd drop from this line, we'd introduce one new one. Thus, we kept getting seduced back into this line even though I knew we had to discontinue it. After two years, I finally solved the problem by telling my staff that if you or your subordinates present me with any new sketch for this clothing line, that person will lose his job.

Major problems (and obstacles) surfaced during implementation that had not been identified beforehand were experienced by almost as many firms, specifically 74 per cent. These can be internally oriented problems brought on by the firm trying something new, insufficient advance planning and strategy formulators not getting actively involved in implementation to name a few. Or they can be caused by externally oriented factors such as the uncertainty involved with a new product or new market, uncontrollable events in the external environment or legal/political complications introduced by new legislation or regulations among others.

Consider what happened to one domestic oil equipment firm that was implementing its strategic decision to construct oil wells in an Arab country. All sorts of problems surfaced that had not been identified beforehand as potential problems. Certain employees could not go into that country to work on the project because of their particular race or nationality. Bringing explosives into that country to blast rock in preparation for building the oil-well foundation was delayed because the host government was suspicious that they could be used against the government itself. Neither of these problems had been identified beforehand by the firm or its Arab partner, who led them to believe it really knew the ropes and how to operate in the host country. In addition, another oil firm already in that country for many years tried to put up administrative road blocks by using its contacts in various governmental agencies of the Arab country.

Clearly, some of these problems could have been identified and resolved had the firm selected a better Arab partner. In addition, some of these potential problems overlooked by its Arab partner could have been identified had the firm talked with other US firms already doing business there. However, it is safe to say that some of these problems could probably never be anticipated beforehand.

The presence of competing activities and crises that distracted attention from implementing the strategic decision was yet another frequently occurring problem. Some 64 per cent of the firms experienced this implementation problem. One aerospace-components firm was starting to implement one strategic decision when along came one order from an airline firm that amounted to 25 per cent of its total sales in a typical year. Obviously, considerable time and attention had to be given to this major order for about three months which clearly had priority over the other strategic decision. Actually, the firm decided to forget trying to implement the new strategic decision for a while and put it on hold.

Given the size of the customer order, this seemed the best way to handle these competing events.

Another firm was trying to implement one strategic decision when the market for its coal-related products collapsed in 1977. Because of this unexpected crisis, pressure was put on managers at all levels to do everything possible to increase sales and profits rather than to implement this new management resource planning system. Still another firm was diverted from implementing a new overall strategy for the division and had to help a very major customer design and manufacture one of its products which was encountering major production problems. This was done to ensure that this delinquent customer would get enough revenues from the sale of its products to, in turn, pay money owed to this firm. Thus, it appears that the number and type of competing activities and crises that can occur are almost limitless.

One of three things typically occurs when competing events exist. Time and attention are taken away from implementing the new strategic decision. They are taken away from other existing programmes which suffer. Or often, some time and attention are taken away from the new and existing programmes.

Some 60 per cent of the firms experienced uncontrollable factors in the external environment that had an adverse impact on implementation. Some of these problems are truly surprise events. Examples of these include:

1. A hurricane tearing off a roof of a new plant which damaged equipment
2. The professional airline traffic controllers strike and the 25 per cent reduction in flights which reduced the demand for a firm's new jet-pull-out tractor
3. A surprising upturn in an industry's sales when a firm was trying to move three plants into one new modern facility.

In example 3, this firm competing in the abrasives industry had planned to make this move during a time of slackened demand. All economic forecasts for 1978/79 suggested a softness in the economy; consequently, the firm thought this would be an excellent time to consolidate operations. Unfortunately, after the move got started, that year turned out to be the best year ever for the industry which caused added problems trying to satisfy high customer demand while moving operations.

While most uncontrollable problems in the external environment cannot be anticipated, contingency plans can be developed for some of them. Then, if that problem does occur, at least the firm will be in a better position to take corrective action to minimize its impact on the firm.

Two somewhat lower rated items, which are:

1. Advocates and supporters of the strategic decision left (the division or company) during implementation (experienced by only 27 per cent of the firms)
2. The key people, who developed and made the strategic decision, did not play an active enough role in its subsequent implementation (40 per cent)

illustrate how two problems can combine to make things even worse. One company president put it this way,

> Our company was acquired by another parent firm with no background in this business. A new group vice president was installed to straighten out the mess here. He and I developed a strategy to break even in about 15 months with proper equipment, but then 6 months later, this group vice president was replaced for reasons beyond my knowledge. His replacement was not familiar with our operations, wants us now to go in about a 180-degree different direction, and only looks at bottom-line results.

In another firm, a company president appointed a key subordinate to be the project manager, directly overseeing the implementation of the strategic decision. Halfway through its implementation, the subordinate got so frustrated with the whole thing that he took a job elsewhere which really ground things to a halt. While the loss of a key person implementing a strategic decision can cause problems and lengthen the implementation time, the loss of the key architect of the decision can potentially stop the implementation forever.

HIGH VERSUS LOW IMPLEMENTATION SUCCESS

The sample of 93 firms was then divided into high ($n = 33$), medium ($n = 29$), and low ($n = 31$) success depending on the relative degree of success in implementing the strategic decision. This was based on an implementation success index made up of an average of three questions rated on a five-point scale ranging from 'low extent' to 'high extent'. These questions sought to determine the extent to which the actual implementation effort:

1. Achieved the initial goals and objectives of the strategic decision
2. Achieved the financial results (sales, income, and/or profits) that were expected
3. Was carried out within the various resources (money, manpower, and the like) initially budgeted for it.

Analysis of variance and student t-tests were calculated for each of the 22 potential implementation problems to determine whether there were first significant overall differences and then specific significant differences between the high-success and low-success groups. In 21 instances, the high-success group in implementing their respective strategic decisions had lower mean scores than the low-success group for the respective problem.

Seven of the same 10 problems shown in Table 21.2 along with five new problems were found to be significantly different with the analysis of variance comparing high-, medium- and low-success groups. Then, in 11 instances (marked by asterisks) as shown in Figure 21.1, the student t-test showed that the mean score for high-success implementing firms (as shown by the solid line) was significantly less than that for the low-success group of firms (as shown by the hatched line). The five implementation problems that had t-test significance at the 0.005 level or above are:

1. Key implementation tasks and activities were not defined in enough detail
2. Problems requiring top management involvement were not communicated to them fast enough
3. Changes in roles and responsibilities of key employees were not clearly defined
4. Key formulators of the strategic decision did not play an active enough role in implementation
5. Major problems surfaced during implementation that had not been identified beforehand.

Thus, Figure 21.1 clearly suggests that the presence of more higher rated implementation problems has a negative effect on implementation success. Low-success firms experienced an average of 12.8 problems rated at any intensity level. In addition, 5.0 of these same 12.8 implementation items were rated as substantial or major problems by low-success firms. Conversely, high-success implementation firms experienced an average of only 9.2 problems, of which only 1.5 of them were rated at the substantial or major level.

PROMOTING SUCCESSFUL STRATEGY IMPLEMENTATION

In the follow-up telephone interviews with CEOs, one major purpose was to understand better various implementation problems that did hinder the implementation effort. However, another reason for these interviews was to get these executives to draw on their extensive experience and speculate on the things that help to promote successful strategy implementation. Although these generalizations are not statistically valid, they were mentioned most frequently by 21 CEOs plus 25 additional interviews with agency heads from federal state governments in a comparison study.

Communication, Communication, Communication

This seemingly simple suggestion was mentioned more frequently by CEOs than any other single item. The reason it is repeated three times is to reflect exactly what was said by a number of these company presidents. They felt that top management must first of all clearly communicate with all employees what the new strategic decision is all about. Hopefully, it involves two-way communication that permits and solicits questions from affected employees about the formulated strategy, issues to be considered, or potential problems that might occur. In addition, communication includes clearly explaining what new responsibilities, tasks and duties need to be performed by the affected employees. It also includes the why behind changed job activities, and more fundamentally the reasons why the new strategic decision was made in the first place. Finally, CEOs mentioned that two-way communication is needed throughout the implementation process to monitor what is actually happening, analyze how to

Figure 2.1 Mean ratings and student *t*-tests for high- vs low-success implementation efforts

	Not a Problem 1	Minor Problem 2	Moderate Problem 3	Substantial Problem 4	Major Problem 5
Implementation problems					

Implementation took more time than originally allocated — 2.39 / 3.23*

Advocates and supporters of the strategic decision left during implementation — 1.30 / 2.06**

Competing activities and crises distracted attention from implementing this decision — 2.00 / 2.74*

High success in implementation

Key implementation tasks and activities were not defined in enough detail — 1.58 / 2.81****

Overall goals of the strategic decision were not understood well enough by employees — 1.76 / 2.48*

Leadership and direction provided by departmental managers were not adequate enough — 2.06 / 2.71*

Changes in roles and responsibilities of key employees were not clearly defined — 1.27 / 2.00***

Key formulators of the strategic decision did not play an active enough role in implementation — 1.45 / 2.42***

Low success in implementation

Major problems surfaced during implementation that had not been identified beforehand — 2.15 / 3.19***

Problems requiring top management involvement were not communicated to them fast enough — 1.36 / 2.16****

Uncontrollable factors in the environment had an adverse impact on implementation — 2.06 / 2.87*

*p = 0.05, **p = 0.01, ***p = 0.005, ****p = 0.001

deal with emerging problems, and in deciding what modifications might be needed in the programme to make it work.

Start with a Good Concept or Idea

The need to start with a formulated strategy that involves a good idea or concept was mentioned next most often in helping promote successful implementation. In a nut shell, what this idea suggests is that no amount of time and effort spent on implementation can rescue a strategic decision that is not well-formulated to begin with. More than being thoroughly planned out, the idea must be fundamentally sound. Thus, this suggests that strategy implementation can fail for one of two reasons. One is caused by a failure to do the things required during implementation to ensure that a well-formulated strategy is successful. The other cause of failure is due to a poorly conceived formulated plan that no amount of implementation effort can help rescue.

Obtain Employee Commitment and Involvement

This third suggestion builds on the first two and interrelates with them. CEOs suggested that one way to accomplish this is to involve affected employees and managers right from the start in the strategy formulation process. On the contrary, when a strategic decision has been developed in a vacuum by a few people, top management should not be surprised that it is resisted during implementation by the affected employees. Top management should not be surprised if the formulated plan has major flaws in it because key employees and affected groups did not participate in its formulation. In fact, just the opposite may be true. Top management ought to be surprised if a formulated strategy, developed pretty much without key employee involvement, is implemented successfully.

Involvement and commitment should also be developed and maintained throughout the implementation process. If middle and lower level managers and key subordinates are permitted to be involved with the detailed implementation planning, their commitment typically will tend to increase. The workability of the specific action plan should also be improved simply by getting the affected employees involved—and committed—early on as well as throughout the implementation process.

Provide Sufficient Resources

CEOs mentioned at least four different kinds of resources. The obvious one is money, which, considering the sizeable scope of many strategic decisions, is a bottom line requirement. Conversely, failure to provide adequate funding may contribute to limited success or outright failure. Manpower is another key resource which can have either a positive or a negative effect on implementation. Technical expertise (or knowledge), as related to the new strategic decision, is still another resource mentioned by some CEOs. The idea suggested here is that firms need to have in-house expertise or hire a few new employees who possess it in order to implement strategic decisions involving new endeavours. A final resource mentioned is time. Sufficient time to accomplish the implementation, adequate time and attention given by top management to the new effort, and hopefully not too many other competing programmes demanding the time of affected employees who will implement this one.

Develop an Implementation Plan

This final suggestion is a plea to develop many of the specifics to be done during implementation. In essence, this details who is to do what and when it is to be accomplished. A few CEOs mentioned that this plan must strike the right balance. If the implementation plan is too vague, it is of little practical use. Conversely, if the plan is too detailed, it may tend to force various functional departments to follow it precisely, even when it clearly needs to be modified.

Several CEOs also mentioned that a part of that plan should be to identify likely implementation problems. Instead of being blindly optimistic that nothing will go wrong while implementing a strategic decision, do just the opposite. Try to identify the most likely problems that might occur and then develop contingency responses for those eventualities.

SUMMARY AND CONCLUSIONS

A number of strategy implementation problems do seem to occur on a regular basis. In fact, 10 of the 22 potential problems rated occurred to at least 50 per cent of the sampled firms. While problems do occur frequently, the vast majority of firms experience them as minor or moderate problems. However, when a firm encounters several implementation problems, rated at the substantial or major level, it can have a very adverse impact on the implementation process.

Surprisingly, some of the traditional strategy implementation factors mentioned in the literature were not judged as frequently to be problems. Rated among the least frequent of the 22 implementation problems were:

Rewards and incentives utilized to get employee conformance to programme were not sufficient (cited as a problem by only 18 per cent of the respondents)

Support and backing by top management in this SBU and at the corporate level were not adequate (21 per cent)

Financial resources made available were not sufficient (27 per cent)

Organizational structural changes made were not effective (33 per cent)

Changes in roles and responsibilities of key employees were not clearly defined (38 per cent)

It may be that firms do such a good job in these areas that problems are prevented. Or it may suggest that other implementation problems identified in this study are more important than the literature has somewhat led us to believe.

High-success firms experience implementation problems to a significantly less extent than do low-success implementation firms. In fact, some 11 problems were experienced to a significantly less extent by high-success firms when compared with low-success firms. In addition, high-success firms experienced problems rated at the substantial or major problem intensity level three times less frequently than did low-success firms. In addition, high-success firms also encountered fewer total problems during implementation.

Successful implementation in part involves preventing various implementation problems from occurring in the first place. It also involves taking quick action of resolve and address problems that do occur. Obviously, the faster corrective action is initiated during implementation, the more likely it can be resolved before it impacts adversely on the firm.

Successful implementation also involves doing the things that help promote success rather than just preventing problems from occurring. Although the five suggestions presented here are not statistically significant, they do help reinforce the importance of satisfying basic managerial tasks to help bring about success.

REFERENCES

1. L. Alexander (1980) *Strategy Implementation Annotated Bibliography*, Harvard's HBS Case Services. Case No. 9-380-797, plus 1983 Supplement
2. K. Andrews (1971) *The Concept of Corporate Strategy*, Dow Jones-Irwin, Homewood, IL
3. J. Galbraith and D. Nathanson (1978) *Strategy Implementation. The Role of Structure and Process*, West Publishing Co., St Paul, MN
4. J. Hobbs and D. Heany (1977) Coupling strategy to operating plans, *Harvard Business Review*, (May-June) pp 119–26
5. J. Kotter and L. Schlesinger (1979) Choosing strategies for change. *Harvard Business Review*, (March-April), pp 106–14
6. P. Le Breton (1965) *General Administration: Planning and Implementation*, Holt, Reinehart and Winston, New York
7. D. McCarthy, R. Minichiello and J. Curran (1979) *Business Policy and Strategy: Concepts and Readings*, Richard D. Irwin, Homewood, IL
8. J. Quinn (1980) *Strategies for Change: Logical Incrementalism*, Richard D. Irwin, Homewood, IL
9. G. Steiner and J. Miner (1977) *Management Policy and Strategy: Text, Readings and Cases*, Macmillan, New York
10. A. Thompson and A. Strickland (1981) *Strategy Formulation and Implementation: Tasks of the General Manager*, Business Publications, Dallas
11. J. Pressman and A. Wildavsky (1973) *Implementation*, University of California Press, Berkeley, CA
12. J. Murphy (1971) Title 1 of ESEA: The politics of implementing federal education reform. *Harvard Educational Review* (February) pp 35–63
13. J. Quinn (1982) *General Motors' downsizing decision*. In D. Harvey, Business

Policy and Strategic Management. Charles E. Merrill, Columbus, OH, pp 669–95

14. L. Alexander (1984) *Pacific power and light: implementation of an innovating home weatherization program*. In A. Thompson and A. Strickland, Strategic Management: Concepts and Cases, Business Publications, Dallas, pp 880–905

INDEX